THE PSYCHOLOGY AND TREATMENT OF ADDICTIVE BEHAVIOR

Workshop Series of the American Psychoanalytic Association

Editor
Scott Dowling, M.D.

THE PSYCHOLOGY
AND TREATMENT OF
ADDICTIVE BEHAVIOR

Workshop Series of the
American Psychoanalytic Association

Monograph 8

THE PSYCHOLOGY
AND TREATMENT OF
ADDICTIVE BEHAVIOR

Edited by

SCOTT DOWLING, M.D.

INTERNATIONAL UNIVERSITIES PRESS, INC.
Madison   Connecticut

Library of Congress Cataloging-in-Publication Data

The psychology and treatment of addictive behavior / edited by Scott
  Dowling.
        p.   cm. — (Workshop series of the American Psychoanalytic
  Association ; monograph 8)
    Includes bibliographical references and index.
    ISBN 0-8236-5562-8
    1. Compulsive behavior. 2. Psychoanalysis. I. Dowling, Scott.
  II. Series.
  RC533.P76 1995
  616.86—dc20   95-2873
                                                          CIP

Manufactured in the United States of America

This Book Is Dedicated
to the Memory of Our Friend and Colleague

Edith Sabshin, M.D.

Contents

Section II. The Discussions

Acknowledgments

This book is based on presentations at two Seminars for Clinicians conferences organized and sponsored by the American Psychoanalytic Association. The first of these conferences took place in Washington, DC, on October 13–14, 1990, cosponsored by the Washington Psychoanalytic Society, and the Baltimore-Washington Psychoanalytic Society and Institute. The second conference took place in Seattle, Washington, on March 16–17, 1991, cosponsored by the Seattle Psychoanalytic Society and Institute. These conferences and this volume would not have been possible without the active cooperation and support of all the organizations involved and by the members of both societies who contributed their time and effort to the undertaking. The hard work and initiative of Mrs. Helen Fischer, Executive Director of the American Psychoanalytic Association, and her staff were essential to the success of these conferences and to the production of this volume.

Contributors

Lance M. Dodes, M.D., Faculty, Boston Psychoanalytic Society and Institute; Assistant Clinical Professor of Psychiatry, Harvard Medical School

David M. Hurst, M.D., Secretary, American Psychoanalytic Association; Director, Training and Supervising Analyst, Denver Institute for Psychoanalysis; Clinical Professor of Psychiatry, University of Colorado School of Medicine

Jacob G. Jacobson, M.D., Training and Supervising Analyst, Denver Institute for Psychoanalysis; Clinical Professor of Psychiatry, University of Colorado, Department of Psychiatry

Edward J. Khantzian, M.D., President, American Academy of Psychiatrists in Alcoholism and The Addictions; Clinical Professor of Psychiatry, Harvard Medical School; Associate Chief of Psychiatry, Tewksbury Hospital, Tewksbury, Massachusetts; Principal Psychiatrist for Substance Abuse Disorders, Department of Psychiatry, The Cambridge Hospital, Cambridge, Massachusetts

Henry Krystal, M.D., Professor Emeritus of Psychiatry, Michigan State University; Lecturer, Michigan Psychoanalytic Institute

Dale R. Meers, Ph.D., Teaching Analyst, The Baltimore-Washington Institute for Psychoanalysis; Past President, The Consultation and Treatment Services of the Baltimore-District of Columbia Institute for Psychoanalysis, Inc.

Wayne A. Myers, M.D., Clinical Professor of Psychiatry, Cornell University Medical Center; Training and Supervising Psychoanalyst, Columbia University Center for Psychoanalytic Training and Research

Anna Ornstein, M.D., Professor of Child Psychiatry, University of
    Cincinnati; Co-Director, International Center for the Study
    of Self Psychology in the Department of Psychiatry

Edith Sabshin, M.D. was a Training and Supervising Analyst of the
    Washington Psychoanalytic Institute, Washington, DC and
    Professorial Lecturer, Georgetown University, Washington,
    DC. Dr. Sabshin died on March 23, 1992.

Leon Wurmser, M.D., Training and Supervising Analyst, New
    York Freudian Society; Clinical Professor of Psychiatry, Uni-
    versity of West Virginia

Introduction

The title of this book and the conferences on which it is based have evoked surprise both within and outside the psychoanalytic community. The nature and treatment of addictive behavior has not been a popular subject of psychoanalytic investigation. There has always been a scattering of analysts interested in addictive behavior, but until recently, there has not been a unified effort by psychoanalysts to examine the psychology and methods of treatment of addictive behavior. JourLook, the database of psychoanalytic periodical literature, lists only 21 references to addiction or addictive behavior. Now, a group of psychoanalytic investigators and therapists has joined forces to reexamine our knowledge and approach to these disorders. These analysts have investigated the development and modulation of affect, of self-esteem, of interpersonal relationships, and of disturbances of self-care in relation to addictive behavior. Their findings have ramifications not only for the treatment and theoretical understanding of addiction but also have application to other disorders of ego development and expression. Their treatment studies enlarge our understanding of group phenomena and provide a model for psychoanalytic participation in multiform treatment programs. We are fortunate to have several of these contemporary investigators and theoreticians among the authors in this volume.

This book explores the psychology of addictive behavior in both drug addiction and other forms of driven, compulsive behavior. We set forth psychoanalytic contributions to an understanding of the inner psychological processes, the mental events, which occur in persons who show addictive behavior, while acknowledging, and in a more limited way, discussing the contributions from other psychological orientations.

The authors of this book use the term *psychoanalysis* to refer to a specific form of psychological investigation, to a body of knowledge which has been gained through psychoanalytic investigation, and to a method of psychological treatment based on these investigations. The two uses of the term with which we are particularly concerned are the first two mentioned. There is no claim that psychoanalytic treatment is, with any regularity, the treatment of choice for individuals who are addicted to drugs. Our approach is that psychoanalysis is a basic science of human psychology. It is a source of otherwise unavailable psychological information about the workings of the mind. A psychoanalyst's concerns are with motives, with affect, with forms of self-deception and self-regulation, with the formation and characteristics of human relationships, and with issues of conscience and self-appraisal as they enter into relationships with others, and into work, play, and other aspects of behavior. Psychoanalytic psychology is developmental, epigenetic, and transformational in that it emphasizes underlying psychological continuity from childhood through old age, expressed through ever changing psychological transformations. The psychoanalytic viewpoint emphasizes that psychological issues and solutions, though showing continuity, may appear in quite different forms in childhood than in later life.

The authors of the six chapters of Part I provide information, case studies, and theoretical conclusions drawn from daily psychoanalytic work and research with addicted individuals. There are important similarities and differences between the six authors in the kind of cases they describe, in the treatment they provide, and in their understanding of their patients' addictions. These similarities and differences are spelled out and discussed by the four discussants in Part II who bring their own integrative points of view to the issues involved. It is our intention that discussion of disparate ideas will provide a better understanding of the issues and of the possible solutions to a problem which is devastating to the afflicted individuals, to their families, and to society.

Scott Dowling, M.D.

SECTION I
THE WORKSHOP PAPERS

Chapter 1

Psychoanalytic Studies of Addictive Behavior: A Review

Edith Sabshin, M.D.

Addictive behavior implies a broad spectrum of behavior, from drug addiction to alcoholism, to smoking, to gambling, to food addiction, to hypersexuality. These behaviors are fueled by strong unconscious forces which give them a driven and demanding, insatiable and impulsive peremptory quality. Addictive behavior includes a wide spectrum of degrees of pathology, from the boundary of normal behavior to severe psychological and biological dependency. Psychoanalytic interest has included occasional commentaries by the pioneers of psychoanalysis but was infrequent and intermittent in the early days. The depth of the psychopathology and the difficulties in treatment seemed beyond the scope of classical psychoanalysis.

In the past twenty years, psychoanalytic study has led to a large body of data and discussion concerning the nature, the origin, and the treatment of addiction. This burst of interest has been due to concern about the increase of addiction that parallels easy access to more addicting drugs such as crack cocaine; to concern about the frequency of addictive behavior in young teenagers; and to openness to change in psychoanalytic theory. This research has led to new theoretical understanding and to devising new and more effective therapeutic procedures.

When assessing patients with severe addictive behavior we ask ourselves to what degree a patient's severe addiction behavior will complicate his or her capacity to tolerate the analytic process. Will the severe addictive behavior impede or prevent the development of the transference neurosis to a degree which makes psychoanalysis or psychoanalytic psychotherapy impossible? Less severe addictive behavior, often termed *casual* or *recreational*, is common and often does not enter into our assessment of the appropriateness of treatment by psychoanalysis or psychoanalytic psychotherapy. It remains unclear whether this casual use of drugs will complicate the use of psychoanalytic treatment, and especially whether it will impede the development of a transference neurosis.

The history of the theory of treatment of addictive behavior reflects the history of psychoanalytic thinking. Positions taken by psychoanalysts in discussing addictive behavior parallel the general lines of the evolution and development of psychoanalytic theory and its clinical application. Present-day psychodynamic therapy subsumes three broad psychoanalytic theoretical frameworks: ego psychology, derived from the classical psychoanalytic theory of Freud and later workers like Hartmann and Jacobson; object relations theory, derived from the work of the British school, including Fairbairn, Winnicott, and Balint; and self psychology, formulated and elaborated by Heinz Kohut through his study of narcissistic personality disorders.

Ego psychology conceptualized the intrapsychic world as one of conflict. As with all psychoanalytic theories, ego psychology emphasizes developmental issues. Freud's early theory is associated with libidinal zones and phases—oral, anal, and genital—as these have been elaborated in ego psychology. Several of the papers I will review utilize the earlier concepts of libidinal zones and phases with particular emphasis on the oral stage. According to ego psychology, drives—libidinal and aggressive—are primary, object relations arising secondarily. In other words, the infant's most compelling agenda is tension discharge under the pressure of the drives. In contrast, object relations theory holds that drives emerge in the context of a relationship, the infant–mother dyad, and therefore cannot be divorced from that relationship. The British school of object relations theory holds that a theory of deficit as well as a theory of conflict is necessary for a complete psychoanalytic understanding of an individual. Thus, both Winnicott and Balint believed development may be interfered with by a mother's failure to respond to her child's basic needs. The object relations point of view has been important in many studies of addictive behavior, including many of the papers in this volume.

The object relations formulations derived from clinical work have been bolstered and elaborated on by the infant observation studies of Margaret Mahler and her coworkers. Through observation of normal and abnormal mother–infant pairs, Mahler has been able to identify phases of development of object relations. Mahler's empirical observations have contributed to our evolving understanding of the developmental pathogenesis of borderline conditions in which behavior is caused by psychological deficits; this group includes some patients with addictive behavior.

In self psychology, as developed by Kohut, the patient is viewed as in need of certain responses from others to maintain self-esteem and self-cohesion. Kohut studied patients with narcissistic personality disorders, patients who complained of nondescript feelings of emptiness, depression, and dissatisfaction in relationships. Their self-esteem was highly vulnerable to slights. As children these adult patients suffered from disturbances of parenting, in particular from a parental failure to empathize with the child's need to idealize the parent. The child, and later the adult patient, has difficulty in maintaining a sense of wholeness and self-esteem. This emphasis on early parental failure to support the child's self-esteem is relevant to more recent work on addictive behavior, and particularly the work of Dr. Khantzian (1972, 1974, 1975, 1978, 1985a,b, 1986, 1987, 1988, 1989, 1990; Khantzian and Mack, 1983, 1989, 1994; Khantzian and Treece, 1985; Khantzian, Halliday, and McAuliffe, 1990).

Many of the early articles consider alcohol and drug addiction in an intermingled fashion. I will start with some consideration of alcoholism and then focus on drug addiction. Often psychoanalytically oriented therapists abandon or avoid efforts to treat alcoholics and drug addicts because of the frustration involved.

Relapse is common and interpretation of unconscious motivation has little impact on the drinking behavior itself. One view of alcoholism is that alcoholics are hedonistic individuals, interested only in their own pursuit of pleasure with no regard for the feelings of others. This view may have its origin in religious or ethical belief that alcoholism is a sinful failure of willpower. It follows that the appropriate way to deal with alcoholism is through legal punishment. Cure with the elimination of drinking is a matter of overcoming weak willpower, a pulling oneself up by the bootstraps.

The tremendous success of Alcoholics Anonymous (AA) supports another common view of alcoholism, that it is a disease. The diabetic is not held responsible for *having* diabetes, though he is held responsible for caring for himself. The alcoholic is not held responsible for *having* alcoholism, though he is held responsible for his actions. In this "disease model" alcoholics have an inherent predisposition to become alcoholics; psychological factors are not so relevant to causation. This view of alcoholism as a disease probably originated as a reaction to moralizing reactions and inhumane or paternalistic treatment of alcoholics, but has recently gained additional support from genetic studies. It is important to recognize, however, that although AA promotes the disease model, its methods actually address psychological needs and facilitate personality change. Abstinence is achieved in the context of a concerned and caring community of fellow-sufferers. This experience with caring figures can be internalized; in a similar manner self-concern, self-control, and self-esteem can be internalized from a psychotherapist. This is one way a psychotherapist can help an alcoholic with the management of affects and control of impulses. A psychodynamic approach can focus or extend therapeutic efforts by facilitating understanding and conceptualization of the changes that the AA method brings about.

Most alcoholism experts would agree that alcoholism is a heterogeneous disorder with multifactorial etiology. What works for one patient may not work for another and all the treatments are surrounded by controversy. No treatment is definitive; each patient must be considered individually. Unfortunately, the disease model of alcoholism has led, for some, to a depsychologizing of alcoholism. Those who emphasize the importance of psychological factors point out that alcoholics not only have difficulty in managing affect and controlling impulses, they also have disturbances in other ego functions, such as maintaining self-esteem and caring for themselves. Alcoholism is not a simple entity. There is not a single alcoholic personality that predisposes to alcoholism. Ignoring personality variables and psychological issues hampers efforts to understand the factors that contribute to relapse in the course of an illness.

Addiction to alcohol, as with all addictions, occurs in a human being, an individual person. An individual may develop alcoholism or any other addiction as the final common pathway of a complex interaction between neurotic conflicts, structural deficits, genetic predispositions, and familial, cultural, and environmental variables. As psychoanalysts we are most competent in delineating the neurotic conflicts and the structural deficits.

Addiction to street drugs also occurs in an individual and may be the final common pathway of a complex interaction between neurotic conflicts, structural deficits, and other environmental variables. A considerable body of research literature describes a frequent association of personality disorders and depression with drug addiction. These studies also suggest that although initiation into the use of marijuana may be related to peer pressure in adolescence, this is not so for the use of and eventual addiction to hard drugs.

The suggestion by early psychoanalytic investigators that all substance abuse occurs as a regression to an oral stage of psychosexual development has been replaced by an understanding that most drug abuse is defensive and adaptive. Drug use may temporarily (I emphasize temporarily) reverse regressive states by reinforcing ego defenses against powerful affects such as rage, shame, and depression. The early psychoanalytic formulations often depicted drug addicts as hedonistic pleasure-seekers, bent on self-destruction. Many contemporary psychoanalytic workers view addictive behavior not primarily as a self-destructive impulse, but as a deficit of adequate internalization of parental figures with subsequent impairment of the capacity for self-protection. Drug addicts suffer from other associated impairments including impairments of judgment, of self-regulation of affect, of control of impulses, and of maintenance of self-esteem. These deficits create corresponding problems in object relations as exemplified by many addicts' incapacity for tolerating and regulating interpersonal closeness. Contributing to these relationship problems is the narcissistic vulnerability inherent in the interpersonal relationships and the inability to modulate affects associated with closeness. The dependence on a drug can thus be viewed as an adaptive behavior to seek relief from painful affects and also to temporarily increase the capacity to cope and to function. It can be viewed as a desperate attempt to self-medicate.

Blatt, Berman, Bloom-Feshback, Sugarman, Wilber, and Kleber (1984) did an in-depth study of narcotic addicts and found the addiction multiply determined by: (1) the need to contain aggression; (2) a yearning for gratification of longings for a symbiotic relationship with a maternal figure; (3) a desire to alleviate depressive affects. These people struggled with feelings of worthlessness, guilt, intense self-criticism, and shame. Dr. Wurmser's work (1974, 1987a) emphasizes that addicts suffer from a tormenting superego from which they escape into drug use. Hence it is necessary to understand the superego pressures felt by an addict much as we seek to understand the superego of severely neurotic patients.

Many clinicians, but not all, believe that abstinence from the substance is a prerequisite to treatment by psychoanalytic psychotherapy. Soon addict and therapist realize that abstinence alone does not automatically lead to change in other areas of life. The underlying problem of modulating affects, regulating self-esteem, and relating to others must be addressed. Alexithymia (Krystal, 1982b, 1982–1983) will often be encountered. Many addicts are unable to recognize and identify their own internal feeling states; the therapist must help the patient identify feelings during the therapy hours.

Each advance in psychoanalytic theory, usually originating from the study of neuroses and less so from the study of psychoses, has contributed to the process of developing a theory of addiction. Prior to 1926, when Rado's first paper, "The Psychic Effects of Intoxicants, an Attempt to Evolve a Psychoanalytic Theory of Morbid Cravings," appeared, the literature referred to specific, separate aspects of addiction, such as alcoholism, alcoholic hallucinosis, delirium tremens, and addiction to cocaine. Theoretical papers centered on libidinal elements, mainly oral-erotic. Clinical papers frequently mentioned other aspects of the problem, especially sadism and masochism, but the emphasis, as in analytic theory generally, was on libidinal elements. In "Three Essays on the Theory of Sexuality," Freud (1905) stated that boys who retained a constitutional reinforcement of lip eroticism had, as adult men, a marked desire for drinking and smoking. In 1908, Abraham developed a detailed account of the psychological relations between sexuality and alcoholism. Alcohol undermined the capacity to sublimate. As a result, previously repressed or defended expressions of infantile sexuality appeared, such as exhibitionism, sadism, masochism, incest, and homosexuality. Abraham suggests that drinking is the alcoholic's sexual activity. Alcoholism ultimately produces genital impotence and on this basis illusions of jealousy arise. Abraham concluded that sexuality, alcoholism, and neurosis are all interrelated and the individual factors must be explored.

In his analysis of a case of paranoia, the Schreber case, Freud in 1911 explains alcoholic delusions of jealousy on the basis of unconscious homosexuality. In 1916, Freud, in "A Metapsychological Supplement to the Theory of Dreams," regarded hallucinations and alcoholic delirium as a reaction to the unbearable loss occasioned by withdrawal of alcohol. Hallucinations stopped when alcohol was supplied. The scolding voices and hallucinosis are attributed by Freud to the ego ideal. Brill (1922) felt that libidinal elements are etiological in addictive tobacco abuse. It is an expression of autoerotic activity and a manifestation of exhibitionism.

In 1925, an article on the effects of morphine appeared for the first time in a psychoanalytic journal, the *International Journal of Psycho-Analysis.* Levy described three patients treated with morphine for serious organic illness and the effects of this treatment. In 1926, Rado, who is frequently quoted by current workers, wrote "The Psychic Effects of Intoxicants, an Attempt to Evolve a Psychoanalytic Theory of Morbid Cravings."

Rado starts with basic concepts of pain, sedation, hypnotic drug effects, and stimulation. He discusses euphoria, including the euphoric effects of morphine. He refers to Abraham's discussion of the erotic nature of morphine euphoria and discusses a pharmacogenic orgasm, as distinguished from a genital orgasm, as one aim of the drug use. He points out that this leads to loss or withdrawal from reality and the emergence of a primitive libidinal organization. This was seen as the final phase of addiction, much like the final stages of schizophrenia as it was viewed in those days. The emergence of a primitive libidinal organization includes the quality of aggressive instincts directed inwardly and outwardly. In a further elaboration in 1933, "The Psychoanalysis of Pharmaco-thymia," Rado coined the word *psychothymis*, meaning an illness characterized by a craving for drugs. He mentions disturbances in libido functioning as an explanation for alcoholism and mor-phine addiction as postulated by Freud and Abraham. Rado was struggling for an organizing concept and a one-disease model. He repeats his 1926 point about drugs that allay and prevent pain and secondarily drugs that generate pleasure. This generation of pleasure is achieved at a heavy cost in suffering, self-injury, and self-destruction. He struggles with the idea of tense depression, which he does not define clearly, but says some people respond to frustration with tense depression and to intolerance to pain. Drugs may produce elation but it is transitory and becomes part of a destructive cycle. This cycle treats the pharmacothymia re-gime as a realistic one. Life becomes impoverished and genital pleasure is replaced by pharmacogenic pleasure affect. Love ob-jects are no longer needed and the addict feels invulnerable, as if nothing can happen to him or her. But then the regime col-lapses and the addict enters a pharmacothymia crisis. There are three ways out of this crisis: suicide, in which the patient believes elation will last forever; a flight into a drug-free interval; or the patient moves into a psychotic state. Rado then discusses how masochistic delusions of self-injury can occur, such as delusions of castration or homosexuality.

The next paper I am going to discuss is by Ernst Simmel, written in 1927, called "Psychoanalytic Treatment in a Sanato-rium." It is a nice description of milieu therapy, with an explana-tion of how transferences work in hospital settings. The medical and nursing staff were instructed by the analyst to assure that approaches to the patient were analytically oriented. Actual envi-ronmental reality can be changed to be supportive of therapy.

Mental reality can be constrained in the resistant phase or expanded in other phases. There is little value in letting patients endure long lonely struggles to achieve abstinence from the drug. Treatment can be dangerous because of self-punishing ideas, suicidal trends, and the tendency to sadistic gratifications. In the sanatorium patients were allowed to kill, devour, and castrate the personnel in effigy. They were given two to three times the usual amount of food. They were allowed to cut off branches from the trees or to indulge in other activities that involved destructiveness. When the patient was completely deprived of the drug he was permitted to stay in bed and assigned a special nurse who encouraged him and looked after his personal welfare. In spite of conscious torments the patient had his deepest longings satisfied, namely, the longing to be a child, to be in bed, to have a kind mother attend to him and feed him, a mother who is always there when he is anxious. Withdrawal from this phase of treatment was understood as a repetition of the weaning period; the patient then went back to regular analysis. Treatment by abstinence only is regarded as leaving the patient with a crippling neurosis which may drive him to suicide. Simmel said addicts with underlying neurosis had good results in analytic treatment and those with underlying psychosis sometimes showed improvement.

Glover (1931), in "The Prevention and Treatment of Drug Addiction," stated that nonpsychological treatment is devoid of value because the importance of the drug to the patient is psychological. The patient can forgo the drug up to the last drop. After that it is difficult because the last drop contains the symbolism. Glover felt dissatisfied with his early attempts at treatment and concluded that there needs to be more research on oral erotism and more recognition of the complexity of the first two years of life.

In his "Outline of Clinical Psychoanalysis," Fenichel (1931) suggested that drug addiction may guard against painful external stimuli as well as against internal stimuli. If the external stimuli can be changed by changing social conditions, special therapy may not be necessary. At that time it was unusual for an analyst to suggest the therapeutic benefit of social change. Fenichel also felt that therapy is less successful in cases with marked pregenital narcissistic components. The more recent the onset of addiction the better the chance for cure. Preliminary treatment helps the patient realize that he is ill. The patient cannot be expected to remain abstinent at the beginning of treatment.

Knight in 1937 reported on "Dynamics and Treatment of Chronic Alcohol Addiction." He attempted to find a specific etiology for the use of alcohol. Although he does not neglect intrapsychic factors, he emphasizes the role of actual parental care and describes a parental constellation which he feels is typical of chronic male alcoholism. He classified alcoholics into two groups with differing prognosis: essential alcoholics are those with a preponderance of oral character traits—passivity, demandingness, and marked dependence, a characterization which also applies to many drug addicts. He emphasized the warm glow in the stomach felt by these alcoholics and the erotization of eating and taking medicines. The second type, the regressive alcoholic, has traits of perseverance and mastery derived from the anal stage. Oral traits are less prominent and precipitating factors play a larger part in triggering the condition. These individuals are compulsive and have as good a prognosis as other compulsive neurotics, whereas essential alcoholism is a severe disorder with a poor prognosis.

There are two other very nice papers, one by Robert Savitt in 1963, "Psychoanalytic Studies on Addiction, Ego Structure and Narcotic Addiction." Savitt classifies narcotic addiction as a malignant transition stage between psychoneurosis and psychosis. He regards narcotic addiction as a symptom complex rather than a disease entity, and as such the symptom complex may be a part of a variety of psychic disorders. The common trait of the addictive process is impulsivity. Savitt emphasizes a point made by Fenichel, that addicts act as if any tension were dangerous trauma. Their principal aim is to get rid of tension and pain, not achieving pleasure. Any tension is felt as a preemptive threat to existence much as hunger is felt by the infant. Savitt insisted that simple pleasure seeking, elation, the high or euphoria, has been overemphasized and that the addict's desperate need to escape from intolerable tension has not been sufficiently recognized. The euphoria is frequently short-lived; sleep or stupor often follows soon after the craving for the drug awakens the addict. The addict alternates between hunger for the drug and narcotic stupor, like the infant who alternates between hunger and sleep. Unless tension is completely obliterated the addict is left with the situation that parallels the undifferentiated state of the neonate in which the infant, not yet able to bind tension, is flooded with stimuli against which there is no adequate apparatus of defense.

Savitt gives vignettes of four patients treated psychoanalytically; one was able to develop a classical transference neurosis. At the beginning of treatment, we do not know how well the psychotherapeutic process will stimulate maturation of the archaic ego of the addict. He emphasizes archaic object relations, unbearable tension, and depression. He asks searching questions: Why don't others with apparently similar hunger needs develop narcotic addictions? Why do others resort to alcohol, or barbiturates, food, or hypersexuality as a way of dealing with tension? Is there a recognizable additional factor determining the form of the addiction? As is true in many other syndromes, the mother–child relationship appears to be crucial. He suggests that while the core of the addiction process exists in all of us, in such benign forms as cravings for food, tobacco, candy, or coffee, the vicissitudes of early ego development and later ego maturation, which facilitate fixation and encourage regression, appear to play a dominant role in predisposing an individual to the crippling, morbid craving of drug or alcohol addiction.

Dr. Wurmser's 1974 paper, "Psychoanalytic Considerations of the Etiology of Compulsive Drug Use," is an important landmark in psychoanalytic understanding of addiction; his thinking is presented in a later chapter of this book.

I will now briefly describe what can be considered a footnote to this presentation. I am referring to Freud's discovery and use of cocaine and to his addiction to cigars as described in Jones' 1953 biography of Freud. Freud's first reference to cocaine is in a letter of 1884 in which he refers to reading about the use of an extract of cocoa leaves by an army doctor to increase the soldiers' energy. Freud obtained samples of the pure drug and tried it himself, taking it orally. He found it turned his bad moods into cheerfulness and gave him the feeling of having dined well, "so there was nothing at all one need bother about," without interfering with his energy for work or exercise. He also offered the drug to a physician friend, Ernst Fleischl, who was trying to free himself from morphine addiction, which he developed in trying to manage an intolerable nerve pain as a result of a partial amputation of his hand. Fleischl began taking cocaine regularly and soon after freed himself of morphine addiction. Even before that happened Freud became more and more enthusiastic, and was viewing cocaine as a magical drug which he used for a variety of ills. He sent some to his fiancée; he pressed it on his friends and colleagues both for themselves and their patients; he gave it to his sisters. Jones writes, "Looked at from the vantage point of our present 1953 knowledge, he was rapidly becoming a public menace." At that time he had no reason to think there was any danger as he could not detect any signs of craving for it in himself. In June of 1884 Freud published his essay on cocoa. In this he described his studies of the effect of cocaine on hunger, sleep, and fatigue, based largely on his observations of himself.

He valued the drug as applicable in those functional states comprised under the diagnosis of neurasthenia, in the treatment of indigestion, and during withdrawal from morphine. In the final paragraph of this essay he refers to the anesthetic property of cocaine on cutaneous and mucous membrane and the possibility of additional uses because of the anesthetic property. Koller and Konigstein, ophthalmologist friends of Freud, went on to use it in the eye and achieved world fame as benefactors of mankind. For a while Freud received recognition and praise for his work with cocaine and for his monograph.

He then learned that his friend Fleischl, to whom he had given cocaine to help cure a morphine addiction, had become severely addicted and was in serious physical condition as a result. In 1886, cases of cocaine addiction were reported all over the world. Freud was accused of unleashing this evil force. He reacted defensively at first but also with much self-reproach and guilt, especially concerning his friend Fleischl. There is occasional reference to Freud's use of cocaine during the years of his relationship and letter writing to Fliess, and he continued to use it occasionally until his later years. But there is no evidence of addictive behavior, behavior that was "driven, demanding, and insatiable."

It is otherwise with his use of tobacco, a lifelong habit that he refused to relinquish even in the face of leukoplakia and recurrent and eventually fatal carcinoma of the palate. By the standards

of the day, such persistent cigar smoking was not considered devi-
ant. Still, it is a confirmation of Freud's humanity and a reminder
of our own that he was vulnerable to a form of addictive behavior
which eventually caused his death. In the words of Peter Gay
(1988), "Plainly there were depths to his mind that his self-analy-
sis had never reached, conflict it had never been able to resolve.
Freud's inability to give up smoking vividly underscores the truth
in his observation of an all-too-human disposition he called know-
ing-and-not-knowing, a state of rational apprehension that does
not result in appropriate action" (p. 427).

Chapter 2

Self-Regulation Vulnerabilities in Substance Abusers: Treatment Implications

Edward J. Khantzian, M.D.

Suffering is at the heart of addictive disorders. It is not primarily the result of marketeering, peer pressure, or the availability of drugs, neither is it the result of pleasure-seeking or self-destructiveness. The suffering that addicts attempt to ameliorate or perpetuate with their use of drugs reflects major difficulties in self-regulation mainly involving four dimensions of psychological life: feelings, self-esteem, relationships, and self-care. This point of view is based on three decades of accumulating evidence derived from clinical work with substance-dependent individuals. Prior to this more recent understanding of substance dependence, our thinking about or reactions to addicts has been governed by early drive theory which stressed pleasure-seeking or destructive motives. Freud's dual instinct theory indicated that libidinal and aggressive drives were prime motivators in the addictions as they were in psychological life in general. Our collective unempathic if not pejorative view of addicts partly evolves out of this early

17

psychoanalytic theory which suggested addicts are pleasure-driven, destructive characters. It is further heightened or aggravated by the judgments we make about addicts based on their behaviors and self-centeredness associated with acute intoxication, or the psychological regression that ensues with chronic addictive illness.

Contemporary psychodynamic approaches to substance abuse problems, guided by structural, selfobject, and developmental theory, has allowed for a better understanding of the factors which protect against and those that predispose to addiction. Individuals are not apt to become drug dependent if they are more or less in touch with and able to bear and express their feelings, if they feel good about themselves, if they have reasonably healthy relationships with others, and if they have an adequate capacity for self-care. It is not surprising that traumatizing, abusive, or neglectful parental environments detract from or do injury in all four of these areas. The developmental trauma or damage that addicts experience in this respect is further accentuated when factors of biologic or genetic susceptibility, cultural norms or oppressive social conditions, further contribute to or amplify the psychological vulnerabilities. Such interactions make it more likely that affected individuals will experiment with and discover the short-term adaptive and pain-relieving effects of addictive drugs.

In this report I will elaborate on the nature of addicts' self-regulation vulnerabilities which affect their capacities to govern their emotions, self-esteem, relationships, and self-care. My understanding is guided by and based on a developmental and adaptive perspective. I consider addiction to be a solution to life problems for individuals who have varying degrees of vulnerability and resiliency, dating back to the earliest phases of development. I will consider some treatment implications based on my understanding of their vulnerabilities as well as their capacities for recovery and self-repair.

Accessing Addictive Vulnerabilities

There are a number of influences that stand in the way of our understanding the addictive process and addicted individuals.

Two of the more prominent ones are, first, the pejorative attitudes we harbor toward substance abusers, and second, the problem of competing ideologies. As I have already indicated, the first derives from our tendency to view addicts as pleasure seekers or destructive characters. The second problem of competing ideologies is at least as formidable an impediment when we try to fathom the etiologic basis of addictive problems. Although psychological theorists (including psychoanalysts) have always had a penchant for polarizing concepts to explain mental life and human behavior, the debates have been particularly intense and in the extreme in the area of substance abuse. The controversies have more often taken on a quality of religious fervor rather than respectful reasoning and discourse. This has been most evident in debates about whether substance abuse is a disease or symptom, whether biologic and genetic factors are more important than environmental and psychologic ones, or whether substance abuse is the cause or consequence of the emotional suffering associated with drug–alcohol dependence. An extensive review of these controversies goes beyond the scope of this report. In what follows here, I will underscore how clinical work and diagnostic studies with substance-dependent individuals provide an important and legitimate basis to conclude that psychological factors are important etiologic determinants in the development of addictive disorders. What is offered here is a perspective based primarily on a psychodynamic appreciation of addicts' self-regulation vulnerabilities. This perspective need not compete with other perspectives which yield different information or conceptualization, such as, for example, a disease concept of addictive illness. This latter formulation provides an appreciation of the progressive, biologic nature of addictive illness and a rationale for emergent intervention and control. A psychodynamic perspective provides a basis to intervene and go beyond symptom control and the disease process, and to access and modify the psychological vulnerabilities that predispose to and perpetuate addictive disorders.

Nature of the Data

The treatment relationships which are established and evolve in individual and group work with addicted individuals provide rich and ample clinical data to understand the nature of addictive vulnerability. Patients repeat in their treatment relationships many of the qualities and characteristics of the lifelong dilemmas and problems they have endured, including those that have left them susceptible to becoming dependent on alcohol and drugs.

In what follows, unless otherwise indicated, we draw on the time-proven clinical context of the treatment relationship to understand human problems in addictive suffering. Spanning three decades of clinical experience with addicted individuals, I have found little or no evidence to suggest to me that this context is not as relevant or valid for understanding and treating addicted patients as it is for patients with other symptomatic and characteriologic problems. Although addicted patients more often have special needs for safety, containment, and control, once provided, clinical work with such patients proceeds and unfolds in surprisingly meaningful and understandable ways and patterns.

The Clinical Perspective

The psychotherapeutic treatment relationship, as all therapists come to know, evokes powerful emotions and characteristic patterns of reaction in patients and therapists. When these reactions occur in the patient we refer to them as transference, and countertransference when they occur in the therapist. In the original, more strict definition, transference–countertransference reactions referred to emotions and ways of reacting that derive from early, unresolved conflicts in the child–parent relationship. More generally, transference has taken on a broader meaning to characterize more or less fixed patterns of reacting in a wide variety of relationships and situations, and, along similar lines, countertransference refers to qualities and patterns of reacting that certain patients and treatment situations evoke in the therapist. When Freud first introduced these concepts there was a tendency to consider transference and countertransference reactions as potential barriers to treatment. As these terms are currently viewed, however, we understand that they provide powerful if not essential cues to what patients' psychological dilemmas are about as well as suggesting what it is about the patient's makeup and characteristic responses that is in need of modification and change.

Except for some early noteworthy attempts (Freud, 1905; Abraham, 1908; Rado, 1933; Glover, 1932), it is only within the past two decades that we have applied powerful and useful concepts such as transference and countertransference, and psychodynamic theory in general, to our understanding of addicts and the nature of their suffering. This has mainly been the result of the growing and widespread drug use and dependency in our culture, which has afforded psychoanalytically trained practitioners the opportunity to understand and treat large numbers of drug–alcohol dependent individuals in a variety of settings. Psychodynamic reports growing out of clinical work with addicts during this recent period, have stressed major developmental handicaps and structural deficits that have left such individuals impaired in their capacity to manage affect, to maintain reasonable self–other relationships, and to modulate and regulate their behavior (Wieder and Kaplan, 1969; Krystal and Raskin, 1970; Milkman and Frosch, 1973; Wurmser, 1974; Khantzian, 1974, 1978).

More recently, these contemporary psychodynamic findings and understanding have been applied more systematically in individual and group therapy with substance-dependent individuals. Luborsky, Woody, Hole, and Velleco (1977) have demonstrated that an individual psychotherapeutic relationship, and the transferences that develop, can help the therapist and addict-patient to understand the meaning of the patient's drug dependence. They have developed an individual psychodynamic psychotherapeutic approach, utilizing a manual, to treat opiate addicts, which allows a focus on such individuals' "core conflictual relationship themes" (CCRT), and how such themes are intimately involved in precipitating and maintaining drug use. Along similar lines, but with an expanded focus, Khantzian, Halliday, and McAuliffe, 1990) at The Cambridge Hospital—Massachusetts have developed a modified dynamic group psychotherapeutic approach for cocaine addicts which allows for an unfolding of their self-regulation vulnerabilities involving problems with affects, self-esteem, relationships, and self-care. The group experience affords opportunities to understand how such vulnerabilities and defenses predispose and cause individuals to relapse to drug use. At the same time that they try to disguise or compensate for their vulnerabilities, addicts betray themselves through their characteristic defenses and behaviors. These responses are played out with the group leader(s) and the other members, and an opportunity is provided for recognition of such patterns in self and other, and thus the opportunity for interruption and modification of the self-defeating patterns, and the development of more mature and less stereotypic responses, especially those involving drugs and related behaviors.

In our approach, as I will elaborate, we have increasingly placed an emphasis on sectors of vulnerability in personality organization related to difficulties with affect defense, self-esteem, relationships, and self-care. Although I will review all four dimensions, I will amplify on primarily two areas, namely those involving affect life and self-care. In my work, starting with opiate addicts and subsequently with other substance abusers, it has constantly impressed me how central these two areas of vulnerability are. My patients have repeatedly revealed that their attempts to medicate or alter their distress, which they experience as intolerable, and their inability to take care of themselves, have combined most powerfully, and more often have been the necessary and sufficient conditions to become addicted. In my opinion it is the deficits in ego–self organization, primarily impacting on affect life and self-care, that is in need of therapeutic understanding and management.

Diagnostic and Empirical Findings

Notwithstanding my emphasis on a dimensional approach which focuses on sectors of psychological vulnerability, there have recently been a series of diagnostic and empirical studies which should be mentioned because they compliment a psychodynamic perspective. Starting in the mid-1970s and over the subsequent decade, a series of diagnostic reports revealed the coexistence of a range of psychopathology among opiate addicts. Reports by Woody, O'Brien, and Rickels (1975), Dorus and Senay (1980), Rounsaville, Weissman, Crits-Christoph, Wilber, and Kleber (1982a), Rounsaville, Weissman, Kleber, and Wilber (1982b), and

Khantzian and Treece (1985) documented a high incidence of depression (mostly unipolar), personality disorder, and alcoholism. In the reports by Rounsaville and associates (1982a,b), the authors concluded that their data supported formulations by Wurmser and Khantzian, namely that depressed addicts used opiates to self-medicate feelings which were dysphoric and unbearable. Studying a similar population of ninety-nine opiate addicts, using projective techniques and ego scales, Blatt, Berman, Bloom-Feshback, Sugarman, Wilber, and Kleber (1984) concluded that these addicts suffer significantly in affect modulation and interpersonal relations, and use drugs to isolate and withdraw. More recently, Wilson, Passik, Faude, Abrams, and Gordon (1989) compared twenty-five opiate addicted subjects to a normal control group using a scale to measure failures in self-regulation derived from the thematic apperception test. They found that the opiate addicts had greater difficulties than the normal subjects in self-regulatory functions, and further ascertained that their dysfunction derived from early phases of development. And finally, diagnostic studies have shown cocaine addicts to suffer with a disproportionate incidence of bipolar, attentional deficit, and narcissistic disorders (Gawin and Kleber, 1984, 1986; Weiss and Mirin, 1984, 1986; Weiss, Mirin, Griffin, and Michaels, 1988), and alcoholics to suffer with significant levels of depression and anxiety (Hesselbrock, Meyer, and Keener, 1985; Weiss and Rosenberg, 1985). These varying patterns of diagnostic findings in relation to the preferred drugs also further supports the idea that addicts differentially select a type of drug based on its ability to ameliorate specific painful affects.

Self-Regulation Vulnerabilities

Psychopathology versus Vulnerability

In my own work, I originally emphasized severe and pervasive psychopathology as predeterminants of addiction, involving major deficits in drive–affect defense, narcissistic disturbances, and significant problems in self-care and impulse control (Khantzian, 1972, 1974, 1978). These observations and formulations, however, were based primarily on clinical work with opiate addicts in a methadone treatment program in which the patients were admittedly more disturbed subjectively and behaviorally. Subsequently, I worked with a broader clientele in private practice and with patients in self-help and outpatient drug-free programs whose choice of drugs predominantly involved marijuana, alcohol, and/ or cocaine. I have been impressed with the high degree of variability in the type and severity of psychopathology and the degrees of resiliency and capacity for recovery in this group of patients. As a consequence, rather than emphasizing severity of pathology and diagnostic categories involved with addictions, I have, as previously noted, increasingly focused on sectors of psychological vulnerability with an emphasis mainly on four dimensions of self-regulation; namely, self-esteem, relationships, affects, and self-care. I will place my main emphasis on the latter two areas of vulnerability.

Self-Esteem, Need Satisfaction, and Relationships

Addicts suffer because they do not feel good about themselves and as a consequence they are unable to get their needs met or establish satisfying or satisfactory relationships. One of the main complications of their self-esteem dilemma is their extraordinary inconsistency in processing their dependency needs. They alternate between selflessness and self-centeredness; demanding and expectant attitudes are often and quickly replaced by disdainful rejection of help and disavowal of need. Cool and aloof posturing often veils deeper layers of shame and feelings of inadequacy. It is little wonder then that the powerful feeling-altering properties of addictive substances are sought after. They can serve as powerful antidotes to the inner sense of emptiness, disharmony, and dis-ease such people experience. For some it is the boost of an energizing drug such as cocaine or an amphetamine that counters states of inertia and immobilization associated with chronic low self-esteem. On the other hand, these same drugs may act as augmenters for those who compensate with more expansive or hypomanic defenses. Yet for those who react to their inner disharmony with agitation or rage, the calming and muting effects of opiates will be welcomed; and for those who rigidly wall off from themselves and others their needs for comfort, contact, and nurturance, the softening effects of alcohol or other sedatives will be experienced as a warming and magical antidote.

The work of the self psychologists, especially that of Heinz Kohut (1971, 1977), has been most helpful in understanding how the developmental–structural deficits of certain individuals impact on self-esteem maintenance, and how addicts in particular use drugs in this respect in a compensatory way. Kohut observed, "The drug serves not as a substitute for loved or loving objects, or for a relationship with them, but as *a replacement for a defect in the psychological structure*" (1971, p. 46; emphasis added). His work has helped us to appreciate how self-worth, or self-love, derives from earliest phases of the child–parent relationship. A basic sense of well-being, inner harmony, and cohesion is established as a function of optimal soothing, nurturance, and protection. Subsequently a capacity for self–other love builds on this foundation through the reactions of admiring and being admired that transpire between the parents and the developing child. When optimal, individuals grow in their sense of self-worth, develop guiding values and ambitions, and establish a healthy capacity for interdependence.

Although Kohut and his followers did not systematically expand on and apply their ideas to addicts, his ideas are germane to their self–other problems. Addicts suffer not only because they experience inner disharmony, discomfort, and fragmentation, or that they are unable to feel good about themselves, and thus, others. They suffer even more because of the defenses they employ to mask these vulnerabilities. Addictive individuals protect the injured and vulnerable self by employing self-defeating defenses such as disavowal, self-sufficiency, aggression, and bravado. The main costs involve a sense of isolation, emotional constriction, and highly erratic relationships. Subsequently, I will explore a major therapeutic challenge, helping such individuals yield on their distrust, shame, and counterdependence by identifying the shaky sense of self that drives them, and by replacing their bravado and counterdependency with a more balanced interdependent approach to self and others.

Affects

Addicts constantly convey that they suffer in the extreme with their emotions. At one extreme their feelings are overwhelming and unbearable, and drugs are used to relieve their suffering. At the other extreme feelings seem absent or vague and thus confusing, and drugs are employed to change their suffering. Whether the intent is to relieve or to change suffering, addicts' drug behaviors suggest lifelong difficulties with regulating feelings; drugs represent attempts to control affects that otherwise seem uncontrollable.

Over the past three decades a literature has emerged describing how character-disordered, severely traumatized, psychosomatic, and substance-dependent individuals share certain qualities and dysfunctions in the way they experience their feelings. The works of Krystal and Raskin (1970) and Krystal (1977b, 1982b, 1988a) have been seminal in developing an appreciation of why and how feelings can be so problematic and bewildering for self and others in such conditions. Drawing on extensive clinical work with victims of massive trauma or alcoholism, Krystal has proposed that affects have a normal line of development which is progressive, but subject to developmental arrest or traumatic regression. As a consequence, certain individuals are unable to differentiate their feelings (e.g., they cannot distinguish anxiety from depression), tend to somatize affect, and cannot give words to feelings. In this latter respect, Krystal (1982b) has borrowed the term *alexithymia,* coined by Sifneos (1967) and Nemiah (1970) in their work with psychosomatic patients, to convey the special problems substance abusers have in processing and expressing their feelings. As he has witnessed with addicts, and as Nemiah (1975) has also described with psychosomatic patients, individuals so affected cannot identify or tell whether they are tired, angry, sad, hungry, or ill when they are asked about their distress. These deficits may manifest themselves as well in the emotional and cognitive realm. Krystal (1982b) cites the work of Marty and de M'Uzan (1963) on operational thinking (pensée operatoire) wherein such individuals might display momentary brilliant thinking, but ultimately reveal that their reactions are more bound to events and facts with little connection to emotions. In other instances, the emotional void is interrupted by brief explosions of violence and rage. Related to these observations, McDougall (1984) has referred to such patients as "dis-affected," and Wurmser (1974) has used the term *hyposymbolization,* to characterize the emotional impoverishment that addicts feel within themselves and interpersonally as a result of such deficits.

In contrast to the developmental problems that cause addicts to have difficulty accessing and expressing feelings, their emotional–developmental impairments just as often cause them to suffer with the opposite problem, namely, that affects are experienced as overwhelming and unbearable. On this basis, early in his writing, Wurmser (1974) placed "defect of affect defense" at the root of addictive disorders, and on this same basis Wieder and Kaplan (1969) referred to drugs of dependence as a "corrective" and "prosthesis." On a similar basis I originally stressed how opiate addicts use opiates to counter the disorganizing influences of rage and aggression on the ego (Khantzian, 1974). These formulations shared an appreciation of addicts' limited capacity to bear or sustain painful affects and an understanding of how addicts used the pain-relieving action of the drugs as a way to cope with deficits in affect defense.

One of the main developments which has evolved from these psychodynamic formulations has been the growing appreciation that an addict's main motivation for drug dependence is to use the effects of drugs to relieve or change feelings that are experienced as painful or unbearable. Although addicts experiment with and may use more than one drug, most addicts, if asked, will indicate that they prefer a particular drug. Despite the aforementioned inability to name or express their feelings, when asked what the drugs do for them, it is striking how addicts can differentiate between drug effects and indicate why they prefer one class of drugs over another. Furthermore, they often directly or indirectly indicate the painful states that are ameliorated or altered by their preferred drug. Wieder and Kaplan (1969) were the first to appreciate this phenomenon and coined the term *drug of choice,* and Milkman and Frosch (1973) documented empirical findings to support, as they called it, a "preferential use of drugs." Most recently, Spotts and Shontz (1987) coined the term *drug of commitment* in coming to similar conclusions. I originally referred to this

28   EDWARD J. KHANTZIAN

differential pattern of drug use among various types of addicts as the "self-selection" process (Khantzian, 1975), and more recently I reviewed and articulated the basis for a "self-medication hypothesis" of addictive disorders (Khantzian, 1985a). In this report, drawing on my own experience and that of others (Wieder and Kaplan, 1969; Krystal and Raskin, 1970; Milkman and Frosch, 1973; Wurmser, 1974) I placed emphasis on vulnerabilities and deficits in ego capacities, sense of self, and object relations which produce psychological suffering and painful affects, and on this basis I proposed that substance abusers discover that the action of addictive drugs counters or relieves the painful states (Khantzian, 1990).

The three main classes of addictive drugs, *analgesic-opiates, sedative-hypnotics* (including alcohol), and *stimulants* (e.g., cocaine, amphetamines), have powerful and different psychotropic effects that can relieve or alter psychological suffering. The motives for initial and subsequent use of these drugs can change as a consequence of biological–addictive factors and chronicity, but psychological factors continue to influence the way addicts employ the pain relieving and pain perpetuating aspects of addictive drugs. On the side of pain relief, over the past two decades I have reported clinical findings which indicate that individuals use the three classes of drugs to differentially "self-medicate" painful affect states that result from a range of defects and deficits in defense and personality organization (Khantzian, 1975, 1985a, 1990). In particular, I suggested that narcotic addicts are individuals who already have shaky defenses; they take advantage of the antirage, antiaggression action of opiates to counter the disorganizing effect of such threatening drives and affects. Sedative-hypnotic or alcohol-dependent individuals are counterdependent; they discover how their drug of choice softens overdrawn and rigid defenses and thus temporarily relieves inner states of isolation, emptiness, and coldness. Stimulant abusers are individuals with deflated (or inflated) ego-ideal structures, and depressive and narcissistic personalities, who use cocaine or amphetamines to treat states of depletion, anergia, and hyperactivity (Khantzian, 1991).

Although addicts make it abundantly clear that drugs relieve their suffering, they also make it amply clear that their reliance on such drugs perpetuates and amplifies their distress. That is, an inevitable consequence of drug use and dependency involves the pain and distress of overdose and side effects, painful withdrawal symptoms, and the pain and dysfunction associated with the personal deterioration and regression of chronic, addictive illness. In part this can be explained by addicts' willingness to endure whatever distress that is associated with their use of drugs to obtain even momentary relief from their pain. More recently, however, I have come to realize that addicts, in part, actively and even knowingly perpetuate their distress when they compulsively continue their drug use. I have likened this pain-perpetuating aspect of drug use to a compulsion to repeat unresolved pain from early phases of development. Schiffer (1988) has independently come to a similar conclusion, emphasizing self-punitive, sadomasochistic dynamics, deriving from childhood traumatic abuse, to explain the painful, self-damaging aspects of cocaine use and dependence. My own explanation for accepting the pain associated with drug use involves motives to master and convert the passive, confusing experience of being alexithymic or disaffected to an active one of controlling feelings, even if they are painful. Drawing on psychoanalytic and developmental theory that attempts to measure the impact of earliest life vicissitudes on affect and personality development (Lichtenberg, 1983; Gedo, 1986), I have speculated that the painful, repetitious aspects of drug use and dependence represent attempts to work out painful affect states for which there are no words, memories, or other symbolic representation. This dilemma is especially germane for those patients I described previously who seem not to have or know their feelings (Khantzian, 1990, 1993). Instead of simply relieving painful feelings when they are unbearable or overwhelming, substance abusers may use drugs to control affects, especially when they are vague, elusive, and nameless (Khantzian, 1990; Khantzian and Wilson, 1993), even if they pay the price of more suffering.

Self-Care

Addicts constantly give the impression that they are self-destructive. The well-known, well-publicized deadly effects of drugs of abuse and all the related dangerous environments, relationships, and activities associated with the drugs do not seem to deter addicts from their compulsion to use them. They act and often speak as if they do not care about such consequences. On this basis we frequently infer or conclude that they harbor or live out conscious and unconscious suicidal impulses. Such a conclusion is bolstered by evidence that there is in fact a high suicide rate associated with substance abuse (Blumenthal, 1988).

In my opinion, and experience, the apparent "not caring," and the suicidality, associated with addictive disorders is a consequence, and secondary to, rather than the cause of the self-destructiveness associated with long-term substance abuse. It reflects more the deterioration, despair, and depression that is the result of an addictive adaptation. The act of using such drugs is less the function of a motivated behavior to actively harm the self, but more an indication of developmental failures and deficits that leave such individuals ill-equipped to take care of themselves. Whether it involves the dangers of drug or alcohol use, or the hazards of daily living (e.g., accidents, health care, finances, etc.), addicts give much evidence that they fail in many contexts to protect themselves. Closer examination reveals that the risks and dangers such individuals constantly encounter are not so much courted or unconsciously harbored, but more often are not anticipated or considered. Based on our experience with these characteristics in addicts, we proposed that substance abusers' self-protective, survival deficiencies are the consequence of deficits in a capacity for self-care (Khantzian, 1978; Khantzian and Mack, 1983, 1989). Although we first described this deficit in opiate addicts (Khantzian, 1978), we subsequently have been impressed that it is present to some degree in all substance abusers.

Self-care is a psychological capacity related to certain ego functions and reactions. This capacity protects against harm and assures survival, and involves reality testing, judgment, control, signal anxiety, and the ability to draw cause–consequence conclusions. The self-care capacity develops out of the nurturance, ministrations, and protective roles provided by the parents from early infancy, and subsequently, out of child–parent interactions. If conditions are optimal the growing child internalizes adequate protective functions and responses to care for him- or herself. The capacity for self-care is evident in adults in appropriate planning, action, and anticipation of harm, danger, or hazardous situations, and involves appropriate degrees of anticipatory affect such as fear, worry, and shame. Such reactions and anticipation are strikingly absent or underdeveloped in addicts. They recurrently fail to consider how their behaviors and reactions fail to take into account situations and conditions that can jeopardize their well-being, especially those involving drug or alcohol use and related activities (Khantzian, 1978, 1990; Khantzian and Mack, 1983, 1989).

Self-care deficits are more pervasive in some addicts than others. For example, it is more apparent in polydrug or intravenous drug abusers where ego capacities in general are more globally impaired. In other individuals, the capacity for self-care is not as obviously deficient, but under situations of stress, distress, or depression there are lapses or deterioration in self-protective responses. For some individuals, marginally established self-care capacities yield to an overriding need to relieve distress with drugs, or to use them to enhance performance or achieve a goal, which drugs can often provide on a short-term basis. Whether self-care impairments are severe and pervasive, or represent temporary lapses in function, addicts reveal their self-care problems when they do not sufficiently worry about or anticipate the immediate and long-term dangerous consequences of their substance abuse (Khantzian, 1990).

We conclude this section by providing a clinical example of how self-regulation vulnerabilities involving affect and self-care deficits combine malignantly to place addicts at risk.

A Case Vignette

The following summary of a group therapy meeting for a group of addicts typifies some of their problems with self-care and their confusion and inability to deal with painful or threatening feeling. Although the extragroup event that gave rise to the group interaction was rather dramatic and traumatic for one of its members, it nevertheless demonstrates their not unusual tendency to

become involved with the details and logistics of an evocative
event or to react with anger and impulsive action.

The member who related the experience was a recovering physician. He began the group by describing an incident in his clinic
in which the boyfriend of a pregnant patient whipped out a knife
and slashed her across her shoulder and chest when he misunder-
stood from the doctor's estimation of gestation that she might have
been impregnated by someone else. The doctor first described his
shock and his maneuvers to position himself next to the door of
the examining room while the boyfriend was angrily screaming
and threatening her. The doctor debated leaving until his nurse-
assistant (who had called the police) handed him his softball bat
and convinced him that the patient's life was in danger. With the
boyfriend's back to him, and without further reflection, the doctor
hit the man's arm with the bat releasing his knife, and as he swung
around, the doctor then hit him across the abdomen and thereby
immobilized him until the police arrived.

Immediately after completing his story, a lawyer-cocaine addict
who was a hyperactive, restless character launched into an ani-
mated monologue on the doctor's potential liability to assault
charges by having interceded. As the leader I tried to slow him
down, to point out his tendency to be legalistic, and to get more
to his feelings. Instead, he and another group member, also a
physician, began to argue whether going to the legal aspects of
the situation was reasonable. I made several attempts to interrupt
by asking them to try and focus on how the story made them feel.
Mostly a tone of irritability pervaded the group interaction, with
the lawyer and the other physician returning to their argument
about the suitability of the lawyer's concerns about the legal implications of the event. The other three members seemed uncharac-
teristically willing to tolerate this exchange. The doctor who told
the story responded to my inquiry about his reactions by telling
me and the group how almost immediately after the episode he
arranged a "three-day break" in Florida, without his family, to visit
a trusted confidant-uncle and ex-marine whom he knew would
provide sanctuary, advice, and wise counsel on what had happened. I pointed out to him that he seemed bewildered about and
unable to describe his feelings but instead described what he had
done. A third physician in the group, in a detached and character-
istically analytic manner, commented on the argument between
the other two members and then went on to suggest that the

doctor had perhaps endangered himself by interceding but also allowed that if he had been involved he might have considered a more devastating blow to the head.

It was only toward the end of the meeting that the fifth member of the group, also a lawyer (the youngest member of the group who was working as a planner and counselor in a drug treatment program as part of his recovery efforts), forcefully interrupted the proceedings and expressed his shock over the event, his anger and sadness, and his worry for the threat that the doctor had been forced to endure. He also allowed that he might have unnecessarily jeopardized himself had he not been as successful in immobilizing the assailant. The young lawyer also correctly reminded the group that they could usually do better with each other's distress and feelings. I pointed out that it was easier for the group members to pick a fight with each other than to stay with the feelings that had been stirred by the story. By the end of the meeting it had become clear that both the doctor who had experienced the episode and the lawyer who first reacted were the least able to describe their feelings. With some defensiveness the lawyer was able to consider that his preoccupation with the legal aspects of the situation served to avoid his confusion about his feelings, and that the doctor had similarly acted on his own by going to Florida.

Treatment Implications

General Considerations

Because addicts have so much difficulty in knowing and tolerating their feelings, because their self-esteem, relationships, and self-care are often so precarious, and because drug–alcohol abuse has so many attendant life-threatening dangers associated with it, treatment considerations for substance abusers must place at a premium their needs for comfort, safety, and control. Self-regulation vulnerabilities predispose to, precipitate, and maintain a reliance on drugs, and ultimately it is these vulnerabilities that need therapeutic correction. Nevertheless, we just as strongly believe treatment must rest on a foundation of stability, containment, and control at the outset, and subsequently, of the often emergent and life-threatening nature of addictive disorders. In this respect it does not make sense to pit a disease concept against a symptom approach to substance abuse. Although the former stresses biological and addictive factors, and the latter attempts to understand and modify predisposing psychological factors, ultimately both are in need of attention.

The need to integrate and appropriately sequence these two paradigms, for example, becomes strikingly apparent when we compare the natural history and evolution of a dependence on cocaine to that of alcohol dependence. Whereas the morbid, life-threatening, and fatal consequences of alcoholism usually develop over a period of two to three decades, they often can develop within weeks to months in the case of cocaine dependence, especially when consumed in its free-base form or intravenously. In this respect, the disease concept, as applied in Alcoholics Anonymous (AA) and related self-help and psychoeducational programs, has been enormously successful, especially initially, because it places such fundamental importance on the need to control the addictive process. As I hope to elaborate subsequently, although the AA/disease concept approaches appear to place an absolute emphasis on abstinence as the core and essential requirement of the program, it goes beyond that requirement to help individuals deal with a broader range of psychological issues that have made their lives and their use of substances unmanageable. I hope to show that clinical-psychotherapeutic and self-help approaches can and need to work in complementary or differential ways to target and modify the self-regulation vulnerabilities of substance-dependent individuals. In this section, I hope to show that effective clinicians can optimally benefit substance abusing patients if they can imaginatively, and oftentimes pragmatically, combine therapeutic elements (clinical and self-help) in meeting such patients' needs.

The Primary Care Therapist

To be effective in managing and treating substance abusers, clinicians need to play multiple roles and be flexible to assure that patient needs are met. The treatment relationship can be a powerful vehicle for influencing and modifying behavior, and addicted patients are no exception. Before the leverage of a treatment relationship is employed to access addicts' psychological vulnerabilities, it can and should also be employed to address the needs for safety and stabilization which extrapsychotherapeutic interventions can often better provide. A nonjudgmental, empathic, and authoritative (i.e., confident, hopeful, and instructive) therapist can quickly establish credibility with addicts to help them accept the vitally needed benefits that confinement, pharmacological stabilization, detoxification, or maintenance can offer, as well as involvement in support groups such as AA or NA and assistance with environmental stressors, particularly those involving family.

Considering the multiple clinical management and psychotherapeutic needs of substance abusers I have proposed that the role of the individual clinician should be that of a *primary care therapist,* especially in early phases of treatment (Khantzian, 1985b, 1986, 1988). I have suggested that operating in such a role, the involvement of the therapist-clinician in referring addicts to and brokering other treatment elements is not only necessary but, if done carefully, can help in building a treatment alliance. Beyond the initial referral and clinical management aspects, the primary care therapist plays important roles in monitoring and modifying reactions to the treatment components that have been recommended and adopted. This might involve countering avoidant tendencies against attending AA or NA meetings in one instance and, in another, to consider that a particular patient's characterologic problem or psychopathology makes such a treatment inappropriate. Simultaneously, the primary therapist remains in a position to gauge how patients make use of and benefit from the individual and group psychotherapeutic relationships that develop. In summary, I have proposed that the primary care therapist can function in direct, coordinating, and monitoring roles to meet patient needs for control, containment, contact, and comfort. Subsequently the treatment relationship can evolve into more traditional psychotherapy. In doing so the clinician is able to maximize treatment retention and assure that what is recommended or provided is effective, and if not, to broker or provide alternative approaches (Khantzian, 1988).

*Alcoholics Anonymous—A Vehicle for Control, Support, and
Understanding*

Alcoholics Anonymous or its derivatives such as NA or Cocaine
Anonymous (CA), serve as powerful containers and transformers
for addictive behavior. People who are resistant to ceasing a destructive behavior and deny vulnerability can be helped to cease
such behavior by *admitting to their vulnerability*. Self-help groups
such as these work not merely by using group pressure to eliminate the offending agent, namely the drug or alcohol, but they
also work because they have evolved as extraordinarily sophisticated group psychologies that effectively address the physiological
and psychological determinants of addictive compulsions.

Alcoholics Anonymous works as a container, or controlling
influence, because it deals effectively with the physiological and
psychological factors that drive the addictive compulsivity. It is
correctly argued that one of the main reasons people compulsively drink or take drugs is the result of physiologic-addictive
mechanisms (i.e., tolerance and physical dependence). This has
not been the focus of this paper, albeit it is an important one to
appreciate. Helping a person stop the regular use of substances
and thus interrupting the physiological basis for desiring drugs
or alcohol, goes far for many in removing their compulsion. What
stands in the way just as often, however, are the predisposing
personality characteristics of human beings, including and especially addicts, that make admission of vulnerability so difficult
when people most need to do so. Denial is not a defense upon
which alcoholics and addicts have sole claim. Nevertheless, it can
have more obvious devastating consequences in their case.

The more alcoholics and addicts lose control of their substances and thus their lives, the more they posture to the contrary.
Alcoholics Anonymous is most ingenious in confronting this penchant by its traditions of initially on a daily basis, and thereafter
in helping alcoholics and addicts admit to themselves and others
that they suffer with a disease or illness and admit that they lost
control of alcohol (or drugs) and their lives (i.e., the first step in
the twelve steps of Alcoholics Anonymous—"we admitted we were
powerless over alcohol . . . that our lives had become unmanageable" (Alcoholics Anonymous World Services, 1976). Stephanie

Brown (1985) has stressed how this focus on loss of control and accepting and maintaining an identity as an alcoholic is a key to AA's success. The steps successively build on the admission of vulnerability and the acceptance of humility and altruism as necessary alternatives to the predisposing and progressive self-centeredness and egoism that has been involved in their addictive illness. These defenses are exaggerated and overdeveloped to counter their self-regulation deficits, especially those involving low self-esteem. The many supportive, active, and guiding elements that the addicts immediately encounter in the program provide structure and support that compensate for their self-regulation vulnerabilities. The aphorisms provide a source of soothing and comfort that they desperately need, and the stepwise approach, counsel, and even admonitions (e.g., "stay in touch, show up, call, don't pick up, go to meetings, ask for help") provide needed consistent guidelines and structure to support and direct individuals to organize their lives, which are often in a shambles. Beyond these practical elements, the use of prayer and spirituality forces the issue of surrendering to a force beyond self, admitting to dependency and the importance of self–other relationships.

As a transformer, AA helps to modify those parts of the self responsible for taking charge and controlling one's life. John Mack (1981) has referred to such a capacity as "self-governance" and described it as a self–other, multiperson psychology. Alcoholics Anonymous compensates for diminished or underdeveloped self-governance capacities that alcoholics and addicts display. Alcoholics Anonymous challenges the assumption of alcoholics and addicts (or for that matter, of all of us as humans) that we are able to govern our lives and behavior *alone.* Beyond challenging the "character defects" (i.e., as employed in AA but similar to that used in psychoanalysis) that mask lack of self-esteem and related interpersonal problems, AA also effectively addresses the affect and self-care deficits by inviting its participants to listen to each other's accounts of how they succumbed to and recovered from their addictive illness.

More precisely, we (Mack, 1981; Khantzian and Mack, 1989, 1994) believe that the story-telling traditions of AA (also referred to as "drunkalogues" or "drugalogues") wittingly or unwittingly are an extraordinarily helpful way for substance dependent individuals to identify in themselves and others how much their dilemmas with feeling life and self-care have caused their problems. As they tell their stories, often with engaging humor and great eloquence, they perceptively identify and disclose their self-regulation vulnerabilities and reveal the self-defeating characterologic defenses that they employ which are so much a part of their difficulties. The stories reveal they not only did not know, tolerate, or express feelings, but they more often absorb themselves with circumstances, events, and action. Instead of admitting to being lost or confused in matters of self-care, their narratives indicate that they responded to life's hazards and those involving substances with denial of danger, bravado, aggressive postures, and counterphobia. Conversely, their stories of recovery beg the importance of yielding on their self-defeating defenses, admitting to their vulnerabilities, and surrendering to the necessity of accepting distress and interdependence as inevitabilities and requirements of adult life.

Psychotherapy

Addicts and alcoholics need and respond to psychodynamic psychotherapy. Contrary to the truisms and negative stereotypes of addicts that they do not come, accept, stay, or benefit from such treatment, there are now at least two decades of experience by involved clinicians with preliminary empirical findings indicating that such pessimism is not warranted. As we indicated at the outset of this report, substance abusers can and do respond to psychodynamic treatment relationships, both individually and in groups. Such treatment allows the characterologic defenses and underlying vulnerabilities involved in addictive disorders to unfold, be examined, and modified in the context of the individual and group relationships that develop. A systematic review of psychotherapy for substance abusers goes beyond the scope of this report, but, in this final section, I would like to highlight some themes central to the focus I have placed on addicts' self-regulation vulnerabilities.

   In my opinion we have better succeeded in treating addicts psychotherapeutically than we used to because (1) we have better understood their vulnerabilities, and (2) we have modified our psychotherapeutic technique in general and in particular to better respond to addicts' vulnerabilities. The traditions of passivity, uncovering techniques, the blank screen, and strictly interpretive approaches, derived from psychoanalysis of neurotic patients, are not appropriate for either understanding or modifying addictive vulnerability. An appreciation of substance abusers' developmental problems suggests they need greater support, structure, empathy, and contact than that provided by classical psychoanalytic treatments. Accordingly, therapists need to be alerted to the requirements for more actively identifying in individual and group therapy the nature of addicts' self-esteem, relationship, affect, and self-care deficits, as well as the need to constantly point out, clarify, and confront such patients with the self-defeating defenses which they use to disguise or deny their vulnerabilities.

   There has been a common thread in our own work and that of Krystal, Wurmser, Dodes, and Luborsky and associates, regarding the advantages of focusing on core areas or sectors of vulnerability, to access and modify substance abusers' problems. That is, these approaches stress dimensions of psychological life, or the quality and nature of addicts' distress and suffering, as opposed to more categorical, diagnostic approaches or those that stress the dynamics of a particular type of psychopathology. Krystal's work has laid stress on the conditions of affect deficit and alexithymia, and how the therapist must be active in explaining to patients how they are different in relation to feelings, and the need to help patients identify and express feelings. Wurmser (1987c) has placed growing importance on the need to help addicts understand their problems with shame and with an archaic superego that causes them to repeat humiliating and self-destructive encounters with substances, relationships, and activities. Dodes (Dodes, 1990; Dodes and Khantzian, 1991) has drawn attention to states of helplessness and reactive narcissistic rage that precipitate relapse and are in need of therapeutic attention. Woody, McLellan, Luborsky, and O'Brien (1986) have explored the importance of the core conflictual relationship themes. In our approaches, we have stressed the four areas of self-regulation vulnerabilities involving affects, self-esteem, relationships, and self-care in understanding how dysfunction in these areas precipitates and maintains drug dependence. All of these approaches share in common an emphasis on activity, support, and empathy and also share the belief that active–supportive methods are not inconsistent or incompatible with expressive approaches which allow for analysis of defenses and the vulnerabilities they mask or disguise.

Conclusion

To be effective, treatment approaches to substance abusers need to constantly appreciate and focus on these patients' self-regulation difficulties. At the outset emphasis needs to be placed on control, safety, and comfort and early treatment needs to be guided by these considerations. We have proposed that initially a clinician must be prepared to act as a primary care therapist to assure that these initial treatment priorities are adequately managed. Furthermore, because we cannot very well predict who will respond best to what modalities and treatment elements, the role of the primary care therapist is needed to monitor treatment responses and to flexibly combine treatment elements to manage the addictive illness on a short-term basis, and the psychotherapeutic needs on a more long-term basis. It will become evident, for example, that some patients are so disabled and refractory with their alexithymia or behavioral difficulties that more long-term confinement or more active self-help, and psychoeducative approaches are indicated. In other cases cooccurring psychopathology such as a severe panic disorder or suicidal depression make the acceptance or suitability of a self-help approach unlikely. The need for an augmented program involving drug therapy to treat cooccurring psychopathology, might also necessitate referral or an expanded role for the treating clinician. In either case, the recovery and psychotherapeutic needs of patients are best met by imaginative and pragmatic employment of a combination of treatment elements. In doing so there must be a readiness on the part of the clinician to conclude, based on his or her monitoring efforts and appreciation of the vulnerabilities involved, that a treatment modality is inappropriate or contraindicated and to then consider alternative approaches.

Chapter 3

Compulsiveness and Conflict: The Distinction Between Description and Explanation in the Treatment of Addictive Behavior

Leon Wurmser, M.D.

The Problem of Addictive Behavior

In the face of clinical reality all the simple answers to a difficult problem such as addictive behavior and its underlying dynamics wither away: "what is simple and unified is not true, can hardly be that. Only what is composite can perhaps be assumed to be that" (Lagerkvist, 1966, p. 230).[1] There is no such thing as "alcoholism is a disease," in the meaning of a unitary entity with clear and singular cause, course, and treatment (Fingarette, 1988). There is no such thing as an "addictive personality" with clear and common dynamics and one preferable treatment approach

---

[1]"det enkla och enhetlica ar inte sant, kan inte garna vara det. Bara det sammansatta kan mojligen tankas vara det."

for all. There is no linear relation between one set of causal factors and the symptoms of addictive behavior. There is no sharp line between specific addictions and addictive behavior in general, except for the contingencies of the physical aspects induced by specific drugs; but there also is no sharp line between addictive behavior and the neurotic process. The experiences with the treatment of the severe forms of neurosis, those that now often are singled out either as "narcissistic" or "borderline disorders" (Abend, Porder, and Willick, 1983), are not principally separated by a gulf from those with the milder forms, and the problems in the treatment of drug- and alcohol-dependent patients to a great extent are simply a special form of these severe neuroses (Wurmser, 1987b,c, 1988b).

Addictus is a legal term referring to somebody being given over, surrendered, awarded; "addicere liberum corpus in servitutem" means to sentence somebody who is free to servitude because of indebtedness; "addictus" is one in bondage because of debts (Stowasser, 1940).

Therefore, metaphorically, addictive behavior refers to a deep, enslaving dependency on some authority, some compelling, constraining force, usually seen and experienced as coming from the outside—a drug, a love partner, food, money, power, gambling—in short, any system or object demanding and getting total submission. It is a seemingly willing subservience to compulsion. In fact, all our psychoanalytic experience tells us that it is neither so "willing" nor that the power is truly on the outside. For us the problem is: What is this compelling force from within that creates such enormously destructive bondage to something on the outside?

The question is not so much, What is veiled by the curtain woven by drug effects and noisy social deviance? Rather it is, What is the power of self-deception that weaves its own thick curtain?

We are struck by the prominence of avoidance and denial, often in the following encompassing way: "I don't have any inner problems. Everything is on the outside and can be corrected by manipulation there." Or: "If only I can get rid of the drug use (or some other obnoxious behavior), everything will be all right." Inner conflict, inner reality altogether, is being denied as having anything to do with life's problems. Most drug addicts and alcoholics show such a vast form of denial for a long time. It results in what I have called *psychophobia*, a disregard for the importance of introspection of any kind and its resolute and self-righteous avoidance; in fact, there is frequently a disdain expressed toward any approach to it.

While in some of my earlier writings the dynamics were highlighted particularly from the vantage point of ego analysis, the point of view shifts here to that of superego analysis. The two perspectives are obviously complementary. I will first give a brief summary of the ego analysis of the dynamics.

Layers of Specificity

The lowest level of specificity, the main, easily visible dynamic features are:

✗ 1. Drugs uniformly are used as an artificial affect defense; that is, they are compulsively taken to bring about relief from overwhelming feelings. Drug use always includes a pharmacologically reinforced denial and affect blocking. This presupposes not only a particular proneness for these particular defenses, but also an inclination to massive affect regression (Krystal, 1970, 1974, 1977c), with some specificity between prominent affect and drug preferred (Wurmser, 1974, 1978).

2. In most addicts a phobic core can be seen, an infantile neurosis underlying the later pathology, typically with fears (and wishes) around being closed in, captured, entrapped by structures, limitations, commitments, physical and emotional closeness, and bonds. The compulsive search of the addict is like a mirror image of the compulsive avoidance of the phobic. Whereas the latter condenses all his dangers into one object or one situation and arranges all of his life around its avoidance, the addict does exactly the reverse. His life's entire content and pursuit, that which he seeks above everything else and that he depends on, has also become condensed in one object or one situation (Wurmser, 1980; Wurmser and Zients, 1982).

3. Where there are phobias, there are *protective fantasies*—fantasies of personal protective figures or of impersonal protective

systems, specifically counterpoised to those threats. This search for a protector against the phobic object and the anxiety situation almost inevitably leads to a compelling dependency once such a factor has been found—be it a love partner, a fetish, a drug, a system of actions, or the analyst. Most typically drug addiction enacts the protective fantasy that most potently defends the phobic core. With the dependency on them, such protectors must be highly overvalued; they are "narcissistic objects," selfobjects, and are experienced in extremes: all-powerful, all-giving, all-forgiving, or all-destructive, all-condemning, all-depriving.

4. The helplessness of being uncontrollably overwhelmed and traumatized is defended against by a thick crust of narcissism—of grandiosity and entitlement, resentment and coldness, or idealization and submission. Often it is papered over by the superficial amiability, friendly compliance, and flirtatious charm of the "sociopath."

5. Torn between the fears of the condemning and humiliating powers on the outside and these narcissistic needs of a defensive nature from within, the personality assumes a strikingly unstable and unreliable quality. Periods of high integrity and honesty suddenly give way to episodes of ruthless coldness and criminality. The discrepancy may go so far that we encounter split or multiple personalities. There is correspondingly a remarkable discontinuity of the sense of self, a global lability without mediation and perspective. It is an unreliability that infuriates others and humiliates and depresses the persons themselves. These "ego splits" or "ego discontinuities" are not a defense but a functional disparity and contradictoriness derived from denial above all.

6. Acute narcissistic crises, feared or real disappointments in others and the self, usually trigger the overwhelming affects described and with that launch the patients into compulsive drug use.

The next level of specificity is of a higher level of abstraction; it concerns the nature of the predominantly used defenses. I single out three of particular prominence:

Drug use always includes a pharmacologically reinforced denial and affect blocking, an attempt to get rid of feelings and thus of undesirable inner and outer reality.

The defense of turning passive into active is a cardinal defense in all severe psychopathology, especially against traumatic reality and against aggression from within, much as repression is found in the less severe forms of neurosis and is used mostly against libido.

With externalization "the whole internal battle ground is changed into an external one" (A. Freud, 1965); externalization is the defensive effort to resort to external action in order to support the denial of inner conflict.

Superego Analysis

Dynamically, most specific and most important for intensive therapy is the centrality of conflicts within conscience (Rangell, 1963a,b), and between different ideals, in the triggering of severely destructive impulsive action sequences, especially those involving compulsive drug use. This necessarily entails a different approach to understanding and treating this type of patient than is usually taken.

I will focus now on these conflicts of conscience, the severity of the feelings of shame and guilt in these patients.

The Need to Destroy Success

Victor, a farmer in his early thirties, sought treatment for severe cocaine and narcotics addiction as well as alcohol abuse, a problem since his middle teens. Both parents were alcoholics, caught in unending stormy fights. His father died at 42, partly due to liver cirrhosis; one older brother succumbed to a drug overdose, the other was also an alcoholic. Victor has been seen, with long interruptions, in psychoanalysis and psychotherapy for eight years, about 600 sessions so far. Much time has been spent exploring his deep conflict between wanting to succeed where all the other members of the family have failed, and his wish to be accepted by those shadowy figures from the past, mostly his late father and brother, hence the conflicts between opposite identifications. There have been conscious wishes to have one or both of his argumentative, querulous, resentful, even violent parents die and be replaced by better people. His conviction that he does not deserve success is firmly rooted in his sense of guilt about his father's precipitous death when he was 13, about the sudden death by overdose of his older brother at a time when Victor was close to him, and about his chronic anger and contempt for his mother, a bitter, quarreling drunk.

Yet, psychoanalysis is the art of the specific. An episode of sleepwalking by his daughter, a child born during his first, unsuccessful marriage to an alcoholic woman, reminded him of similar episodes from his own childhood. His sleepwalking was associated with nightmares or dissociative states during which he saw himself surrounded and pursued by huge, threatening, white birds fluttering around him and attacking him. He himself related this image to scenes of intercourse between his parents and to a memory of tiptoeing to the threshold of their bedroom, just as his daughter had done the night before. He recalled how he had feared to enter, yet had wanted to, and, at times, had done so. His fantasy was that his father might kill his mother in some violent fight and *he* had to enter and protect her by killing the father. He was afraid to go in: "I was speechless, frozen by fear. It is as if it had been me who had killed my father. And toward my mother I feel: 'I hate you and I hate myself for being the cause of his death.' As if it had been in my power and my fault . . . 'May God strike you blind!' "(session 368).

A few sessions thereafter he came back to the memory of his father's sudden death, allegedly caused by a stroke (he had been hypertensive and, although only 42 at the time, had signs of cardiac decompensation and severe liver cirrhosis). What was curious, though, about that event was the following. The patient had been playing that morning with a friend at some distance from his parents' farmhouse. His mother came by and asked him whether he had seen his father, she couldn't find him. His answer was: "Have you looked in the bathroom?" She went there and discovered her husband lying on the floor, dead.

"Why did I tell her that? How could I have known? Somehow I did know!" The more he pondered this, the more certain he was that, earlier that morning while upstairs, he had heard a thud from below. He had perhaps gone downstairs to check and detected something suspicious or ominous (it is not clear if he actually saw his father lying on the floor with blood flowing from his ear, as one image suggested, or merely heard something frightening). Instead of taking any action he had then gone outside and away from the house, down to the barn, so as not to face what had happened. Still he had perceived enough to tell his mother where to look for the father: "I knew something was amiss, but I blocked it out the instant I knew it. I denied it. Then I felt guilty for not having spoken. Perhaps something could still have been done for him!"

After this "life secret" had been uncovered and put into words he felt very relieved, as if a big load had been lifted from his shoulders. Not long after that he decided to interrupt his analysis, which by then had lasted about two and one-half years (400 hours). He resumed treatment five years later, two to three sessions a week, on the couch. For eight years after treatment began, he did very well; he had abstained almost completely from cocaine and narcotics, and over the years had gradually given up marijuana and alcohol as well. He was managing his large farm virtually alone and did so successfully. After eight years he suffered from a kind of resistant "flu," with weird symptoms. One month later the diagnosis of auto immune deficiency syndrome (AIDS) was made; the usual treatment effort with AZT and similar drugs proved very dangerous because of serious liver damage.

I continue to see him regularly, we work on the inner and outer issues raised by the terminal illness. He stated: "I am disappointed: I have been healing myself by work and therapy, and then suddenly to be physically ill, the unfairness of it all. Yet I brought it all upon myself, unknowingly. The irony is so cruel. I am again confronted by death. It is frightening. The ultimate price must be paid. The bill of guilt must be settled."

The Defense Against Conscience

Ingmar, a polydrug user, commented about his sense of shame: "I am exposed by being with people—at work, in school, in the congregation, even just standing in line in a store or walking on the mall, especially by going to an interview. I feel the same way when I express feelings toward my mother or mention not feeling well at the family table. All this is exposure, it is shame. When I begin to speak I lose the train of thought; I fear I will say something stupid.'' What ensues is a feeling of shame about shame, an embarrassment about his inability to talk and think. Cocaine helps him to feel in control again; it is a powerful antidote against this overwhelming sense of humiliation. Alcohol works in a parallel fashion: ''When I don't carry out my tasks, when I'm irresponsible, alcohol allows me to forget about it. Without it the guilt becomes unbearable.'' Cocaine specifically counteracts his shame, alcohol his guilt. It is not just an easy excuse when he adds that, ''having too much of a conscience is a heavy load to bear.'' The use of drugs is a flight from conscience.

During the episodes of vague tension, there was an increasing sense of crisis, spilling over into impulsive action, and an overbearing inner authority with impossible ideals which became intolerable. The anxiety he felt about the pressure of these demands was overwhelming, and the sense of guilt or of shame about having miserably failed the peremptory demands, was particularly harsh. There followed a kind of defiance against and temporary overthrow of one part of the burdensome inner authority figure. He hoped to reach a fantasied identity free of that inner tyrant (Rangell, 1974, 1980).

What lies behind such a compulsive, temporary, and self-defeating overthrow of conscience, however, dynamically speaking, is a defense against the superego (Freud, 1924).

When I started working with Ingmar, he was a 26-year-old divorced laborer, a burly, thoroughly pleasant man of convincing innocence and compliance, very bright and articulate, the second of five children. He had one older brother and three younger sisters, all born at two- to three-year intervals. His older brother is said to have molested two of the sisters when baby-sitting.

Both parents are prominent, intelligent, and successful people, the father in public life, the mother in the health care field; they are described as kind and caring, but also as very reluctant to show their feelings or to accept open discussion of anything negative, like difficulties or failure. The father is seen as very judgmental: ''He seems to attack everyone; he finds fault with everybody. Yet he neither picks on us nor does he lift us up. But how could he avoid doing it to us if he did it to everybody else? I tell him what he wants to hear" (session 37). "Mother is sweet and kind but can't touch anybody. If I try to hug her or tell her I love her she gives no answer and turns away."

The patient was always a shy, frightened child, afraid to go to nursery school (age 4) and later to elementary school, never able to "reach his potential," which was the refrain from his teachers. They chided him: "Why can't you be more like your brother?"

When he was in the second grade, he repeatedly pulled the fire alarm. The entire school building had to be evacuated, and fire engines arrived. This recurrent experience, without his being detected, gave him a sense of magical power and provided him with an antidote against his pervasive sense of shame and resentment about his weakness and inferiority.

In high school he once stole the teacher's grade book because he was failing in his classes. He changed his grades but was detected. His parents arranged a brief period of help with a child psychiatrist.

After the first semester of college and when working at some odd jobs he went on a spree with a friend, shooting out windows in cars, trucks, an army recruiting office, and a supermarket, partly in order to take revenge on someone who had fired his friend, but, more particularly, in order to get back at people who had been kind to *him*, but in front of whom he had felt so much pressure to perform. At the time of the shooting spree he was on "speed" and drunk. He was arrested and was seen for a while by a psychiatrist, again to little avail. For the following seven years he was drunk most of the time and often high on cocaine. He shunned marijuana and LSD because they induced a loss of his sense of control. An avid gun collector and hunter, he had to sell many of his weapons to buy his drugs.

For approximately one year he was without work, "because of the panic attacks and low self-esteem, I thought, 'I'll screw up anyway. So why should I try?' It's as if I were forced from within; my body thwarts all my plans. I've always had the fantasy of being someone else, somebody whom people would respect. Yet I cannot accept it when people *do* respect me. I'm setting myself up to fail."

Besides the prevalent anxiety in his childhood, he described "the most humiliating thing that ever happened": When he was 5 years old, he was spanked by his father on his bare bottom, once for having stolen a toy gun, the other time after having harassed a little girl.

What we noticed was a fairly typical sequence:

1. He is chronically under a severe inner pressure: "I'm more critical about myself than anybody else is. Often I don't begin doing things because I tell myself 'You won't succeed anyway!' "
2. When he attains some success, he feels "fantastic."
3. Then, the "trance," an altered state of consciousness, suddenly and unaccountably comes over him; he feels lonely, unloved, and humiliated, is overwhelmed either by guilt or by shame, and is paralyzed by panic.
4. This forces him to impulsively try to find relief with the help of alcohol or cocaine.
5. Before long, suicidal depression overwhelms him, he calls frantically for help, and is profoundly contrite and debases himself.
6. Eventually he reaches a point of relief and relaxation: "I'm welcomed back, I'm forgiven." He tries hard to be "good" and to overcome his demonic state. Once again he submits to his "inner judge" or "inner dictator," and the cycle begins anew.

The denial, the blocking out of perceptual reality, assumes such an important role that we can really speak about a split personality. It is as if the patient were possessed; a demon takes over.

Yet where does this fantastic weight of conscience come from, an inner force which perverts every intent, every plan, into a crushing command whose absoluteness he cannot oppose for long? Every ego decision is at once transformed into a superego command.

Ingmar believes that, "Out of that dictatorship that controls my life comes the attraction to cocaine: When I do cocaine I'm in control. It's only temporary and imaginary but it feels good for a while." Nothing he plans or does escapes the fate of being turned into a command given by the inner dictator. The question is therefore: "Why am I absolutely bad unless I carry out an inner command? Why should it have become such an absolute dictate?" (session 40).

It points back to one deeply repressed and yet massively influential conflict: the clear opposition between needs to belong and needs to be himself, belonging and merger versus separation and individuation. The sharpest and clinically most important version of the conflict about union and separateness is this: "If I separate, I wound or kill the other; in turn, I will have to die for breaking away." The issue of separation guilt, "not having the right to one's own life" (Modell, 1984), is often an important motive in severe pathology. Its antipode is: "If I am passive and dependent, I have no control over anything, over myself; I am a nothing, a wimp—hence I must be deeply ashamed of myself." Thus the two antithetical affects of extreme separation guilt and of equally deep dependency shame come to form one of the basic polarities in the structure of the conscience.

What about Ingmar's intense shame? "The family structure is sick," he said some time later. "Everyone has his secrets and is slowly dying within. The parents don't want to know that my brother has not only molested my sisters but actually had intercourse with them and enforced their silence by threatening to inflict harm upon the other sister if the secret was revealed" (session 86).

Another area of secrecy and denial concerns the earlier life of the father. Although little is known about the details, it has been hinted that he had a shameful wartime experience. He was part of a commando group which had to operate behind enemy lines in Korea. He was ordered to blow up a bridge, but first he had to eliminate the sentry guarding it. He killed the guard, then discovered he had killed a woman. This is one of the topics that cannot be mentioned. Another is the fact that about half a year before onset of the therapy, the (maternal) grandmother was murdered by a boyfriend of the mentally retarded sister of the mother. He killed her mother after she refused to continue giving the daughter money left to her by her father. A third topic of silence concerned the rampant, even fatal alcoholism on both sides of the family.

One has to wonder whether such hidden themes of guilt and shame and such a conspiracy of silence is poisoning the entire family; to what extent is Ingmar's pernicious inner judge fed by borrowed guilt and hidden family shame?

The evidence points to the likelihood that the sudden switches in his mood, and hence the initiation of the impulsive action sequences, are triggered by an exacerbation of anxiety. More specifically, this takes place when he sees himself confronted by unsolvable conflicts of conscience between conflicting obligations, between opposite loyalties, or, very prominently, between the submission to one obligation and his own pride or his wish to be faithful to himself. An example of the latter is the conflict between the gratitude toward his employer and his indignation about the wanton and degrading way the latter was treating him and his coworkers; or between the commitment to come to the analysis and to continue his work task; or to submit loyally to his father's commands and fundamentalist values and the need to respect himself and expect such respect also from others. There are clearly sharp contradictions within his superego and between the defensive efforts made in behalf of one superego part against another, and it is these that exert a determining effect upon the impulsive actions.

About eleven months after beginning the analysis (after the 172nd session) he was abruptly and without any forewarning told by his mother that, after the current month, she would no longer pay for the analysis.[2] Ingmar said: "My mother says there are many people who have problems, and they deal with them. My situation is no different than that of others. Psychoanalysis is a luxury." No discussion was possible. "She does not understand the severity of my problems." Right after that the spiral of regression, which had not been present for nine months, set in again, with uncontrolled recourse to alcohol and drugs and loss of his job. His family insisted that he break off the treatment with me and enter treatment with behavior modification and medication. I have not heard from him since.

---

[2]He had turned over his entire income to his parents and had done much of the work in the parental household, as partial payment for his room, board, and treatment bill.

Return of the Denied

The conflict solution attained by drug use, and more generally, by addictive behavior, is precarious and self-defeating. Its untenability is spelled out by the *"return of the denied"* (Waelder, 1951). What should have been warded off in that solution reappears in distorted but powerful form, and in a more primitive shape than when it was originally fended off. I will briefly sketch the way this defense against the superego and the return of the denied takes place:

1. Instead of an ideal of himself that he aspires to reach, the patient looks for a state of ideal gratification, grandiosity, and pacification here and now.
2. Instead of having the corrective of self-criticism and self-punishment within, the patient provokes chastisement and penalty from without.
3. Instead of a finely tuned, functioning capacity for self-observation, there is great readiness and often immense sensitivity to shaming and humiliation felt or provoked from others.
4. Instead of accepting limitations imposed by reality and by previous commitments, he both flees and searches for them. He is claustrophic, yet paradoxically, seeks out confinement and restrictions.
5. Instead of the self-care and self-protection vested in the superego (Schafer, 1960; Khantzian, 1978, 1987; Khantzian and Mack, 1983; Krystal, 1978c, 1982c) he is recklessly negligent about his own safety and survival, while doing everything to have others assume responsibility and care for him.
6. Instead of the inner stability given by the internal authority of the superego (Jacobson, 1964, 1971), there are strange flip-flops, an utter emotional unreliability, yet a craving for a person on the outside who will be trustworthy and not succumb to the disappointments and betrayals perpetrated by the patient (Wurmser and Zients, 1982).

What lies behind such a compulsive, temporary, and self-defeating overthrow of conscience? To answer this we must first step back and broaden our view by asking the epistemologic question:

What is the nature of causality specific to psychoanalysis (Grün-baum, 1984), and what place does this issue of compulsiveness have in the causal nexus?

Core Phenomena of the Neurotic Process—The Leap from Description to Explanation

When we review our experience with severely ill patients who show "addictive behavior" we find that "addictive behavior" is synonymous with severe "compulsiveness," insofar as it refers to outside factors and entails severely self-destructive consequences (Wurmser, 1987b,c).

Compulsiveness belongs to the essence of the neurotic process. We are forced to rethink the question of description versus explanation: What are the hallmarks of the neurotic process, appearing in a less pronounced way in the milder forms of neurosis and in a much sharpened and more poignant way in the severe forms of neurosis, the "borderline" disorders? What is the essence of the neurotic process? What would we describe as neurotic or more generally as "sick," without trying to explain it? And in turn: What do we as psychoanalysts consider in our work and hence in our theory as causal, and how are our interventions effective insofar as they alter the balance of such causal factors in a way the patient and we can recognize as effective in the long run.

The first and major criterion I have mentioned. As Kubie (1954, 1978) stressed, the stamp of the neurotic process is its compulsiveness—its insatiability, automaticity, and endless repetitiveness. The second one consists in the polarization of the opposites, the dichotomizing of the judgments of good and bad, of pure and impure, of sacred and demonic, of God and Devil, the extreme quality of love and hate, of trust and distrust.

Closely connected with that is the third criterion: the experience of absoluteness and globality of most experiences, the claim of totality for affective or cognitive comprehension of self and world. Wishes and affects have a particularly overwhelming, global, all-encompassing nature; they cannot be contained. Put in different words: there is an overvaluation, an overestimation of self or others; it is a transgressing of the limits, a dissolution of the boundaries, in value, truth, and action.

These three characteristics are basic in any description of the neurotic process and are glaringly obvious in severely regressed patients. Yet each of these criteria has been selected not only as a major attribute, but also misleadingly used as the explanation of what was encountered in the severe neuroses: The first criterion, repetitiveness, was hypostatized in the form of the "repetition compulsion," or, in somewhat different form, as "primary masochism" or the "death instinct." What could not be successfully treated by analysis was ascribed to the intensity of that enigmatic, probably inborn, force.

Alternatively, the second descriptively useful criterion of the polarities and radical dichotomies was taken and hypostatized in the form of the concept of "splitting," which was supposed to serve as a major tool of explanation.

The third criterion is the narcissism that is observable in any neurosis, though much more pronounced in some than in others. Here again, the valuable singling out of one descriptive aspect has been turned into the principal cause of neurosis: the basic forms of such narcissism, of such globality, especially the wishes for omnipotence, grandiosity, and entitlement, were declared the ultimate factors of explanation for the neurotic process, at least in a large group of severely ill patients. In the model of ego psychology these phenomena of globality and absoluteness were attributed to a supposed "deneutralization" of psychic energy.

Clearly each of these explanatory models, as presented for example by Melanie Klein, Kernberg, Kohut, and the adherents of ego psychology, reflects an important part of the truth; opposite perspectives complement each other. They go wrong in the leap from description to explanation. They end where the work is supposed to begin. The patient, faced with any of these three criteria taken as basic and ultimate insights, answers: "I know all that. That is what I am suffering from. That is why I came to see you. And you simply tell me this is what I should accept. The problem is that I cannot accept it and I do not know why. Please, help me to find the reason why I am so compelled, why I live in such radical opposites and feel so torn within, and why I am so

overwhelmed by feelings that flood over everything like a storm
surge."

The question remains: What is truly explanatory in psychoanalytic work? Where must we stop in the exploratory quest for inner
causality? What are the crucial, the mutative insights, hence the
causally most effective interpretations?

I would like to turn to another case as a paradigmatic illustration for the answers I shall come up with, a case of a different
type of "addictive behavior." It is also a completed analysis which
allows us a more careful study of the underlying dynamics.

The Compulsion to Commit Adultery

About twelve years ago I was consulted by a lady in her forties,
Dilecta, who, for a number of years, had been involved in one
dangerous secret liaison after another. Her marriage to a much
older husband was not unhappy, but it did lack excitement. She
professed she wanted to have fun and resented being enclosed
in a conventional marriage, a home life with two children, and a
routine job. When she engaged in serial and often concomitant
affairs she felt beset with guilt and often overcome by depression
after the exultation and triumph of sexual success. She also was
given to episodic alcohol abuse and to buying sprees that she
herself described as being of an addictive quality. But my focus
here is clearly on the issue of her "love addiction."

She was the only child of an intellectual, a spritely and dapper
but unsuccessful and alcoholic man, and a mother who was described as capricious, self-centered, and always complaining that
the birth of the child, after a series of induced abortions, had
crippled her. For many months after the birth the mother had
not been able to take care of her, and there were long, separate
hospitalizations of mother and child.

Both parents led a life given to entertainment and frivolity,
both were sexually quite seductive toward the girl, but at the same
time cruel and rejecting. From early childhood on she had been
an industrious masturbator, and the fantasy with it was that two
men or a man and a monster were fighting over her; the one

man or the monster would be killed and she would be given over as prize to the victor.

The analysis of this patient was extremely difficult. It was interrupted many times and was filled with acting out and intellectual insights that had little effect on the emotionally, socially, and physically dangerous behavior. While her husband was dying of colon cancer she was involved long distance with his best friend. She continued that affair although she had increasing evidence that her lover was bisexual and suffering from an ominous infection. Although she suspected he might have AIDS she continued having sexual relations with him. Around the same time she started another affair with a married man although aware of his blatant lies to his wife and eventually to herself as well. When the other lover died of AIDS, she was surprised to learn that although for years she had been the only one with whom he had had intercourse, it had not been because she had been special but because he had been protecting his wife and other women. In spite of that calamity she was unable to break the equally dangerous and humiliating affair with the other man. Eventually we both had to accept that as long as she continued the affair the analytic work was doomed.

About one year later, eleven years after beginning the analysis, she returned to wrap up her work with me after having broken off the liaison in rage when she saw herself again most massively deceived by him.

Up to now, her wild acting out of resentment and entitlement, in the form of a complex narcissistic scenario with double reality and massive denial, had been understood as the enactment of a triadic scene. Her symptoms seemed to have a direct oedipal quality with repeated triumph over the rival woman and successful conquest of the forbidden man. It appeared that both in childhood and in adulthood, her genital was viewed as a secret treasure better than any phallus. We now learned that what had appeared as an enactment of such a triadic scene had a quite different core.

Her masturbation fantasy included a battle in which she changed from being the victim to being the prize of the fight. It turned out that this fantasy was already a disguise of a masochistic beating fantasy in which she was the suffering one. Only if she accepted pain, humiliation, disregard, even contempt, would she be accepted by her cold, distant mother; only if she underwent sadistic teasing and taunting by her father could she get his admiration and physical closeness. Suffering was thus the condition for acceptance, love, attachment and respect. But that was not all. As in other cases of masochistic perversion, there was a complex layering of denials and reversals; most poignantly, the patient tried to alter reality through omnipotent magical means, as if to say: "By being beaten I transform suffering into pleasure, anxiety into sexual excitement, hatred into love, separation into fusion, helplessness into power and revenge, guilt into forgiveness, shame into triumph, passivity into activity" (see also Novick and Novick, 1987, 1991; Wurmser, 1993). In the overt masochistic perversion the suffering is conscious, the aim of the transformation is unconscious. In the self-destructive acting out of a love addiction and perhaps in other addictions, the suffering, including the superego responses, are defended against; only the seeming victory, the successful triumph, the narcissistic entitlement and grandiosity, appear in manifest form.

Behind the oedipal conflicts, behind the "anal" conflicts about power and control, behind conflicts about merger and individuation and self-assertion, an issue loomed up that could barely be put into words, and yet had to be reenacted in untold versions of the masochistic scenario: Better to be painfully touched than not to be touched at all, than to be lonely and isolated, than to be helplessly overwhelmed by grief and feelings of loss and the terror of aloneness—storms of affects that could not be contained by any symbolization. Her angry defiance, her narcissistic entitlement and spite, her thumbing the nose at outer and inner authority, all were ultimately attempts to defend against her horror and pain of profound separation, reaching back to the early months of infancy.

Only the analysis of this underlying masochistic fantasy and the conflicts behind it removed the compulsive acting out. The analysis could now be completed within two months.

Core Conflicts

What were the major conflicts that came together in this fantasy and the compulsive, "narcissistic" reenactment? I will briefly summarize the most prominent ones:

Although the entrance into the fortress of the neurosis, especially with severe cases such as this patient, can come through many gates, I have found that access through the superego conflicts is particularly helpful. I specifically refer to conflicts between opposite demands of conscience, between opposite ideals, commitments, and obligations that allow relatively quick access to intense inner conflicts. As so often occurs, the superego had become the repository of the brutality and horror of the traumas suffered and of her struggle against that suffering.

As in the previous case, there was an issue of severe and manifold loyalty conflicts, both vis-à-vis her parents, who often were locked in bitter combat, and between them and the other relatives who functioned, in her words, as a "Greek chorus," warning her parents about their profligacy, their negligence, and waywardness. The voices of both sides were replicated by her—in action!

I also refer to the opposition between guilt and shame. The conscience has become the executor of archaic versions of guilt and shame and thus dramatically split. Originally shame and guilt are antithetical: shame refers to weakness and powerlessness, and guilt refers to strength and power. They cannot be reconciled. In her instance the dilemma was supposedly solved by a consistent attempt to turn weakness and humiliation around, turning passive into active. She inflicted on others what she feared suffering herself, inevitably burdening herself with severe guilt—in reality.

Two fantasies dealt with these superego conflicts, beside the central masochistic fantasy:

The first fantasy equated all kinds of limitations and restrictions, hence the superego, with a sense of being entrapped by a claustrum. The need to burst out of the claustrum was a flight from conscience that failed.

A second core fantasy, the centrally narcissistic one, claimed that by blurring interpersonal boundaries, by overstepping limits, by achieving fusion with others, and by excluding the differences between the sexes she could attain a sense of redemption. She sought relief in this narcissistic fantasy from an overweaning superego and protection against profound, traumatic helplessness.

Narcissistic problems and disturbances always involve superego conflicts. Clinically, it is far more helpful to treat narcissistic conflicts as results of superego conflicts than the other way around: to see narcissistic disturbances as more fundamental.

What I just outlined points to another deeply repressed and yet massively influential conflict in this patient as in the case of Ingmar: the clear opposition between her needs to belong and the needs to be herself, separation and individuation versus belonging and merger.

The fierce oedipal competition was condensed in the feeling of being the excluded third and in fantasy scenarios to reverse this. The wish to have the father for herself, to become his wife, and to kill off her mother, had remained close to consciousness; its elaboration did not diminish the compulsiveness of her reenactment. This wish was countered by the rage at her father's belittling of her mother and herself.

The primary fantasy in this context was that of resentment, *Ressentiment*: "I have been cheated. I have been loyal and expected justice, but I have been dealt with unfairly." This fantasy led to insidious attempts, in fantasy and action, to rectify the balance of justice, to redress the grievance by deposing the unjust authority within or without (Wurmser, 1988a,b).

All these conflicts got their virulence from a conflict transcending them. The elucidation of this fourth element and its embodiment in the hidden masochistic fantasy completed the puzzle and allowed the reduction, perhaps the full disappearance, of the compulsion.

It was a conflict of a particularly archaic nature, namely, between clashing overwhelming affects that could not be contained—the overwhelming terror of being separated, alone, untouched, unseen versus shame and rage. There is also the conflict between the tendency to spiral down into overwhelming affects and impulses versus the desperate effort at controlling them.

I have the impression that such overwhelming affects are a kind of psychoanalytic bedrock, transcending the power of verbal and symbolic mastery (Lichtenberg, 1983; Stern, 1985). These affect storms that are being fought off by the compulsive action scenarios are reactions to severe traumatization beginning in earliest childhood and renewed in many forms again and again. Her consistent way of dealing with being the victim was by turning the tables, turning passive into active, in the masochistic fantasy that ostensibly was to end in a narcissistic victory, yet never did in any lasting way. The compulsively attained oedipal triumph covered the hidden suffering, a triumph that never achieved its real aim: to undo the traumas. The traumas were accessible only as part of those conflicts, not directly, and only in the mirror image of their reversal.

It is only the whole "concert" of these conflicts in their specific formulations, as recast in fantasies and eventually manifested in the phenomenological features, that gives us the entire structure of causality. But what is decisive for us is that their foundation, the causality we need to get to, are those core conflicts. The recognition of them and the new attempt to resolve them brings about the effective change, the recognition of their place in the inner chain of causal connection. Outer events, constitution, biological factors, are important causal factors, but they remain outside of the domain of the psychoanalytic exploration. Analysis deals with them insofar as they are filtered through the conflicts.

The form of cause and effect specific for psychoanalysis is conflict causality. The specifically psychoanalytic path from description to explanation proceeds from the core phenomena of the neurotic process—compulsiveness, polarization, and absoluteness—as they typically are reflected in preconscious conflicts, affects, and self-protective behaviors, over the bridge of those core fantasies, to the unconscious core conflicts. Beyond those we may glimpse, over the border to other fields, core affects, of a traumatic or physiologic origin, often determining the severity of the conflicts we deal with.

The Question of Judgmentalness

> "Those who are clever and keen-minded are close to death, because they love to judge the others"
>
> (Lao Tzu)

This view of the centrality of conflict causality and the special role in it of conflicts with and within the superego corresponds to a shift in therapeutic emphasis: in the treatment of patients with "addictive behavior," as well as with "severe neuroses," special care has to be given not to assume much of a real superego role, especially not to be maneuvered into the dilemma between permissiveness and punitiveness, between collusion and prohibition, but rather, as far as this is possible, to analyze the externalized or projected superego functions, as they are manifested in the transference; instead of using the superego transference, it should be analyzed, especially in its more subtle forms (Gray, 1987, 1990, 1991). This entails avoiding being judgmental, the exertion of authority, as far as possible, explicitly or implicitly. It means in particular that aggression is not treated primarily by confrontation nor direct drive interpretations, but by defense and superego analysis. The focus is on the many layers of conflicts and on the specific range of affects they lead to. The traumas, which are refracted by those conflicts, are accessible only through such conflicts.

There is no assumption of a superego defect, a superego lacuna (Brenner, 1982), but of severe conflicts within the superego. Nor is there an a priori assumption of visible, deep ego defects, except for the intolerance toward certain specific affects; only at the end of thorough conflict analysis is it possible to pinpoint possible ego defects.

Deficit psychology and conflict psychology are two different visions of man; they are complementary to each other, not an either-or, but they set very different goals and dictate quite different approaches.

Much importance is given to a rational alliance and hence to a therapeutic atmosphere of kindness and tact which facilitates such an alliance. In most cases, auxiliary measures such as medication, marital or family therapy, self-help groups, even behavioral treatment are needed because of the severity of affect intolerance and flooding, and hence the severity of conflict and superego pressure. Almost without exception a treatment strategy combining several simultaneous modalities is needed. We should realize that the success rate of Alcoholics Anonymous and Narcotics Anonymous is 14 to 18 percent, if all patients who seek help from them are counted. This does not detract from the value of these self-help groups, only from the claim that they are a panacea.

Chapter 4

Disorders of Emotional Development in Addictive Behavior

Henry Krystal, M.D.

The early analysts applied the newly developing psychoanalytic techniques with care and wisdom, contributing important insights which remain the framework that is used by all workers in this field. Some of the contributions of the early analysts such as Abraham (1916, 1924), Simmel (1930, 1948), and Rado (1926, 1933) have become such a deeply ingrained part of the American psychological, psychiatric, and medical lexicon that one frequently encounters their ideas and terms used as commonplace expressions without recognition by the speaker of their origin. Many of our old terms are no more put in quotation marks than phrases from the Bible or Shakespeare. These early successes had a built-in naiveté, however, which had to bring our "beginner's luck" to an end. The original weakness consisted in the early analysts approaching all patients with the insights, models, and techniques developed in their work with neurotics. Once a successful way to work was established, the original theories were used to explain those behaviors that fit the model. There was not an organized or persistent effort to search for new and unique problems of a radically different nature. Quite the contrary path was followed. We became keener and more sophisticated in elaborating the neurotic patterns, conflicts, fantasies, and symptoms, and tended to overlook and leave untouched the extraneurotic parts of our patients. We have, for example, spent fifty years getting over our original preoccupation with the discoveries related to anality in toddlerhood and have finally "discovered" the equally important separation and individuation of the baby in the same age period.

In a similar fashion, considerations of epigenetic development were expected to pertain to partial drives. After a new model of the mind became available, one based on where we see conflict, it was exciting and fruitful to follow defenses, the development of "the ego," and even some object relations. Amidst all that progress and excitement, it is amazing that no psychoanalyst until 1953 made any comment or inquiry about how the emotional expressions and experiences changed from birth to death. After his immigration to the United States, Schur seems to have worked for a while as both an analyst and a dermatologist. One of his patients (who developed itching whenever her husband appeared on the scene) inspired him to consider whether her symptoms represented a regression in the physiological aspect of the affect of anxiety (Schur, 1953, 1955). After a delay of about ten years, a number of analysts contributed reports describing evidence of the genetic view of emotions.

From this beginning we have built up the story of affect epigenesis, regression, and developmental arrest. Among the early pioneers we can list Engel (1962a,b, 1963) and Schmale (1964). Valenstein (1962) had an insight which he mentioned (in a footnote), but did not elaborate. It consisted of his impression that emotions evolved from precursors: "Uraffects."

I did a retrospective study of 1098 patients who had been treated for withdrawal from opiates (predominantly heroin), at the Detroit Receiving Hospital between 1956 and 1959 (Krystal, 1962). In 875 patients the records were detailed and complete enough to conclude that although these patients complained of all the physiological symptoms usually associated with anxiety or depression, they never recognized nor complained of any unpleasant *feelings*. So, I reflected at the time:

> The present work suggests that this regressive phenomenon causes the addicted person to experience anxiety and depression in two ways similar to the reactions of an infant. 1) The reaction is somatic, with little reflective awareness of it, as if this self-perceptive function of the Ego were inactivated. 2) As in the infant, there is little or no differentiation between depression and anxiety. Instead, one sees a generalized "unpleasure" response, primarily on a lower than adult level of integration [Krystal, 1962, p. 61].

Since I was also director of an alcoholism clinic, and finding the same problems there, I made a number of attempts to communicate these findings to my colleagues (Krystal, 1959, 1963, 1966, 1974). What followed was an exciting development, the impact of which can be fully appreciated only in retrospect. While this work was going on, I became involved in working with a large population of Holocaust survivors including almost 900 former concentration camp inmates. My observations of such a large population indicated to me that severely traumatized individuals showed the full picture of affective disturbance. Not only did the Holocaust survivors appear to show what Minkowski called "Affective Anesthesia" (1946); on closer inspections and follow-up, most of the patients had no use of their emotions as signals to themselves. Their affects were undifferentiated, and, for the most part, either the physiological component alone was manifest or no aspect of emotions was registered in response to disturbing circumstances or memories. Only the physiological components of chronic hypervigilance (a variety of muscle tension states, readiness to startle, insomnia with repetitive anxiety dreams), along with a spectrum of depressive and masochistic character traits could be observed. The patients did not complain of problems with "feelings," just listed the physical symptoms. When questioned about "nervousness," they admitted that they were irritable, jumpy, or very worried (Niederland, 1961, 1964; Krystal, 1968; Krystal and Niederland, 1968, 1971).

Eventually these patients blossomed out with a wide variety of psychosomatic illnesses and virtually all developed serious addictive problems (in part secondary to sleep disturbances), fear of their dreams, multiple chronic pain problems which were sometimes called "palindromic arthritis" (Krystal, 1970), but which I now think of as chronic fibrositis and myositis due to tension states. If we add headaches and symptoms secondary to diaphragmatic hernia, we get a picture of people who never have a day without serious pain. Naturally, the management of physical and emotional pain (of an undifferentiated nature) requires medication or at least a lot of attention. Most of the posttraumatic patients showed psychophysiological reactions in place of emotions, virtually without regard to their pretraumatic condition. It seemed reasonable for me to see this reaction as a confirmation that this phenomenon represented a regression in affect form from the adult, mostly verbal, expression to the infantile, undifferentiated, and totally somatic affect form (Krystal, 1971). In the meantime, the picture of the developmental line of affect expression, consisting of vocalization progressing to verbalization and desomatization, became clear. There was a reciprocal explanatory interaction between the observations of affect regression and the reconstruction process of adult catastrophic trauma (Krystal, 1970).

We found two confirmatory findings indicating that we were on the right track. One was that the veterans of World War II, particularly ex-prisoners of war, showed a high incidence of psychosomatic problems as well as other symptoms which we now consider part of posttraumatic stress disorder, which includes evidence of the affective problems mentioned above (Brill and Beebe, 1955; Archibald, Long, Miller, and Tuddenham, 1962; Archibald and Tuddenham, 1965). The other striking finding was my own: I found that although the overall incidence of psychosomatic complaints in concentration camp survivors twenty-five years after liberation was 30 percent, by separately examining the group of survivors who were teenagers during the persecution, that rate went up to 75 percent (Krystal, 1971, p. 22)! It seemed that teenagers were more susceptible to this type of regression than were adults. At about the same time, a group of French psychoanalysts working with psychosomatic patients concluded that these patients could not participate in psychoanalytic treatment because they showed some peculiar disturbances not found in "good neurotic" patients. Their work was brought to our attention by Sifneos (1973). Nemiah and Sifneos (1970a) had been in contact with the European researchers and had a number of associates working with them, testing the cognitive and affective characteristics of psychosomatic patients, and exploring their responses to psychoanalytic psychotherapy. While their work stimulated a wide and fruitful response in this country and abroad, American psychoanalysts were, for the most part, unaware of it. Aside from a general disinterest in psychosomatic and addictive patients, this lack of awareness occurred because the reports were not published in the major psychoanalytic journals.

Alexithymia

A vast literature has appeared, initially stimulated by the reports of Marty and de M'Uzan (1963) and Marty, de M'Uzan, and David (1963), which directed the attention of a significant number of European workers to the cognitive and affective patterns that seem to be most conspicuous in addictive, psychosomatic, and posttraumatic patients. The early writing of Sifneos (1973) and Nemiah (1970) gives the most helpful and comprehensive descriptions of the issues involved. The Beth-Israel group applied the work of the French analysts, which tended to stress the cognitive problem (operative thinking), to their psychosomatic patients as described by Marty and de M'Uzan (1963). They found that there was an equally consistent affective disturbance. The biggest block to the possibility of engaging the patients in psychoanalytic or any anxiety provoking therapy was the nature of their emotions (Sifneos, 1967, 1972, 1972–1973, 1973, 1974, 1975; Nemiah, 1977; Nemiah and Sifneos, 1970b). The affective disturbance described above consists of a regression in affect form rendering them unsuitable for signal function. On first impression, the patients strike observers as especially practical (they like to think of themselves as "action people"). In actuality, they have a "thing" orientation as opposed to a people (and self) orientation.

Affect Components

To understand these extraordinary discoveries we have to conceptualize a broader view of affects than is usual. Freud made an error in thinking that affects are only a physiological reaction and therefore are never unconscious. He adhered to this view all of his life, even after he described an unconscious sense of guilt (Freud, 1916). In order to appreciate the complexity and subtleties of the problems we are about to consider, it is necessary to identify all components and aspects of emotions. (See schematic chart, *Information Processing View of Affects.*) All the components have to be considered because, in the normal individual, they operate together as a functional, though not an anatomical, entity.

We are most familiar with the cognitive and expressive aspect of affects. The cognitive (or idea part) of an affect consists actually of two identifiable parts. Whenever a person experiences an emotion, the emotion has a meaning which is always recognizable, albeit with some effort in those not used to do so. For instance, both fear and anxiety tell us that something bad is about to happen. The cognitive element also includes "the story behind it." Although both fear and anxiety signal impending danger, the story behind each of the two emotions is very different. In fear, the danger is external, veridical, and *avoidable.* Anxiety reflects danger, experienced as coming from "within," which is, for the most, partly unconscious. In psychoanalytic psychotherapy we try to reconstruct in the present the psychological circumstances which have produced the sense of danger. Through his associations, the patient may help us reconstruct previous occasions and circumstances when danger was generated. Because we invite associations, and interpret them according to our own psychological understanding, analysts have constructed a variety of models to organize these associations. The structural theory is a model of the mind based on the conflicting interest of aspects of the personality, while the dynamic view stresses opposing forces. But ultimately, in dealing with anxiety we come back to the question: What is the danger?

Depression signals that something bad has happened already; the subject must accept responsibility for it because of his or her badness or helplessness. Anger, by contrast, also signals that a bad thing has happened. The bad thing was done by a "bad" person whom we are entitled to hate, punish, to exact revenge.

INFORMATION PROCESSING VIEW OF AFFECTS

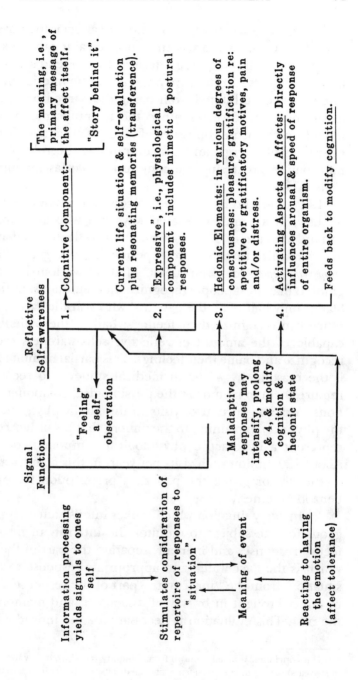

The other well-known component of affect is the physiological one which we analysts are accustomed to calling the "expressive" component, following usage derived from Freud's mistaken notion that affects secrete drive energies to the interior of the body when they are inhibited from being discharged or "expressed" to the outside. If we renounce the hydraulic model, that is, a model which focuses on issues of accumulation and discharge of quantities of energy, and concentrate on the role of affects in information processing, we come upon two fascinating observations:

1. People who have these two components of affects simultaneously, in an undisassociated way, and who are capable of a certain amount of self-observation or reflective self-awareness, may recognize that they are experiencing *feeling*; a feeling is the *subjective experience* of an affect. Medical wisdom has taken for granted that most people recognize their emotions. In the United States, only half of all the patients[1] who visit the average doctor's office can recognize their feelings; half of the patients are not capable of the amount of reflective self-awareness required to recognize and name their feelings. This partial numbness to affect is the reason why we teach medical students to recognize and require them to memorize the physiological components of emotions. A major portion of visits to the family physician end with the physician explaining to the patient that his or her complaints represent a hyperactive physiological component of an affect. About 120 million such visits per year, in this country alone, end in the doctor giving the patient a prescription for one of the benzodiazapines.

2. In every situation which evokes intense affect, it is advantageous for the subject to monitor the intensity of his or her affective responses and mentally separate the part of the response which is the "accurate" and appropriate response to the *present* situation, from the "inaccurate" part of the response, reinforced by affect brought in by way of *associations* and memories out of the past. This evaluation is necessary for the individual in order

---

[1]This conclusion is based on my informal inquiry (conducted now for approximately thirty years) asking doctors, residents, and medical students their experience in this respect.

to select the most appropriate and the most adaptive response to the disturbing stimulus out of a whole repertoire of possible responses. Whether a person is able to do this determines whether he can act according to his best judgment. Otherwise, his life is apt to be dominated by infantile responses. This observation takes us to the area of "affect tolerance."

Affect Tolerance

The question of how a patient experiences his emotions and how he reacts to having them, occupies a lion's share of the time I spend working with any patient with an affective disturbance. For normal mental functioning it is necessary to maintain affects at a tolerable intensity, allowing us to get the maximum information from them. In treating patients with affective disorders, whether they are overt and are the problem presented to the doctor, or are a covert part of the problem, as we see in psychosomatic diseases, addictions, autoimmune illness, anorexia-bulimia, and many more situations, it is essential for the analytic therapist to find out *how* the patient experiences his emotions, and how he or she reacts to having the emotion. That first question, how does the patient experience his emotions, may lead to the secrets of the preverbal and preobject disasters that befell the individual. I have become so accustomed to recognizing the aftereffects of infantile psychic trauma, that on occasion I make a direct statement that this person experienced some terrible experience in the first two years of life which they barely survived. I have in mind some combination of events tied to a failure to thrive, or marasmus. The picture I see is similar to the one documented by Engel and Reichsman (1956), Engel (1967), and Dowling (1977) in cases of esophageal atresia.

I explain to a patient who, as an infant, almost died of marasmus, that when some unbearable distress or illness could not be relieved, or maternal care was not available, their emotional reaction was almost unbearable, and they barely survived. Infantile psychic trauma sets in when the mothering parent, who ordinarily would be viewing these reactions as a call for help and would give instant congruent responses, was not able to relieve the infant. The patient may be caught in an involuntary, compulsive need to repeat the pattern of selectively retained excessive reaction to a specific affect or to the alexithymic undifferentiated affect pattern, and keep repeating the catastrophe of working himself into an unbearable state. The addictive person then becomes driven to search for the relief-giving substance or activity which enacts the reunion with the ambivalently loved primal object. The more self-destructive this process is, the more irresistible it is to some "very sick," highly aggressive addicts. When I worked at the Receiving Hospital in Detroit, I was able to recognize these individuals. Tragically, no matter what I tried at the time, everything failed to slow down the process, and some of these patients destroyed themselves within a year. In 1959 I did a study of a large population of patients with delirium tremens. An incidental finding was that 40 percent of the patients had serious physical injuries. When the patient presents himself to us with an affective disorder such as anxiety or depression it is relatively easy to determine that he or she arrives on our doorstep at the end of a vicious cycle of maladaptive responses to their own emotions, often triggered by mental events which are not identified by the patient as connected to the presenting problem. If we include infantile psychic trauma in the conditioning precursors of addiction, we gain an appreciation of Rado's prescient concept of posttraumatic "traumatophilia" (1933). The first, and perhaps most important writer about affect tolerance was Zetzel (1949, 1955). Not only did she concern herself with the practicalities of helping patients to improve their ability to keep emotions within bearable range, but she categorically stated that individuals who could not bear anxiety or depression could not use psychoanalytic treatment (p. 87). Joffe (1969) worked on problems related to envy. He felt that some people have an inborn problem with intense envy, while others, either naturally or with therapeutic intervention, improve their ability to manage their envy comfortably (p. 543). Limitations of space do not permit a full discussion of the therapist's need to keep the problem of affect tolerance in mind and to keep working on it with the addictive patient—at all stages of the therapy.

So far we have actually only discussed the cognitive and "expressive" element of an emotion. There are two more aspects of affects, the hedonic and the activating; these aspects are essential for normal living, a disturbance of either or both is a *major* component of the predisposition to drug dependence.

The Hedonic Element of Emotions

Ordinarily, we assume that some emotions have a pleasant quality and that other affects are distressful. Whether a given affect is experienced as pleasurable or distressful to a given individual in a defined situation cannot be taken for granted by an observer or even by the individual himself. My experience indicates that if we are going to talk about drugs, we have to accept evidence from many sources that *pleasure* is not the same as *gratification*, and *pain* is different and separate from *suffering* (Krystal, 1981). All four of those qualities may be experienced in relation to appetitive or gratificatory motivations and activities. All four may be conscious or unconscious. In fact, when one uses these words in connection with affects, one becomes aware that our usage is very sloppy, and that these terms are very coarse approximations of reality. I recently read a new book by a couple of old experts who state that newborns and infants have six different states of consciousness (Brazelton and Cramer, 1990). Should we expect that the adult variations in states of arousal and consciousness are fewer than that? We now know that there are at least six spectra along which consciousness and arousal varies (Krystal, 1981). In some cases, it becomes an exceedingly difficult and complex issue to describe and define the nature of the "state of consciousness" of a given person at a specific time.

We certainly cannot maintain the simplistic view of consciousness if we consider psychotropic (not to mention psychedelic) drugs, all of which influence consciousness selectively. In fact, virtually all medications, and other factors (e.g., allergic responses) influence consciousness. In addition, there is the clinically well-established phenomenon of state-related memory, and last but not least, there are well-established anatomical and physiological apparatuses involved in hedonic regulation of the organism which, as Rado told us long ago, we have to be able to reconcile with the rest of psychoanalysis (1964, 1969).

I would like now to consider one of the "addictive mechanisms," which is made possible if the idea of pleasure is separate
from gratification and suffering is not an inseparable part of pain.
These differentiations help us to understand what happens when
we treat a patient with an incurable disease with a phenothiazine
preparation: the patient still has the pain, but he doesn't mind
it, for it has lost the quality of suffering. It is similarly conceivable
that a person derives unconscious gratification from an experience which is consciously painful. We have long been aware that
something like that had to take place in obsessive–compulsive
neurosis, we used to call it sexualization or erotization of thinking.
It is helpful to clarify our definitions by stressing that the pleasure
in a "masochistic perversion" operates on a neurotic basis; pain
is accepted as a self-sacrificial superego bribe, after which sexual
pleasure is experienced in an unmodified way. Since the gratification comes from pleasure, I think of it as a corruption of the
superego only. In cases where the gratification is derived from
pain, we witness a true perversion of pleasure regulation of the
organism. A related "perversion" of the usual survival promoting
action of the pleasure regulation of the organism occurs when
we use a substance as "problem solvent." Instead of addressing
ourselves to fixing the disturbing problem, we anesthetize part
of ourselves, and become unmindful of the unsolved and still
potentially dangerous problem. It is commonly considered a perversion of the pleasure regulation if a hungry person chews coca
leaves, which produce a numbness of mucous membranes,
allowing the individual to ignore his hunger (Krystal and
Raskin, 1970).

The Activating Aspect of Emotions

It is curious that although in some ways we are familiar with the
influence of emotions on the state of arousal and pacing of the
organism (for instance we all know about the psychomotor retar-
dation in depression and the hyperactivity in mania), we tend to
ignore the role of affective influences on the tendency to addiction which is related to the regulation of the state of arousal of
the organism. In our present context this aspect of emotions is

directly connected to the state of *animation* of an organism, and one's monitoring of this important measure becomes quite impressive when patients relate that they feel "dead" or "empty." We know that such words may be the only clue we will ever get as a warning in a suicidal teenager. So, we can imagine that such self-perceptions may be a predisposition which initiates the search for a means of blocking this state by activities or drugs. In addition, Stern has added an important insight in stressing the essential role of the mothering parent displaying "vitality affects," while in contact or even within the observational range of the baby (1985, pp. 53–61). This is one of the hitherto poorly understood phenomena of infantile psychic trauma which I have stubbornly maintained must be appreciated as the major historical factor in a predisposition to substance dependence (Krystal, 1974, 1977a,b, 1978a,b; Krystal and Raskin, 1963, 1970). It has been my impression that the activating aspect of emotions has not gained the same degree of recognition as the other components. It is essential to distinguish the "expressive" aspect of emotions which involves the autonomic nervous system plus facial muscles and tips of digits. This aspect of emotions, which we used to call the "expressive one," is related to the genesis of the commonly recognized psychosomatic diseases. On the other hand, the activating aspect of emotions is the link of mental function with all of psychobiology, and it regulates the whole-organism activation or deactivation. Many studies in this area were performed by a group of psychologists, among whom Duffy (see Duffy, 1951, 1957, 1972; Duffy and Freeman, 1933, 1948; Duffy and Malmo, 1959; Duffy, Pribram, and McGuines, 1975) was most famous and productive (for a review, see Krystal [1982a]).

The distinction between these two aspects of emotion are especially cogent in understanding the difference between isolation and the regressive nature of alexithymia. In isolation of affect the cognitive and "expressive" aspects of affect are defensively separated (Engel, 1962a), while in regression of affect, deverbalization and resomatization of affect may result in chronic hyperactivity of an organ (or organs) which is usually part of the physiology of emotion. This may go on silently until lesions are produced. For some reason, many people have difficulty in conceptualizing the responses that occur with regression of affect.

There are other manifestations of regression of emotions besides alexithymia (Krystal, 1978a,b, 1982a,b, 1985). The most common regression is the loss of the sense of time when we experience intense pain—physical or emotional. It is powerful medicine to remind the patient with a recurrent condition that the present depression, even if they believe it to be "the worst one ever," is not so different from last year's depression, which got better after a while, as will their present suffering.

In 1974 I pointed out that pain cannot be differentiated from the general "distress response" in the young infant, due to the overall immaturity of the nervous system. To put it in a psychological frame of reference, we cannot have an adult-type, localized pain until we develop a body image.

Finally, we have the currently very popular DSM-IV diagnosis of Panic Reaction (APA, 1994, pp. 397–403; NIH Consensus Statement, 1991). The defining symptoms do not correspond to the actual meaning of the word *panic*, but consist of a mixture of symptoms of the physiological components of anxiety, depression, and other dysphoric affects which is the perfect illustration of affect repression, similar to what we see in withdrawal from drugs (Krystal, 1962, 1966). Another similar picture used to be presented by patients in methadone clinics. If these patients had a physical or emotional problem, they would present themselves with palpitations, hyperventilation, constipation or diarrhea, cramps, or chest pains, explaining to their doctor, "Doc, the Meth is not holding me." Further evidence that "panic reaction" represents a regression in affects is that although the symptoms respond poorly and partially to a variety of drugs, they respond best to a low dose of an antidepressive medication. In the beginning, these patients tend to complain of the side-effects more than patients who take much higher doses of the same drugs. Breasch (1990) and Traube-Werner (1990) commented on the peculiar responses of these patients. Taylor (1986) demonstrated that panic disorder had a rich cognitive element which was missed because, in sensitive people it can be precipitated by the injection of various stimulants as well as lactates. The reason we did not catch on to the cognitive nature of the "panic reaction" is that we were accustomed to looking for sources of anxiety in the oedipal situation. As Taylor (1987) pointed out, and I have been able to confirm many times in my practice, the anxiety here is derived from much earlier sources. The work of Hofer (1978, 1981a,b, 1982, 1983; Hofer and Weiner, 1971) demonstrated the "hidden" components of attachment. The problems of attachment involve complex reactions and the cognitive element of "panic reaction" goes back to that period. The difficulty here is derived from early conflicts related to attachment, and that early kind of transference can be demonstrated in these patients, but we are still in the infancy of learning to do so.

It is inconvenient to continue to adhere to Freud's assumption that every affective response has to involve a cognitive element. The work of Jones (1982) has led us to more careful observation of babies, which is in harmony with the view proposed by Stern (1983) that infants have amodal affect responses which precede the availability of verbal or symbolic components, and that these responses are often retained in memory in that form. In working psychotherapeutically with addictive and psychosomatic patients, it is useful to assume that a major portion of the psychic residues preserved from the period of the relatedness on the basis of "affective attunement" with the mothering parent, and the affects related to the early self representations (and self attachments), remain intact in sensorimotor type of memory. Stern (1983) states that verbal development is built up "on top" of the prelanguage memory traces. The common wishful thinking, shared by many analytic colleagues, is that we can just sit back and wait and all the early, "necessary" infantile material will present itself through verbal and symbolic derivatives. This expectation is not warranted by our experience.

The belief persists that all experience can appear in verbal or symbolic form because when we are dealing with "healthy" neurotic patients, the early material can be ignored. For the rare patient who ventured into psychoanalytic treatment with conspicuous addictive or psychosomatic problems, or otherwise needed to deal with the residues of infantile psychic trauma, we can only envy those colleagues who are naturally talented, or have enough experience with direct observation of infants, to be able to recognize and use the memory traces of the early period in their analytic work. But it is not always possible to get to that material. I just learned about the father of one of my patients who had a "successful" analysis which lasted over a dozen years. Recently, he has become a severe alcoholic. We have all had successfully analyzed patients who later develop psychosomatic diseases or depression.

One important consequence of noting the finer details of affect components is the recognition of the difference between activation and excitability on the one hand and vitality on the other. Duffy (1957) observed that "these two characteristics are more likely to be negatively than positively related. The tendency to be frequently aroused leads, no doubt, to fatigue and to a consequent reduction in vitality" (p. 266). This is a characteristic trait of the addictive personality who swings from artificial highs to totally depleted and devitalized "lows."The casual observer tends to think of emotions as occasional phenomena which, as members of the self-help group "Recovery, Inc." reassure each other, "Emotions are self-limited in duration, and are painful, but never dangerous." Without taking issue with that fine group, I must assert that what is a useful emphasis for them is not the whole truth about affects. They are concerned with improving their affect tolerance of emotions intense enough to attract attention. Actually, our information processing operates on subliminal emotions, which are our information-processing "switches," without calling attention to themselves. I think a living person can no more be in a state of "no emotion" than the outdoors can be in a state of "no weather" (Krystal, 1978a). But, to be suitable to function as subliminal "switches" in all our information processing, emotions have to be capable of being reduced to subliminal, signal intensity.

One of the issues related to the state of emotional arousal of an organism is that when graphed against performance, it has an "inverted U" curve. Performance increases up to a certain point, and then falls (Freeman, 1948). The dimensions of that curve are influenced by a number of factors, including affect tolerance. Therein lies one of the confusing clinical phenomena related to drug use, particularly conspicuous in regard to alcohol; that patients can use the same drug for opposing purposes. Some people drink to relax after work, others drink to relax so they can work. Some people drink to suppress their sexual urges, others drink to be able to perform. Some people drink to numb or control their rage, others drink to work up "dutch courage" to be able to be aggressive or assertive. But the most confusing paradox is that some people drink to numb their emotions while others drink to be able to "cry in their beer." The experience of therapists is that the affects expressed in a drugged state, no matter how intense or sincere, are useless for psychotherapeutic purposes (Krystal, 1977b). As our understanding of both emotions and alexithymia deepened, I tried to describe this problem in greater detail (1978c, 1982–1983, 1988a). In the meantime, other researchers contributed important insights, particularly Hoppe's studies on "split brain," which showed that the anatomical or functional dissociation of the brain hemispheres produces alexithymia (1977, 1978, 1984).

Sifneos (1973), Von Rad (1983), Overbeck (1977), Desmers-Derosiers (1982), Gottschalk (1978), and Ten Houten, Hoppe, Bogen, and Walter (1985a,b,c) and particularly Taylor and his associates and John H. Krystal have developed instruments to measure various aspects of alexithymia (for a review, see J. H. Krystal [1988]). These tools will help us to identify patients who cannot use classical psychoanalytic treatment, and perhaps will also provide a measure of the progress of their alexithymic difficulties.

Operative Thinking and Alexithymia

The work of the Paris group of psychoanalysts led by de M'Uzan clarified the findings of earlier investigators (Ruesch, 1948; MacLean, 1949; Shands, 1958, 1971, 1976, 1977) concerning the type of cognition used by some psychosomatic patients. They discovered that these patients could not describe their feelings. They were prevented from having fantasies, and, therefore, could neither form neuroses nor develop neurotic transferences (de M'Uzan, 1974a, p. 462). They could not benefit from psychoanalytic psychotherapy.

Moreover, the same author soon realized that the situation was even more tragic because these patients experienced people around them as "meaningless reduplications . . . stripped of truly

personal traits and indefinitely reproducible according to a ste-
reotyped form" (de M'Uzan, 1974b, p. 106). I have previously
reviewed the problems of transference (1982–1983, 1985, 1988a;
Krystal and Raskin, 1981), which can be summarized by describing a few of my conclusions.

Infantile psychic trauma has a number of tragic consequences:
one thesis is that it interrupts prematurely the illusion of symbiosis
which seems to be very important despite the fact that the newborn is able to recognize his mother from day one (Stern, 1974,
1983). The illusion of symbiosis permits the infant to indulge
the fantasy of omnipotence. The premature interruption of this
contented state by long-lasting, unrelievable distress confronts the
child with an uncontrollable "external" object, and at the same
time, aggression of extraordinary intensity. It seems that the intensity of the child's affects is, even under "good-enough" circumstances, the greatest threat to harmonious development and
that the externalization of it, "the creation of an external object
representation," is the first act of the life-saving use of one's imagination. But in distress approaching trauma, the object representation is rigidly "walled-off" and the relation takes on a
permanently idolatrous nature. All goodness, all authority to exercise soothing, healing, and even regulation is attributed to it.
The self representation is left diminished of all hope of volitional
control of vital and affective functions. It is possible to imagine
all the blame and badness being attributed to the self representation. The idol can never give the worshiper the desired magic so
it must be further propitiated and appeased, and the relief from
suffering must be purchased at an ever increasing price. History
teaches us that idolatry ended up each time in human sacrifice,
usually leading to the sacrifice of the most precious ones, children
and the hearts of virgins. In our practice, these problems manifest
themselves in having to demonstrate to patients that self-sacrifice
is still a form of human sacrifice. Long ago, certainly by 1970
when Raskin and I published our book on drug dependence, we
resolved that if drug dependent and other alexithymic patients
could not use psychoanalytic psychotherapy, then we would devise
a preparatory phase of the treatment and get them ready to participate in their treatment. First, I was going to explain to them the
nature of their affective disturbance. This I did, and it worked

fine. It turned out that some patients had a vague recognition of their problem and were relieved to have it explained. Working on affect tolerance is an important psychotherapeutic task with applications to many kinds of patients; it is an issue which has to be addressed with virtually every patient who has an affective or addictive disturbance. Helping patients to recognize and name their emotions, just like parents and child analysts have always done, is an interesting and instructive experience, but mostly for the therapist. In the process of working on these issues, I discovered that many addictive, alexithymic patients had severe inhibitions in regard to self-soothing, self-caring, and even self-regulation.

The most clear-cut example is a case I would like to borrow from Edgecumbe, which she called "the patient who could not talk to herself" (1983). In an advanced stage of analysis, Edgecumbe, as a child analyst, had helped the patient to use her emotions as she used to do with child patients. The patient made great progress over several years in various respects, but then her ability to relate a story on her own became worse, and she had to be questioned by the analyst (as well as her husband) or she could not relate even the events of the day.

Edgecumbe had been aware of the life-long psychosomatic and addictive nature of this case, still she was puzzled about how this "attractive, reliable, young professional woman, who competently looks after her husband and home, as well as holding down a job and working for her parish church," felt that all the authority and power of "goodness"and caring for her was reserved for the analyst. When the patient became overwhelmed with her (undifferentiated) emotions, she had to search for Edgecumbe, and "when she found me she did not know what she wanted from me, the best she could explain was: 'I just want you to be there!' " (p. 5).

In considering this case, I felt that it represented a perfect example of *idolatrous* transference, because the patient fashioned the analyst like an idol to whom all the goodness, and the power to care for, comfort, and even *organize* her thoughts were attributed, while her self representation was impoverished, and access to her own powers was prohibited as the threat of a fate worse than death. Because this is such an extraordinary claim, I feel compelled to supply more information about the case.

The patient presented herself to Edgecumbe with a multitude of psychosomatic diseases and severe alexithymia.

> [Edgecumbe described her patient as] out of touch with her feelings. She was unable to distinguish between nausea and most other physical or mental feelings. . . . She could not describe her own state when away (from the analyst) beyond calling herself "useless," a term she also applied to herself when she was sick. . . . She often sat crying and helpless, unable to pull herself together to do anything.

When the patient was with her analyst, she expected to feel better, but instead often felt "peculiar"; for example, "her heart was pounding, she was trembling, she felt cold, when I [Mrs. Edgecumbe] said that it sounded like fear, she responded that "she could not understand why she should be afraid" (p. 1).

The following are the things that the patient learned gradually: (1) How to distinguish and name her own feelings. (2) How to link them with events and interactions with other people. (3) How to stop complying with her mother's childhood injunction: "Don't think." However, when doing this, she sometimes ended up developing "severe abdominal pain." (4) The childhood history from age 3 to 4 was of frequent nausea and vomiting, constipation, sleep disturbances, food refusal, and asthma. (5) At age 7, she developed performance inhibitions; sometimes she even refused to walk. (6) Relative to the capacity for self-care: "It took 9 months for her first statement of what she wanted, because she was terrified to say it aloud, and anyway it hadn't occurred to her that anything could be done about it." (7) "Throughout her life, she had stifled any form of creative or imaginative thinking. She could not draw or write." (8) "At her seventh birthday party, she became excited and sick. From then on she avoided all kinds of excitement and feelings and she was restricting her thinking, for fear that she would get sick. By the time she reached adolescence, she could no longer understand what her girlfriends were talking about when they discussed sex" (p. 8).

Now, I want to repeat Edgecumbe's words in describing the conversational disturbance which developed in the third year of analysis:

She never took the initiative in conversation, always asked to be asked questions. The most she could ever manage was a brief mention of events that were important to her. She then left it to the other person to pursue the topic or not. If the analyst or the husband didn't ask the questions, she could not *organize* the story (emphasis added).

Edgecumbe described some of her interpretations:

I told her (at various times) that she seemed to feel incomplete at times when she was apart from me, since I had to be the part of her which did the thinking and the feeling [p. 1].

Even now her mother tries to usurp her function of judgment and anticipation by saying: "You won't like that," "You don't want to do that" [p. 2].

"To be independent and *separate* in her thinking is too lonely and frightening, so she tried to get me to do her thinking for her to be the part of herself that tells her what to want and feel [Edgecumbe, 1983; emphasis added].

In trying to explain to myself the idolatrous nature of this transference, to consider how the patient experienced the analyst as her primary maternal love object for whom all life giving and sustaining and regulating functions ("powers") were reserved, including organizing a narrative of the day's events, I suddenly also understood why alexithymics presented their trivial accounts of what happened since the last session in a chronological order. By doing so, they used time as a "crib sheet" to deny their responsibility in organizing their thoughts. My idea about the kind of transference these patients were experiencing was confirmed in working with patients who were also in biofeedback training, while they remained in psychotherapy with me. From them I learned that they believed that if they took over the control of their vital or affective functions, which they believed to belong to mother, that would be a "Promethean" transgression, punishable by a "fate worse than death." When I learned to decode the whole message, I understood that "the fate worse than death" meant the return of the infantile trauma state. I then understood that all descriptions of Hell referred to the same fear, and the timelessness of infantile trauma accounted for the religious certainty that the torture of Hell went on "forever and ever." I also understood that whenever anyone suffers severe mental or physical pain, they *regress* and become convinced that this "time" (e.g., spell of depression) is the worst one ever and will never go away, an illustration that regression of affects is an ongoing phenomenon. The other example is that many patients, especially alexithymics, experience physical pain along with or instead of emotions. Their regression to the infantile state puts them back in a state when pain could not have yet separated from the total distress pattern.

Thus I acquired more tools for helping with affect tolerance, and I realized why it was that biofeedback training could not live up to its theoretical potential. In other words, in trying to help drug-dependent and other alexithymic patients to "get in touch with their feelings," I ran into primal object transference which posed some novel and unexpected challenges. The maternal transference turned out to be manifest in the feeling that all vital and affective functions are universally experienced and are reserved exclusively for mother. Individuals vary in the degree in which they feel that all self-caring, self-soothing, and even, as we have seen, self-regulating functions are reserved for mother, and can only be carried out "under a franchise" from a maternal transference object. It is indeed an amazing observation to ponder that we "normal," successful analysts believe that we have no power to, say, lower our blood pressure although we know that we could do it in a hypnotic trance or when given a placebo. That means that we have the capacity to exercise such function, but we have an inhibition of precisely the same kind as a hysterical paralysis. And yet, neither in regard to ourselves nor our analysands do we have the slightest inclination to get into analyzing this obvious and glaring inhibition. What could be the reason for this amazing phenomenon? This transference is different than the transferences that are uncovered and reconstructed by analysts interested in preoedipal conflicts. Recent progress in psychoanalysis, neuroscience, and cognitive psychology has opened huge areas of development so that we dare to question the meaning of the Promethean complex. These patients' inability to take care of themselves was also especially reported by Zinberg (1975) and confirmed by Khantzian and Mack (1983), a subject which is further elaborated by Khantzian in this volume (see chapter 2).

Adult Catastrophic Trauma

In adults, when the self-perception changes from one of impending *avoidable* danger which is signaled by fear or anxiety, to a conclusion that the danger is *unavoidable*, overwhelmingly destructive, and additionally, is evaluated as a situation which one is helpless to modify or escape, the affect changes from fear to the catatonoid reaction. This reaction is part of an ancient pattern of surrender common to virtually all animals. This surrender pattern contains a painless "self-destruct" mechanism, with the heart stopping in diastole (Richter, 1957; Seligman, 1975; Krystal, 1978b). The reader may recall my emphasis above that fear, anxiety, and anger are activating emotions. But when an individual decides that the danger is unavoidable, and he surrenders to it, then the affect changes from fear to the catatonoid reaction, an occurrence which marks the beginning of the traumatic state. The subject stops fighting or resisting, obeys orders, and "freezes." The more he obeys orders or remains in a helpless state, the "deeper" or more profoundly or irreversibly the trance-like submission develops. All these reactions may be continued as components of posttrauma sequelae (Krystal, 1978a,b,c, 1979, 1982–1983, 1985, 1988a). As the traumatized state progresses, there is a numbing of the registration of pain and painful feelings, followed by a progressive constriction of cognition including perception, conscious registration, memory and recall, scanning, problem solving, judgment, and planning. This picture was called "psychic closing off" (Lifton, 1968). The loss of memory and recall deprives the victim of access to "benign introjects." Among the aftereffects that concern us here are irreversible changes of self representation which may include the shattering of predominant, grandiose ideas often based on identification and making the maintenance of coherent self representation impossible.[2] The

---

[2]This is the "Narcissistic Blow" which Wurmser discovered to be the start of the self-destructive "Heptade" of the addict (1978).

traumatic situation may be absolutely incompatible with the "perceived acceptability or visibility" and handled by primary repression creating a "hole," the very existence of which may become
the dominant personal organization which Cohen and Kinston
call "an Object-Narcissistic state." It may become the imperative
determinant of the defensive style for the future (Cohen, 1980,
1987; Kinston and Cohen, 1986, 1987). Also, in the adults surviv-
ing a severe cognitive constriction, the last step before psychogenic death includes complicated consequences of the
confrontation with death such as inability to restore the denial
of death, identification with death, or with the dead (Lifton, 1976,
1979). But the part of the trauma process which continues for
life, and which I am stressing, is the affect regression (i.e., the
affect component of alexithymia and probably closely related
problems of anhedonia). It should be kept in mind that although
I am not going to trace the aftereffects of these other factors
in this essay, the serious student who wishes to understand the
modifications which make psychotherapy with addicts possible
has to include them all in the picture.

Infantile Trauma

After I learned to recognize the signs of posttraumatic sequelae
in adults, I realized that alexithymic, anhedonic patients, particularly those with severe and widespread inhibitions in self-caring,
were suffering from the aftereffects of infantile trauma. This type
of trauma occurs in early life, and is caused not by the perceived
meaning of helplessness and surrender, but by the nature of infantile affect precursors, and the nature of the infantile, imma-
ture mind. Although the infant reaches a state of distress in which
it becomes virtually impossible to comfort and soothe, unlike the
adult, it does not die, for it has a natural protection so that eventually it goes off to sleep. But, repeated severe traumatization results
in a failure to thrive and the states of apathy and withdrawal,
known by many names such as marasmus or anaclitic depression
(Spitz, 1946). If attachment to a single mothering parent is prevented, the baby dies. If the child is saved and survives the trauma,
it can be later identified by a fear of all affects and sometimes

a profound distrust of all people, a "doomsday expectation," a profound belief that no matter how well things go, security will suddenly collapse. They tend to have severe inhibitions in all self-caring functions, and they are the kind of people who need someone "to help them make it through the night." They have severe alexithymia and anhedonia. They have, in contrast to the adult group, often no recollection of the trauma, and no one in the family may have an idea that anything went wrong. What was pure hell to the baby may have been in accord with the best judgment of the caretaker or the recommendations of a physician or religious authority; for example, those favoring the "breaking of the spirit of the child" as the surest prevention of a future "sin of pride."[3]

Operative Thinking

One of the difficulties that I avoided discussing so far is the severe inhibition in the alexithymic–addictive individual's capacity to form wish-fulfillment fantasies. As will be recalled, this was the characteristic discovered when the Paris and Beth-Israel psychoanalytic psychosomaticists discovered that these patients could not use psychoanalytic psychotherapy. Of course, their impairment in the ability to form fantasies and to use them defensively prevented them from becoming neurotic in the first place. So, it became evident that the reason they could not be induced to form a good neurotic-type transference, which we have been trained to work with, was because they needed to form another type of transference which was so strange to us that it seemed like no transference at all.[4]

What is striking is the very slight interest that the patient shows in the analyst. The relationship is courteous and correct, but libidinally very poor. The organization of this relationship seems to be

---

[3]Among the difficult problems to understand is the problem of shame which in the addict is of deadly intensity—denoting a state of being a "reject" in the eyes of the mother, God, and the patient himself (Wurmser, 1981a).

[4]This is so crucial that I will repeat this quotation, for we are going to apply it to broaden the context.

conventional and personalized to such a small degree that the
neurotic mechanism seems to be lacking. A sort of inertia, noticed
during the preliminary interview, persists and results in a stagnant
situation [de M'Uzan, 1974a, p. 462].

In my earlier work, I spelled out the details of the alexithymics'
problems in psychotherapy and their presumptive genesis (1971,
1979, 1981, 1982–1983, 1985, 1988a). I will just review a few clinical problems without going over the history of the laborious way
they were derived.

The aspect of infantile psychic trauma, which I discussed before, has another tragic consequence because it interrupts prematurely the *illusion* of symbiosis which seems to be very important
despite the fact that the newborn is able to recognize his mother
from day one (Stern, 1983, 1985). The illusion of symbiosis permits the infant to indulge the fantasy of omnipotence. The premature interruption of this contented state by long-lasting,
unrelievable distress confronts the child with an uncontrollable
"external" object, and at the same time, aggression of overwhelming, disorganizing intensity. In a number of my previous studies
of this subject, particularly in my paper entitled "Self Representation and the Capacity for Self Care" (1977b), I pointed out that
the severity of inhibition of self-care seemed proportional to the
history and difficulty in handling aggression in early childhood.
This point was also noted by Khantzian (1978) and Zinberg
(1975). I concluded, in a manner not too dissimilar from Melanie
Klein, that the intensity of rageful feelings the infant makes the
mother experience is very dangerous (1946). Unlike Klein, I
found evidence that the maternal object was "externalized" and
"walled off," instead of the rather early access to the maternal
representation as if the mother was external, but easily available,
and could be used at times as if she was a selfobject, or part of
the self, or even food. In the addicts, the maternal representation
was rigidly walled off, and all the goodness was attributed to it.
This operation constituted a precursor of the later addictive orientation, one where an "external" object is necessary to obtain
any succor. Transgression of the walling off of mother's goodness
is experienced as a "promethean" crime punishable by a fate
worse than death. It seems that the intensity of the child's aggression is, even under "good-enough" circumstances, the greatest

threat to harmonious development. The externalization of the aggression through "creation of an external object representation" is the first act of life-saving use of one's imagination. The "taming" of our early affects, and the joint creation of the maternal and the paternal object representations by the mother and the baby together is difficult even when it takes place in a timely and reassuring setting (Dorsey, 1971a,b; Winnicott, 1971; Arvanitakis, 1985). In situations of threatened, impending, or actual traumatic state, the object representation is rigidly "walled off" and the predominant object relation is likely to take on a permanently idolatrous nature. All goodness, all authority to exercise soothing, healing, and even regulation is attributed to it. The self representation is left greatly diminished of all hope of volitional control of vital and affective functions. If it is possible to imagine, all the blame and badness is attributed to the self representation on a nonverbal level. The more severe the child's suffering the greater the shift to self-blame. Under these circumstances, there is created a need for an "addictive object"—some thing or act which is external to the self representation. It can serve to soothe one, but cannot be made or felt to be part of one's self. Our increasing awareness of the severe consequences of the abuse of older, verbal children leaves no room for doubt about the nature of the possibility and my pictures of the early reactions. The major additional problem in dealing with the survivors of infantile trauma is that the significant "problem" transferences are preverbal, amodal, sensorimotor. As already mentioned, our work indicates that Stern (1985) is right in assuming that the object relation and memory traces derived from preverbal, presymbolic affective attunement remain in their original state, and the verbal relations and memories are built up "on top" of the infantile foundation, the translation into the verbal, which most analysts are trained to expect is minimal (Krystal, 1988a).

One observation that illustrates this point goes back to an observation of McDougall back in 1974, confirmed many times in my own and others' experience with the treatment of alexithymic patients. Once safely ensconced in the treatment, they are perfectly satisfied to keep coming, giving a trivial and boring recitation, without complaining about the lack of progress. The therapeutic zeal displayed by the analyst in such a case betrays the therapist's failure to comprehend the nature of idolatrous transference. The basic defect of the addict is his or her inability to see themselves as complete, self-reliant, self-evaluating individuals. No matter what the presenting diagnosis, when we discover that at the core the patient's self-image is an incomplete creature, requiring someone to love them (always), we are dealing with an addict. The patient's assumptions are: "If you loved me, everything would be perfect. If things are not perfect, you do not love me, you hate me, you despise me, I am worthless, and you have changed into a cruel, evil witch." The old saying of Fenichel that we must understand the patient's "object addiction" (1945) comes back, but in much darker hues. The idol must be propitiated, and the relief from suffering must be purchased at an ever increasing price. The biblical struggle against idolatry reflects the victory of sublimation over the need to sacrifice the first-born son (Menninger, 1938; Simmel, 1927). One of the major yields of our studies on the genetic development of affects was the realization that in infancy affects have not matured enough to serve in the formation of the early self and object representation in the adult fashion, and that the hedonic component of affects develops early and serves alone in the earliest formation of the object image. This "naked" rule of the pleasure and punishment regulatory functions accounts for the extreme force and implacability of the drivenness of the "true addict" (the kind we used to call "oral character," as opposed to the "neurotic addict"). In these patients, distress or deprivation is automatically judged as a state of great peril, and one indicating to them the helplessness and worthlessness of the self (Wurmser, 1981a; Hadley, 1983, 1985; Krystal, 1981, 1988a).

So the answer to McDougall's riddle is that the disaffected is not in analysis to reclaim the alienated parts of his soul. Far from it; he lives in the dread expectation of the return of his infantile traumatic state. He is still engaging in appeasing the idol by human sacrifice in its most common and most popular form—self-sacrifice. Why are we bothering him with our countertransference preoccupation with the need for progress? No thanks, he tells us, things are going about as well as can be expected. And, they add, "One can trust a 'thing' much more than a person."

When this was understood, I was still puzzled. Why is there a cognitive disturbance in alexithymia in addition to the regression in affect? In order to understand this, we had to wait for the progress in child development. Bowlby's (1969, 1977, 1980) emphasis on the process of attachment as a primary need of every baby (and all mammalian young) replaced the older view that because the mother gratified the infant's partial drives, there was (secondarily) an attachment to her. This change in emphasis resulted in a tremendous expansion in developmental psychology and physiology, with advances in our understanding of various early interactions, particularly of the nature and centrality of transitional object precursors.

Attachment is an intrapsychic act. It is manifest by all "attachment behavior"; that is, the actions whose effect it is to keep the primary object near. Besides these "visible" manifestations of attachment, there turned out to be another "hidden," and far more important attachment behavior for us to ponder. The work of Hofer and others showed that the mother and baby acted like one open system, mutually influencing each other's physiological regulatory systems, a process which is essential to the development of the young, and the maintaining of maternal behaviors in the caregiver (Hofer, 1978, 1981a,b, 1982, 1983, 1990; Hofer and Weiner, 1971). There was simultaneous development of the appreciation of the role of early *transitional object precursors* (Gadini, 1975, 1987), an integration of physiological and psychological developmental processes in the preparation and practicing of the somatic and ego apparatus essential in the creation of the self representations and the representation world (Hadley, 1985). We also learned and have a lot more to learn about the things that can go wrong with the transitional object development (Tustin, 1980, 1981; Deri, 1984). Finally came the illumination of the discovery of the essential function of the transitional object in *solacing* all the rest of one's life (Horton and Sharp, 1981, 1984; Horton, Gewirtz, and Kreutter, 1988). From this work, and the work of other developmental psychologists, an amazing story emerges.

Early human development depends on tactile, vestibular, and a multiplicity of other physiological stimuli. Suckling provides not only nutrition, but a variety of essential regulations to the physical

and psychological development of the infant, including preparation of the framework for creativity and solacing. The early transitional affect precursors may be parts of one's self (sucking on
one's tongue or cheek) before the infant masters the finger-to-
mouth connection, which is accompanied by a multitude of direct
into-the-mouth transitional objects which are direct mother substitutes. They provide for physiological regulation and direct his
physical and mental development just as a good mothering parent
does. If this process is not interrupted by infantile traumatic experience, the transitional objects become increasingly abstract, so
that a nursery rhyme, a song, and eventually highly abstract mean-
ings, melodies, colors, and harmonies, the appreciation of order,
security, and *love* can be developed and used for a lifetime of ever
increasing inner resources (Krystal, 1988c).

The traumatic events of infancy can interrupt all of these.
Creativity is not cultivated and the imagination cannot be put in
the service of solacing and gratification. The operative thinking
becomes the last line of defense against the reemergence of the
split, idealized, but also vilified object. In analysis it is too dangerous to reopen the free fantasy life, for the analyst, like the primary
object, may turn out to be the evil witch who delights in torture,
and whose objective is "soul murder" (Shengold, 1989). If the
infant's early experience is traumatic, if there is a poor match
between the mother and the baby's temperament, or its psychic
apparatus is too irritable, even a good mother cannot achieve a
way to soothe the baby and help the infant to discover his own
soothing potential. If she cannot establish comfortable mutually
shared rhythms, the potential transitional object may become an
"autistic object" used especially to exclude the primary object
(and with it any hope for a benign world). We can recall that this
is just a magnification of the turn from mother to things which
we saw in infants who are inadequately mothered (Greenspan,
1981) and which we rediscover in alexithymic, addictive individuals. The profound ambivalence, fear, and preference for short-
acting intoxicants as compared to taking a chance on a person,
were all well known to us before we understood their infantile
roots (Krystal and Raskin, 1970). I believe that there is universal
recognition, rarely consciously faced, that *the most* addictive substances contain the reunification and concretization of the object

of the quest of the "hero" on his journey; the yearning to be reunited with the mother-lover-goddess found in all myths and fables. She offers gratification and punishment, oblivion, love, and death (Campbell, 1989).

Discussion

In emphasizing the special problems of the posttraumatic, alexithymic, anhedonic, addictive individuals, I did not mean to suggest that all drug-dependent individuals conform to this model. In the first place, I feel that the individuals identified as addicts represent a small minority of people who actually depend on a variety of drugs. In my opinion, everything that we say about "addicts" refers to the unsuccessful drug users, whom we call pejoratively "abusers." These individuals are not able to handle the drugs for many reasons, some of which Rado pointed out in 1926, and elaborated further in 1933. The major problem is one of severe ambivalence, and consequently fear and guilt for taking the drug. Rado emphasized that the habitual use of drugs to improve one's feelings, in the place of solving a problem or accepting a painful reality (the addictive pattern), also signifies the giving up of the "reality-oriented regime of the ego." Because of the ambivalence, guilt over aggression accompanied by magical thinking, there is an ever deepening dysphoria which requires an increased use of the drug which ends in the development of a "pharmacothymic crisis" in which the drug can no longer lend relief. A paranoid panic results, or so much has to be taken, that an overdose, sometimes a deadly one, results. Now we can add that in these individuals all forms of self-gratification are forbidden and generate the kind of guilt and expectation of such terrible punishment that most people cannot even imagine the nightmarish inner life of the addict. Another thing we have to add to Rado's conception is that he thought that the reaction to the loss of the ability to get relief would be rage, fear, helplessness, and affects that we could discuss with the patient. Already in 1961 I found that the reaction consisted of the physiological component of infantile-type, undifferentiated affects which were not useful as signals. My youthful expectation that I was going to start my psychotherapy on the remorseful and miserable addict in withdrawal who could see that drugs did not work for him, did not materialize.

Luckily, most drug users are successful, do not lose control of their "rituals," and never come to our professional attention. But to return to the "unsuccessful addicts"; in addition to affective problems I described, there are the problems for which the currently popular term is *dual diagnosis*. If I cannot tell how many of these patients could also be classified in other categories, I can say that just about all Borderline Schizophrenic individuals are among the hardest mixed drug users to treat (Southwick and Satel, 1990), and their periods of successful drug use are short, the crises severe in line with their rages, splitting, idealization, and vilification of their object representation. The point is that since their views of themselves and their object relations are virtually totally fantasy dominated, the disappointing object instantly turns into the poisonous evil witch and the pharmacogenic crisis is often a matter of life and death.

The proliferation of medical committees "on the well-being of physicians" has brought to our attention the fact that in addicted doctors, the most common *surface* problem is severe compulsiveness, driven by an unrealistic perfectionism. In this group, the inclination to view one's self as a machine induces the physician, or related professional, to regulate their body and daily activities without paying attention to their own condition, but to use a multitude of drugs to turn themselves into the most effective, most efficient "robot" possible. The doctors, including psychiatrists, are doing this mechanistic control treatment to such a degree that they also "fine tune" their patients to their highest chemical potential. We have even caught athletes in our chemical mechanical orientation and fortified them with the shaman's magic disguised in our chemical and mechanistic art. We have been using anabolic corticoids with athletes, and every self-respecting team should also have a team hypnotist who can break records and ignore the athletes. A patient of mine, a doctor who was aware that he was having "a little coronary," but resolved to finish his night's work in an industrial clinic, was merely one of the most successful products of present-day medical education in which we push memorization, require our apprentices to work enormously long hours with little undisturbed sleep, and pile upon them an increasingly heavy bureaucratic burden of paper work. We pay no attention to the fact that while these wretches are dragging themselves through the day in a semistuporous condition, they are also at least weekly receiving visits from attractive retail drug representatives who are their most charming and generous with free drugs for their future partners in the "Health Industry," together with whom they will be soon experienced as a problem, if not a menace to society. As in the family, the things we teach which may be most important are not in anybody's official curriculum.

This problem reminds me that in our 1970 book, Raskin and I called the addict's relationship to the drug "a case of extreme transference" in which, because of the ambivalence, the conspicuous activity was the attempt to take in the object substitute. But the drug turns out to be evil, poisonous, and painful. Considering the bigger picture, we find that the addict labors on the riddance of the evil object (with whom, unlike the schizophrenic, he cannot maintain a permanent fantasy of fusion), and their rituals and symptoms, as well as implicit fantasies, are the "poisoned apple" from the witch-mother, which produces the pain of hangovers and withdrawal. Here we need to remind ourselves of a common experience known to all those who put in years in methadone clinics. Frequently, when the addicts who were successfully maintained on methadone ran into any kind of problem, physical or verbal, bad luck, financial, social or romantic, they would start to develop symptoms of withdrawal from the drugs. These symptoms are also the very mixture of undifferentiated, mostly physiological components of affects which they were trying to "block" or numb with the drug in the first place. The social dimension of their problems is brought up here to remind us that the treatment of drug dependence does not address itself to the actual problem, but a pattern of failure to help one's self.

We are all in agreement that we must work with all the people with something to offer, especially Alcoholics Anonymous, Narcotics Anonymous, and related groups; no single therapist solves all the problems. As a matter of fact, I found rather early that certain types of addicts (approximately the ones we might call "junkie") do better in a clinic than working with a solo therapist

because they need to be able to "split" their ambivalent transferences. There is some positive transference to be found in the
relationship so the treatment can continue (Krystal, 1964).

The latest estimation is that about 30 percent of addicts have
serious, significant affective disorders that require treatment—all
other things being equal (Kleber and Gold, 1978; Mirin, Weiss,
Soloqub, and Jacqueline, 1984). Let me reemphasize that with
the constant proliferation of psychotropic drugs by the "ethical"
as well as bootleg pharmaceutical industry, individuals in all walks
of life will be found to be heavy and steady drug users. Many are
drugs prescribed for muscle relaxation, disturbances of attention,
and antihistamines. The over 100 million prescriptions per an-
num for benzodiazapines will eventually produce many "normo-
paths" who have to be withdrawn gently while the underlying
problems are being reconsidered. Addictive mechanisms should
be in the analyst's mind with all patients.

Conclusions: On a Few Therapeutic Problems

The emphasis in this paper on the posttraumatic factors in the
starting and maintaining of drug dependence necessitates that
we say a word about the perceptual and defensive functions in
trauma prevention. Freud accurately inferred that the determination of total helplessness and surrender to it, which starts the
traumatic process, is a subjectively determined act. This view has
withstood the test of time and the present-day explosion of studies
on posttraumatic problems. On the other hand, Freud's view of
perception was that it was superficial, and accurate even in traumatic situations. Freud simultaneously proposed two definitions
of trauma in 1893. The first definition is that trauma consists of
an individual being confronted by overwhelming emotions. The
second definition is: "When the incompatibility forces itself upon
the ego . . . and at which latter decides on the repudiation of the
incompatible idea. That idea is not annihilated by a repudiation
of this kind, but merely repressed into the unconscious" (p. 123).
Freud envisioned that the repressed perception was perfectly perceived and preserved in this perfection in the state of repression.
This view was retained in the second volume in the Workshop

Series (Rothstein, 1986). In my opinion, it is not compatible with the tasks and experiences in working with posttraumatic patients, and it has an important bearing on the question of applicability of psychoanalysis to drug addiction (Krystal, 1988b). In my book review, I noted the crucial importance of Dowling's contribution. He emphasized that it is the psychic experience and interpretation (i.e., the *meaning attributed to a percept*), which had the traumatic potential. Thus, "Reconstruction of trauma is, like reconstruction in general, an effort to present to the patient the events, feelings, fantasies, and thoughts that make up the experience" (Dowling, 1986, p. 215). This point was also made by Brenner. As I already mentioned, by retaining Freud's original model of perception, the effect of the whole volume was to perpetuate the original error of our approach to the addictions; we were trying to view and treat the addicts with methods and theories that are "good enough" for the neurotics. The outcome has been tragic, and the time has come to bring our knowledge and practices up to date in the areas where progress has been made.

I will only mention a few examples of such opportunities.

1. We know now that perception is a complex, multistep process, with a reworking of the early, vaguest, unconscious registration to the "final" stimulus-proximate registration in regard to which, in the small minority of percepts which become conscious, we can expect "intersubjective" agreement.
2. Simultaneously with the reworking of the percept, a parallel operation is going on to answer the question, What is that? This part of the processing of perceptions as well as impulses and ideas is achieved by bringing in associations. The associations, like all mental elements, carry with them signal affects (i.e., affect of subliminal intensity). These signal affects mobilize defenses, often of the type related to the predominant characterological traits types, which determine how, and where, in what state of consciousness, an idea or percept shall register (Westerlundh and Smith, 1983).
3. If the percept is experienced as dangerous ("painful," Dorpat, 1985), then, in Dorpat's model, denial is activated, which initiates defensive distortions, and maybe repression of the idea. At any rate, the mental element is not left in its pristine form, and cannot

be expected to be recovered with the expectation that it will give us an accurate retrospective view of "external reality."

4. There is evidence in the work of a number of authors (for a review see Krystal [1985]) that a traumatic perception may be experienced as incompatible with self-survival and may be destroyed and leave behind it a "hole." This imaginary vacuum is threatening to one's integrity; certain defenses are built around it, which Cohen and Kinston call "Object Narcissism"; which they allow, may be equated with alexithymia. But the critical point is that *structures* are damaged or destroyed; therefore, claim Cohen and Kinston, the kind of reconstruction that needs to be done is the reconstruction of structures. If that goal is achieved, and the reliability of the therapist is tested by serious, sometimes life-threatening crises, then the therapist and patient working together may, for the first time, jointly create the missing mental elements. To this I have added that such an event most likely takes place in a state of altered consciousness (Krystal, 1988a).

5. Lastly, I want to mention once more that in the addictive individuals who suffer the aftereffects of infantile psychic trauma and have severe inhibitions in self-care, we can expect an idolatrous transference, which means that we have to prepare ourselves to deal with residues of early preverbal memory traces, and need to find out how to deal with the reexperiencing of amodal, sensori-motor transferences and affects.

Chapter 5

Erotic Passion: A Form of Addiction

Anna Ornstein, M.D.

There is a tendency nowadays to refer to an array of symptomatic behaviors that do not involve the use of drugs or alcohol as "addictive." Anorexia and bulimia, sexual excesses, gambling, all have been referred to as "addictive," primarily because these forms of symptomatic behaviors are driven by strong unconscious imperatives and are subjectively experienced as obligatory and peremptory. If this use becomes indiscriminate, however, it may eventually make the word *addictive* useless in the clinical situation.

In the clinical example I shall describe, it was the compulsive nature of the patient's love relationships that had "addictive" qualities. The paper will focus on those significant pathogenic factors which could be reconstructed in the course of the analysis and helped explain the source of the patient's "sexual addiction."[1]

---

[1]A psychoanalytic answer as to what motivates a particular addictive behavior can only be found by the in-depth study of an individual case. Generalizations regarding the pathogenesis of the disorder cannot be made since the findings of psychoanalysts will differ, depending on their theoretical orientation. In this instance, the analysis was conducted in keeping with the principles of psychoanalytic self psychology.

101

Clinical Example

At the time of referral, Mrs. Holland was a 35-year-old married
woman with two young children. As an aspiring artist she did
some painting in her home. Though considered gifted, she never
took formal instruction. As I was to learn in the course of the
analysis, the biggest obstacle to her being an accomplished
painter was her self-image. She felt that her paintings were not
good enough for her to attend a school and, at the same time,
she was convinced that her work was superior and therefore she
ought not to need instruction. In fear of criticism, she did not
dare show her paintings to anyone but had elaborate fantasies of
being "discovered" one day.

The patient was referred for analysis by her husband's analyst.
Her husband was concerned with this wife's erratic behavior: she
would impulsively leave the house (though never jeopardizing
the children's safety) and had periodic, rather severe depressions
during which she spoke of suicide. The patient welcomed the
referral as she felt herself to be "on the brink" of something
dangerous. Her husband was unaware of the extent of her difficulties as she performed functions related to his position without
too much difficulty. She was bored by these social events and did
not make meaningful contact with anyone that belonged to their
"official" social circle.

The Course of the Analysis and the Nature of the Transference

The patient is a very attractive woman. She came to the sessions
casually dressed but with that special flair that one associates with
people who have an extraordinary sense for bringing out the best
in their appearance.

Though in her initial presentation, Mrs. Holland blamed her
husband for their marital difficulties (he was too "straitlaced,"
lacked humor, and treated her as if she were a child), she soon
turned to talking about her fear of destroying her marriage and
taking terrible chances with losing her children in the process as
well. Her concern was related to the nature of her extramarital
affairs: throughout their marriage, she had been involved with

other men, either in fantasy or in reality. The preoccupation with her affairs and the various deceptions that were related to these, kept Mrs. Holland emotionally isolated. She also worried about her increased use of nicotine and marijuana and her occasional use of cocaine. Other than her addiction to nicotine, the patient was less concerned about her drug abuse than she was about her relationships with men; she used drugs only at the request of her lovers. It was in relation to the analysis of her extramarital relationships that the addictive features of her personality emerged. After several trials and with great determination, she stopped smoking cigarettes in the third year of the analysis. After this, her use of marijuana greatly diminished. Like many "ex-smokers," she began to dislike others' smoking.

In the first year of analysis I learned about the imperative nature of her affairs. Most of these liaisons started rather innocently and would come about under very ordinary circumstances. She would see a man in an elevator, meet him in a bank, or at a party, or she would see a gas-station attendant and experience not only sexual excitement but would also quickly develop the conviction that having this man in her life would eliminate her feelings of emptiness and depression. The fantasy that would follow the encounter would not be restricted to a desire for sexual intimacy, though the quality of the sexual experience (the level of arousal and strength of orgasm) played an important part in the subsequent fate of the affairs. The most important aspect of the attraction was the way the man would respond to her overtures. If he smiled back at her and his glances indicated that he found her desirable, this would profoundly affect her emotional state: she would feel energized, more able to look after her family, and generally function more effectively. With each new promise of an involvement, she would be sure that this would be the "perfect relationship" of her life, the one that would undo her periodic depressions and the chronic sense of emotional isolation.

The need for this kind of an involvement could not be explained simply as physical lust. My patient felt tenderness, admiration, and all other emotions that we ordinarily consider to be indicative of "being in love." The conscious desire was not for a fling but for a lasting union. Yet, regardless of how passionate these initial feelings were, and how hopeful she might be at first that they would be enduring, her feelings rarely lasted more then a few months; at times only a couple of weeks. Just as fast as they developed, they would equally speedily disappear, only to be repeated, each time with the same intensity.

In the course of the analysis, I witnessed numerous such encounters and eventually I could discern a certain pattern: (1) An obsessional preoccupation with the object of her desires; she would become determined to have this man respond to her regardless of the reality of her situation or his. (2) Once the man responded, she would become possessive of him. She would insist on either seeing him daily or on having several phone contacts. If he was unable to do so, she would become desperate, at times suicidal. These were the times when her self-image as a worthless, "shitty" person would most strongly emerge, a feeling that could only be dispelled by the positive response of the man who was the object of her idealizations at that time. (3) Most of the time the relationship would end because Mrs. Holland would feel that some aspect of the man's behavior indicated that he was not "completely there" for her. She would detect some coldness in his voice or he would fail to return a phone call when she expected one. Such experiences would make her feel as if she had been "hit over the head"; she would become disillusioned and withdraw into self-pity. It would be then that she would, rather abruptly, end the relationship.

From time to time, the patient became desperate about the way she would repeat this pattern. She would then, not necessarily with a sense of despair but with a sense of resignation, decide to give up hope for change.

Mrs. Holland was the oldest of two children, the only daughter. She described her father as a dashingly good looking man, who, early in the patient's life, became a heavy drinker. He had a violent temper, was highly unpredictable, and frequently threatened suicide. While they engaged in frequent rough-housing together which had definite sexual overtones (she remembers brushing against his erect penis and realizing how pleasing this was to him), he could also, without any forewarning, turn against her. His personality changed drastically after he quit alcohol and the generous use of sleeping medications. This, however, did not occur until the patient was in her midtwenties.

It was around the time that her father sobered up that Mrs. Holland became aware of the special nature of their relationship. It was with her rather then with her brother or her mother that the father shared some of his most intimate thoughts. They had similar interests and enjoyed the same things. Most importantly, she realized how dependent her father was on her emotionally. As she related instances of the ways in which he would expect her to cheer him up or to comfort him, she would become enraged at how thoughtlessly he had exploited her emotionally. The sense of exploitation was most strongly related to the way in which the father teased her sexually. She grew up feeling that her father definitely preferred her sexually over her mother—though she could not recall overt sexual behavior between them. In the course of the analysis, she would frequently muse about the way her "privileged position" had exposed her more keenly to her father's fluctuating moods than other members of her family. She was "the chosen one"; her brother envied her for her position, but neither he, nor anybody else knew what a "curse" this turned out to be for the rest of her life.

Mrs. Holland described her mother as a "mousy woman," very quiet and ineffectual in relationship to her controlling and violent husband, but she too could lose her temper and would then attack the children either physically or verbally. It was difficult for Mrs. Holland to remember many interactions with her mother, though she recalled that mother had frequent headaches and would spend a great deal of time in her bedroom. "Was she depressed?" she wondered. Retrospectively, the patient also thought that her mother must have been jealous of her relationship with her father. Some of the most poignant moments of the analysis related to her intense desire to be close to this woman and to feel loved and appreciated by her.

(I suspect that interpreting her history at this point would keep our focus on the possibility that the patient suffered the consequences of an unresolved Oedipus complex. Only the unfolding of the process of the analysis could reveal the disturbances in the deeper layers of the psyche and help us recognize that while oedipal issues were represented in the manifest material, they did not constitute the essential elements of the patient's psychopathology.)

Mrs. Holland became interested in matters "sexual" at an early age. Around the age of 13 and 14 there were frequent masturbatory activities with Carl, a somewhat older boy, and genital explorations with her girl friends. At times of loneliness and depression later in life, she would try to make herself feel better by masturbating accompanied by fantasies of having intercourse either with Carl or with her father. These fantasies were the most potent means by which she could relieve boredom or depression; they were either enlivening and energizing or soothing and comforting. "It is a fantasy world. I don't feel lively or alive without it . . . but it also depresses me that this is what I need to make myself feel better. . . . "

Some aspects of the pattern that she repeated compulsively with men also appeared in the transference. In the early part of the analysis, the patient was convinced that I had sexual feelings toward her as had many of her female friends. Her sexual fantasies in relation to me always involved some sort of intense experience: totally abandoned love making that would obliterate any differences between the two of us. One of these fantasies involved her sucking on my breasts and watching my face as it would become enraptured. The fantasy would not progress to genital contact. Rather, its most important aspect would be my response to her seductions and stimulations. If I responded by becoming eager to make contact with her, this would comfort her since I would now be completely under her spell. We came to understand the fantasy as one in which she "used"sex to elicit the desired response from me. For an adult to induce erotic excitement in the "other" is the most powerful means by which to assure exclusive attention. Since it would be she who would elicit such rapture in my face, she could be convinced that she was lovable and desirable. An experience such as this can be compared to one in which a baby is successful in eliciting a smile on the mother's face (see Winnicott, 1971). The fantasy of this kind of intense sexual involvement was eventually replaced by fantasies in which I would take care of her as if she were a baby. When feeling depressed and hopeless, she wished she could get off the couch, sit at my feet, and put her head on my lap.

At first, the periods of depression were regularly accompanied by death wishes. "If I could only die without causing my family a

great deal of pain," she would say. She hoarded a supply of sleeping medication and insisted on keeping these for "safety's sake";
it made her feel good to know she had a way out. She would
become worried at times that she scared me with her preoccupation with death and that I would stop the analysis. Though I took
her suicidal ideation seriously, I never considered Mrs. Holland
unanalyzable. My judgment regarding analyzability was based on
the patient's ability to develop a cohesive selfobject transference.
An archaic merger transference had become firmly consolidated
in the second year of the analysis which had deepened the analytic
process. Once that had occurred, Mrs. Holland rarely spoke about
wishing to be dead, doing so only when she was disappointed in
me or when she failed to secure an enthusiastic response from
the man she happened to be attracted to. The patient's mood,
her self-perception, and her self-esteem were totally at the mercy
of the responses of her transference objects.

A good example of this was the hour during the second year
when she told me of having fallen in love with a man she had
recently met. After a few pleasant exchanges in which she felt
that he too was attracted to her, the patient made an overt appeal
for a more intimate contact. At first the man responded but eventually declined her advances. Mrs. Holland immediately lost interest in her work and could not concentrate on her daily tasks, felt
nihilistic, and depressed. She became convinced that she had lost
her sexual appeal, the only thing she felt she had to draw people
close to herself. As the patient described how she felt about herself at times like these (hopelessly damaged and dead inside), she
was convinced that either I did not understand what it was like
for her, or, if I did, I would not accept the unfeeling and dead
parts of her; feelings that made her wish she were dead. I said
that I could see how difficult it would be for her to feel my acceptance when she herself could not be accepting of these feelings
in herself. "Yes," she said, "how could anyone know what it is
like to live in a gray area? . . . Just for a moment I felt again that
you do not know what it is like for me, but almost simultaneously
I also felt that you do. And that sense that you do know is extraordinarily liberating." Mrs. Holland's next associations went to Carl:
the poignancy and the keenness of the sexual excitement she
had with him remained the prototypical one for her. She felt

completely "absorbed" by him and he by her. "This was not a simple sexual experience" she said, "but more like I got lost in his body and he in mine." These were the experiences she wanted to have with her lovers and was hoping that she could have with me. Her next associations went to a friend's description of what it was like to be on cocaine, "as if the substance stands for a lover or someone who gives you the feeling of being alive." Could I understand why, when she feels rejected, and ready to give up on life, masturbating with the memory of the experience with Carl would be the only way she could calm herself? "When I feel like this, I realize how far I had gotten from anything that could be intimate. . . . " This was a reference to the way in which sex alone, without the feeling of "being in love" could become a way in which she would try to overcome the sense of emotional isolation and inner deadness.

The selfobject experiences the patient was seeking with me and her lovers had merger as well as mirroring aspects to them: the intensity of the erotic and sexual experiences assured her of feeling herself one with an other. At the same time, these experiences reassured and validated her: she would be the one to create such a joy in us and we would be completely focused on her. The archaic nature of the transference was also indicated by the imperative quality of her need to be responded to in the desired manner and in the way in which she attempted to control these reactions. It was the obsessional, imperative quality of her determination to secure these responses that brought the association "addictive" first to my mind.

In spite of expectable, periodic disruptions in the transference, Mrs. Holland felt that I "heard" her and was able to respond to the little girl in her who wanted not only unconditional acceptance by others but also intensely and explicitly expressed validation about being lovable. A dream expressed this rather poignantly. In the dream someone spoke two languages: one of the languages was for the "outside," the other, for the "inside." "Funny that I did not feel left out," she said, "more that the inside language was for me . . . you speak the language the baby inside of me understands. . . . The other day I spoke to someone, saying that there is a child in everyone of us . . . the child in me is from Bangladesh . . . but the baby in the dream was a healthy, well-developed baby." (I thought, the dream indicated that my acceptance and responsiveness to the damaged and emotionally starved baby made it possible for her to begin to feel—at least in a dream—as a healthy and well-developed baby.)

Mrs. Holland brought the same intensity and vivid description to her angry feelings toward me as she did to her sexual and tender ones. When in a particularly vulnerable state, she would become enraged at me whenever I failed to recognize even momentary shifts in her mood or whatever she expected in terms of a response. These were times when nothing I said was "good enough" and she felt that she would have to live the rest of her life searching for responses that were intense enough to calm the agitation and fill the empty depression inside of her. When frustrated in her expectation for "a perfect response," her rage would surface suddenly and with great force; the intensity of her anger would render her speechless at times. However, only once did she feel that she wanted to walk out on me. The patient considered it to have been an accomplishment of the analysis when she was able to tell me calmly that she felt like killing me when I was "completely off."

Three years into the analysis, Mrs. Holland began to experience her sexual encounters more and more as only temporary measures which put her in a very precarious position. She had a dream which she herself interpreted as indicating that this was a very dangerous way of making herself feel better. She was on a mountain walk, the ground began to feel slippery, and she held onto a rock. But the rock too began to slide and it looked as if it was about to fall into a ravine; she could barely hold onto the dirt underneath it. As the rock moved, it exposed some scary creatures underneath it. "The rocks are my short-lived relationships," she said, "they give me temporary support and safety. In my dream I had to let go of them because they were about to pull me into an abyss." She thought that the scary creatures underneath the rock were her feelings about herself. She could hide them only as long as she was able to experience a "high" in a relationship. But the relationships, like the rock, were dangerous in themselves, her sense of well-being temporary, only an illusion.

Eventually, the frequency of the affairs dropped off without the patient loosing a sense of her liveliness. She found that she could calm herself with the fantasy that I would tuck her in and wish her good night. Such experiences in the transference could—retrospectively—best explain her increased ability to regulate her tension states and make the repetition of the symptomatic behavior less necessary.[2]

Discussion

As I indicated in my introductory comments, my listening perspective, the way I organized the data, and the manner in which I articulated my interpretive comments—these were all determined by my self psychological theoretical position. With the unfolding and deepening of the analytic process, I found myself asking the following questions: What were the sources of Mrs. Holland's apathy, her dysphoria, her depression, and suicidal thoughts? Why could she not maintain a relationship over a period of time and be more focused on her painting which she enjoyed and had a talent for? What would best explain her symptomatic behavior, "the final common pathway" by which she tried to overcome her distressing affective states? This last question was related to the function and the meaning of the responses her lovers *had* to have in order for her to feel alive, vigorous, and energetic. Was there something special about these men physically in terms of their appearance or manner that could so readily ignite my patient's passions and initiate an elaborate fantasy of a permanent union? And, finally, why did the experience with Carl retain such power that its memory could help her overcome depression and apathy?

The imperative need for the responses that would help her remain functional, pointed to a primary self disorder which is characterized by impairment in affect and tension regulation, lack of vitality, proneness to fragmentation and hypochondriasis.

---

[2]Kohut (1971) related the changes that take place in the course of an analysis to the accretion of psychic structures via transmuting internalization. The process of transmuting internalization is indicated by the patient increasing tolerance for the analyst's absences, for the analyst's occasional failure to achieve immediate and correct empathic understanding, and an increase in the patient's sublimatory capacity. Such structural changes lead to the eventual reduction of the symptomatic, "addictive" behavior.

The difficulty in tension regulation could be seen (1) by the imperative need to have her "fix," which took the form of a delighted and desirous look on a man's face, and (2) in the manner in which Mrs. Holland reacted to slights and inevitable frustrations. Her rage was quick to rise, and her behavior under these circumstances could become totally unpredictable. Her fear of criticism and the grandiose ideas she maintained about her unusual artistic talents also indicated that her infantile grandiosity has not undergone adequate transformation; she has remained extremely vulnerable to the responses of others.

Since her lovers could not meet her archaic expectations and their responses could not be controlled, the patient's initial infatuations would be quickly followed by disillusionment and a new man with "the look on his face" had to be found. This was the cycle of repetition from which Mrs. Holland could not escape. Only in the analysis could the archaic quality of these needs be recognized, accepted, and empathically interpreted.

The nature and the extent of the defects in the self suggested that her difficulties did not begin with the noisiest aspects of her past, namely, with the sexually seductive, unpredictable, volatile, and demeaning interactions with her father. These defects were most likely the legacy of still earlier, developmentally detrimental, experiences. I suspect that in her infancy, Mrs. Holland developed what Kohut and Wolf (1978) called an "understimulated self." The experiences with her father, in spite of their exploitative nature, were, in many ways, restorative; they had two important aspects to them: (1) the excitement of the interaction itself was enlivening, and (2) it was then that she felt most appreciated and valued. The tragedy was that the experiences that helped her overcome her apathy and listlessness were the very same ones which created the symptomatic behavior later in life. These prematurely sexually overstimulating and incestuous encounters became the prototypes by which she tried to overcome her depression and suicidal thoughts in adult life.

Kohut and Wolf (1978), in discussing the function of erotization and sexualization, described individuals whose nascent selves have been insufficiently responded to early in life, who will then use any available stimuli to create a pseudo-excitement in order to ward off the painful feeling of deadness that tends to overtake

them. Children will use whatever methods they have available:
in infancy, they bang their heads; in latency, they masturbate
compulsively; in adolescence, they pursue daredevil activities.
Adults have at their disposal a greater array of self-stimulating
activities—in the sexual sphere, promiscuity and various perversions, and, in the nonsexual sphere, such activities as gambling,
and drug and alcohol-induced excitements.

As the patient and I were putting these pieces together, she
would ask, "What came first, Carl or my father?" I thought that
the two experiences served the same psychological function, they
both helped her overcome the feeling of emptiness and depression. In relation to Carl, during puberty, when sexuality is experienced most keenly and poignantly, she discovered that sexual
excitement and release could both calm and stimulate her. The
playful interactions with her father and their more intimate moments provided not only exhilaration; she also experienced a
sense of belonging and her own importance to someone. Carl
must have been as grateful to her for providing him with sexual
excitement as she experienced her father to have been. This
made her feel valued and appreciated by both of them. The close
physical contact also provided an important aspect of the experience with Carl as well as with her father.

I believe the need for an intense involvement with a man had
become "the final common pathway" for Mrs. Holland in which
she hoped to reexperience the same sense of exhilaration and
the sense of union with other human beings as she had with Carl
and her father. But these attempts at self-healing were bound to
fail, and as one of her dreams so poignantly expressed, these
liaisons gave her only temporary relief and had caused serious
complications in her adult life.

At first, I believed that the sexual aspects of these relationships
were the decisive factors in both calming and enlivening her.
And, to a degree, that was indeed true. With time, though, I
learned to appreciate the fact that only when Mrs. Holland was
unable to find a man she could fall in love with and when she
felt very depressed and suicidal, only then did she turn to the
memory of the sexual excitement with Carl and her father; she
could then be satisfied with a purely sexual relationship with a

man. There were two elements intertwined here, both being important but having different selfobject functions for her. When Mrs. Holland felt relatively well, not threatened by fragmentation, but still not able to focus on her art work, and generally dull and apathetic, she would then pursue a man with the hope and expectation that falling in love, being loved with passion in return, would undo her life-long apathy and depression. When she felt suicidal, and feared that her level of agitation might signal an oncoming psychosis, she would then, in order to restore threatened self-cohesion, resort to compulsive masturbation accompanied by sexual fantasies related to Carl or her father.

Ethel Person (1988), in *Dreams of Love and Fateful Encounters*, describes the subjective experiences involved in romantic love: "Being in love provides for intimacy, for priority, for exaltation," Person says. Subjectively, the preoccupation with the other is experienced "as a high, a liberation, the greatest pleasure . . . " (p. 38). Idealization and merger experiences are central to this experience. Because of the importance of idealization, disappointments in the beloved can be devastating. Person compares the single-mindedness of a lover to that of a child who wails for his mother. And like the child, the lover may feel that the sheer strength of his desire must be enough to achieve its demand; the need to control the feelings of the other is part of a normal love relationship.

If this is the description of normal adult love, how much more true this must be when the desire for the experience is being pursued for the sake of overcoming a sense of emotional deadness? My patient pursued the state of exaltation and "the high" that was provided by this, with determination and single-mindedness. Once this could not be maintained, the relationship was over. Person describes people with this particular kind of problem as "love addicts, whose lives are parsed out in rapid alternations of erotic excitement and disappointment" (p. 49).

It was difficult to say what the physical attributes were of the men who were most likely to attract my patient's attention, but there was something in their manner that she could identify. The men had something "playful" about them, they were never as serious and down-to-earth as was her husband. What she interpreted as playful could be the way in which they cocked their heads or smiled back at her, generally, a flirtatious, seductive manner; attributes that were most likely to reactivate experiences she had with her father and Carl. What makes one person attractive to the other belongs to the mysteries of "erotic aesthetics," says Stoller: "We make a mistake if we think that what excites us erotically is a permanent and universal heritage of our species, not bound by culture and one's private history. There are few eternal verities in art or erotics. It is all in the interpretation and interpretations vary" (1985, p. 48).

Summary

In a highly condensed clinical report, I had attempted to trace the source of a patient's "addiction" to a sense of exhilaration, which she experienced by repeatedly and compulsively seeking a particular kind of intimacy with men. The reconstruction of archaic merger-mirror selfobject transference in the analysis, suggested that the patient's symptom was related to a fairly severe defect in the self that had originated in the earliest periods of her life related to her mother's chronic depression. The sexually overstimulating interactions with her father during latency and with Carl during puberty had become effective ways in which she overcame her childhood depression. The symptomatic behavior in adult life represented a continued effort to recreate these experiences in order to remain functional and to avert apathy, depression, and suicidal thoughts.

Chapter 6

Sexual Addiction

Wayne A. Myers, M.D.

The clinical material presented in this paper is derived from my analytic work with patients who exhibited sexually addictive behavior. Their search for sexual release possessed the driven quality that one normally associates with the behavior of the addict. These patients illustrate the value of working analytically with such people.

Clinical Material

Case 1

Alex entered analysis with me at the age of 33, after several earlier attempts at treatment had aborted due to the deaths or departures of the previous therapists. The prior treatments had paralleled his early life, inasmuch as his mother had divorced both his biological father, who managed to be in the mother's life only long enough to impregnate her, and the first stepfather who shared their household when the patient was between the ages of one to 10. The mother's third husband was despised by the patient and had little contact with him. The family patriarch,

Alex's wealthy maternal grandfather, was the only constant male figure in his life.

Unfortunately, both the grandfather and the mother interacted with Alex as if they lived in different galaxies. There was little attunement to his emotional needs and practically no close encounters physically of any kind. The patient grew up with the perception that he was inadequate, the "wrong boy," and constantly feared that he would be replaced by a more idealized "right" one.

While Alex consciously scorned the first stepfather, he was aware of the fact that the man's penis seemed gigantic in comparison to his own. Though he attempted to deal with both the first and second stepfathers with indifference, his own envy of their penises would occasionally break through, and he would be left feeling bereft by the invidiousness of the comparisons.

In his midtwenties, after finishing college, the patient spent a good part of each and every day frequenting the gay bars, bathhouses, and bookstores of New York. Inasmuch as he did not have to work, as a result of the money meted out to him by his grandfather, he was free to pursue his never ending quest for attractive men with large penises. In the ten years prior to his entering treatment with me, he had at least one (and frequently several) different sexual contacts per day. I emphasize the word *different* to underscore the fact that he was rarely interested in having sex with the same man on more than one occasion. As I came to recognize after working with Alex for a while, his object was to "have" someone, not to hold onto them.

What also became apparent to me, shortly after starting the analysis with him, was that there was an intensely driven quality to Alex's quest. It hardly seemed sexual in nature, despite the fact that most of his encounters culminated in orgastic gratification for both partners. Rather, the aim seemed to be one of forcing the other man, who was almost always chosen on the basis of the presumption that he had a large penis, to admire Alex's erect phallus. Once the patient sensed the aura of acknowledgment of this fact in the other man's eyes, his mission was accomplished and the sexual release (if it occurred) was merely an extra bonus.

One of the tragedies attendant on Alex's life-style, was that he felt an overpowering need to "neutralize" every man whom he saw (or imagined) as having a large penis. If he had just been with one man and encountered another whom he wanted, he felt humiliated if he was unable to produce an erection. In order to avoid this "disaster," he began to carry a photograph of himself with his penis erect to flash at other men so that they might admire his erect phallus. I have described this particular aspect of Alex's behavior elsewhere (Myers, 1990). What is of interest to note here, is that carrying the photograph quickly intensified his anxiety. It simply meant to him that the whole universe of men with large penises was now available to him. Whereas in the past he might have reluctantly passed up an opportunity with a stranger if he had just had sex with another, now he felt compelled to "get them all."

The impetus for many of Alex's sexual encounters was related to anxiety which was aroused in his transference relationship with me, as when he felt me to be rejecting or indifferent to him during periods of weekend or vacation separations; interpreting this simply served to enrage him. He perceived such efforts as trying to force him to acknowledge the importance of me and of the size of my penis for him. His rage was secondary to his feeling "minimized" by me on such occasions, as if his ideas and feelings, his very life, had no significance and only mine and my "transferential phallus" counted for anything. In this regard, I was seen as reduplicating the narcissistic mother and grandfather, in my exquisite lack of attunement to the validity of his thoughts. When I finally formulated this thesis to him, he visibly relaxed, and the therapeutic alliance began to become solidified.

In this setting, the patient began to relate dreams in which I was perceived as a benevolent parental figure, one who could comfort him when he was anxious. In these dreams, and in conscious fantasies as well, my sexuality seemed indeterminate and of no great importance to him. What he seemed to wish from me a those times, which continued for a good six or seven years, was for me to be a soothing presence who could ease his anxieties at those moments when he had failed to neutralize a particular man. The thought that someone had not sufficiently studied his photograph or had not stridently enough proclaimed the virtues of his actual erect member, caused him the tortures of the damned. His anguish was intense at such times and he frequently likened his torment to that of an addict who had been denied the satisfaction of his daily "fix."

Only after I had performed the soothing function for Alex for many years, was he able to deal with me and with his life in a different manner. He began to write stories and essays for homosexual publications, which accorded him a certain degree of notoriety and acclaim in those circles. It was as if his printed words had begun to replace the need for the photograph and the exhibitionism in the bars and baths. Ever so slowly, he began to experiment with missing a day or two on the "circuit." Though he still felt considerable anxiety, he was better able to tolerate the deprivation and the attendant feelings of depression with the aid of fluoxetine.

At this time, he began to have different types of dreams about me. In these, I was frequently seen as a potential sexual partner. And though he would still assure me that I was really not his "physical type," the object of our encounters in the dreams seemed loving as well as sexual in nature. What he wanted to get from me was a sense of my love and admiration of him, as a more complete individual and not simply as an erect penis. Historically, we were able to relate this wish to his desires to have been admired by the first stepfather, in the hope that the man would then prevail upon the mother and grandfather so that they would also come to love the patient. On a couple of occasions, he felt quite tearful in associating to such dreams and would not tolerate any interventions from me at all. Exposing his feelings was tantamount to presenting himself to me in a flaccid state and was intolerably difficult for him to do.

Despite these problems, Alex has persisted with the treatment and with his writing career. While he has not yet relinquished his cruising behavior in toto, he has begun to modify it in a significant manner. The adjunctive use of the fluoxetine in combating the intense depressive affect has been quite helpful in this phase of the treatment.

Case 2

Burton entered treatment with me in his late twenties, after having "trashed" the room of a prostitute he had visited. The precipitating incident occurred when the woman in question resisted masturbating him after they had already, that evening, had intercourse twice. In describing what had happened, the patient mentioned that the earlier sex with the "hooker" had not brought about the "release" that he was looking for and he felt a driving need to get "something more" from her. When she resisted his request to masturbate him, an intense feeling of rage welled up within him and he took it out on some of the inanimate objects in her room. He was deeply frightened by the consequences of his actions, however, as the young woman's pimp had rushed into the room and pulled a knife on him. Only by judiciously flashing a roll of bills at the man, was the patient able to extricate himself unharmed from the "scene of the crime."

Historically, Burton was the only child of an older manic-depressive father and a much younger, attractive mother, who frequently paraded around the house in little or no clothing. As a youngster, he came to believe that his mother participated in sex with his father only for the monetary rewards of their relationship. He did not feel that she loved the older man, but this did not provide much comfort for him as neither she nor the father were especially warm in their interactions with him. In addition, they frequently left him in the custody of nannies when they went off on lengthy jaunts around the world.

From his earliest years, Burton recalled holding onto his penis when he was alone in his room. He quickly came to recognize that this behavior accorded him some sense of comfort and relief from the anxiety which he experienced when his parents were away or when the nannies were busy doing other things or were asleep. When he reached puberty, the penile caressing led to ejaculation and to the added bonus of relief of tension, and he began to pursue this behavior in earnest. For a number of years, he masturbated between six and twelve times a day. Then, when he was in college, he discovered the underworld of prostitution and began to visit these women as many times a week as his finances would allow. While he would often take whatever woman was available at a particular massage parlor or hotel, his preferences went toward large breasted women who were older than he was. Sexually, his tastes were relatively mundane, with his desires running to straight intercourse in the male or female superior position in order to bring about the desired sensations of relief and release.

In his personal life, Burton had not had any relationships of any real significance. In high school, he had idealized a female teacher in her thirties but their actual verbal contacts had been few and far between. Though he fervently wished that this woman would love him, she never became incorporated into his actual masturbatory thoughts. In his twenties, though he had a few dates with women, most of his time after work hours was spent in his pursuit of prostitutes with big breasts.

The treatment began as a twice a week psychoanalytically oriented psychotherapy and then progressed into a four time a week psychoanalysis. I was initially wary of the potential for a psychotic transference in this borderline patient, but when he managed to experience strong feelings of anger within the treatment setting in periods of separation from me, and did not decompensate, I suggested switching over from the chair to the couch and he concurred. What was also apparent to both of us was that Burton was quite psychologically minded and had a strong motivational desire to change his life for the better.

Much of the early part of the therapy focused on Burton's ongoing need to relieve his sense of inner agitation, which stoked the flames of his passionate pursuit of prostitutes. The lexicon he used to describe his lustful acts was quite chaste, however, and was replete with words more often associated with the intake of food than with the practice of sex, such as starvation, hunger, appetite, and satiation.

Whenever he was short of money at night and could not find any to purchase the desired release, Burton would find himself torn between feelings of rage and despair. On a couple of such occasions, he destroyed furniture in his own apartment, and on a number of others, he experienced episodes of depersonalization-derealization which were quiet frightening to him because of the increased sense of distance which he felt from people.

These episodes were similar to ones which he had experienced during his adolescence when he had felt abandoned by his mother or by a nanny whom he was especially fond of. Even though it became apparent to both of us that Burton's pursuit of prostitutes was anchored in his fantasy that his big breasted mother had sexually serviced his father solely for the monetary rewards, this insight did little to alleviate the driven quality of the patient's quest.

In the transference, I alternately became the abandoning prostitute-mother who only serviced him for a fee, or the ungiving father who was unwilling to pass on to him my phallic powers. In whatever guise, I was seen as not giving enough and he was seen as not getting enough, the needy child who was either starving for injections of my masculinity or desperately trying to keep abreast of the latest ministrations of my maternal sexuality. On weekends and during summer vacations, the sensation of being abandoned made him feel worthless and enraged and the only solace he could find to combat these feelings lay in the repetitive encounters with the women of the night or in compulsive masturbation. Again, though he was able to recognize that the masturbation allowed him to become for himself the comforting mother which he had never had, through his identification of his entire self with his penis (via a body–phallus equation), he was unable to modify the driving sense of urgency or the frenetic frequency and addictive nature of this behavior for many years. During the summer vacation after Burton had completed his fourth year in analysis, another prostitute complained about the inordinate quality of his sexual needs and refused to comply with his requests for a sexual encore after a couple of earlier performances. On this occasion, he became quite depressed and in the weeks that followed he experienced weight loss and early morning awakening. He transiently attempted to medicate his own mood disturbance with cocaine, but the sensation of loss of control which he experienced frightened him and he stopped the drug.

On my return, it was apparent that he was suffering from a clinical depressive episode and I placed him on a tricyclic antidepressant (nortriptyline) which ameliorated this disturbance after several weeks. I initially placed him on one such medication (imipramine), but because this led to erectile impotence and to interference with ejaculation, I changed to another. It is of interest to note that even at the height of his depression, Burton still "cruised" for prostitutes on a three times a week basis. This underscores the fact that much of the sexual activity in such patients is not fueled solely by the need to lessen libidinal desires, but is equally propelled by the desire to dampen aggressive tensions and to overcome feelings of anhedonia.

After recovering from this depressive episode, the patient became fearful of stopping the antidepressant medication, lest he be precipitated back into the depths of despair from which he had just emerged. On a number of occasions, he called to ask for an extra session in order to be certain that I was still going to be there for him, no matter how angry he felt at me or how ashamed he felt of his own dependency needs. In a series of intensely upsetting dreams at this time, he had recurrent images of being rejected or abandoned by a woman and then of reaching down to comfort himself by touching his penis, only to find that his organ had become shrunken and he was unable to make it become erect. At such moments, he would turn to an older man for help and his penis would return to normal size once more. In his associations to these dreams, he saw me as being the powerful, loving "father figure" whom he had always wished his own father to be, in order to mitigate his dependency upon his mother and the nannies.

The feelings of dependency on me made him feel inadequate as a heterosexual man, the equivalent of the shrunken "faggot" penis he felt himself saddled with in his dreams. The affects he experienced following such dreams were despair and impotent rage, and he would often resort to frantic masturbation or the pursuit of prostitutes in order to relieve the sense of depression.

During the fifth year of the analysis, Burton met a woman some years older than he was and formed a surprisingly good relationship with her. She owned a business in another city and soon invited the patient to work for her there. With this woman, he was able to tolerate absences and to relinquish his inordinate need to control her every movement. Though his intense sexual needs were still far from muted, she seemed pleased with this aspect of their liaison, and the frequency of their sexual relations led to a marked decrease in his need to seek out prostitutes or to masturbate, though he was unable to totally give up these practices. As the summer vacation approached, he told me that he had agreed to move with her to the city where she lived.

In his transference expectations at this time, he imagined that I would be angry with him for his "rejection" of me. In addition, his dreams were filled with images of massive retaliation by me because of his "forbidden relationship" with the older female figure. When he saw that I was not going to enact these frightening transference fantasies with him in reality, he briefly became depressed again about the idea of losing me. "I don't want to lose you," he said, "and yet if I go with Margo I have to give you up. And you're the only one before her who's ever really been there for me and been able to calm me down."

At this time, I had to again place Burton on the antidepressant medication. In addition, his masturbation and prostitute seeking increased in frequency. The driven quality which had characterized it for so many years returned for a short while, until the medication had a chance to take effect, though the intensity seemed markedly muted. Eventually, he was able to see that my loss was not equivalent to the loss of his masculinity, his identity, or his capacity to experience feelings of pleasure and of being alive and he was able to come off the medication again. He was finally able to leave the treatment, which he, too, likened to a daily "fix," although he telephoned a number of times from the other city and came in to see me on a few occasions. Though the driven quality which had been part and parcel of the "hooker habit" was markedly diminished, the activity itself had not totally disappeared. The patient, however, was quite different from the young man who had begun the treatment with me some six years earlier.

Case 3

Charles came for treatment at the age of 26 at the request of his wife. What had begun for him as the occasional use of pornographic videotapes to produce sexual arousal in the early days of their marriage, had inexorably progressed to the obligatory usage of such tapes by Charles after he and his wife had been married for about two years. His spouse was deeply disturbed by the fact that her husband was no longer able to be sexually aroused by her at all. Provocative disrobing dramas and the use of high heels and erotic lingerie had managed to excite him for a short period of time, but these accoutrements were no longer effective. The only thing that worked for Charles now, was the use of constantly changing pornographic videotapes.

In probing Charles' past history, we learned that, like his 5-year older sister before him, he had spent the first five years of his life ensconced in the parental bedroom where he was undoubtedly exposed to the primal scene on a number of occasions. The next six years of his life were spent sharing a bedroom with the sister, until his troubled older sibling ran away from home on the eve of her sixteenth birthday. The parents spent little effort in looking for the runaway girl and she essentially disappeared from the family's sight from that time forth.

Charles dated a number of young women during high school and college but none of the relationships lasted very long. The occasional sexual encounters which he had during those years were marred by his difficulties in attaining an erection and achieving penetration, and for a long time he worried that he might be homosexual. He met his wife shortly before they were both to graduate from business school and Charles was finally able to effect penetration with her. In the first flush of this success, the couple married and moved to New York, where Charles had been offered an excellent job in an investment firm.

The long hours at work seemed enervating to the patient and his sexual desires for his wife quickly began to wane. In this setting, he suggested that they watch a pornographic tape together. The instant arousal he achieved was immediately translated into a sexual encounter with her, which served to dispel whatever transient reservations she may have had about watching the films. Over the course of the next year, however, the use of the tapes moved from the adjunctive to the obligatory category. As I noted above, Charles' wife attempted to arouse him by other means, such as by performing sexy dances or by wearing provocative clothing, but the tapes soon became the only means of bringing on the desired erection for him.

Shortly after starting analysis, Charles began to demonstrate his curiosity about me. He expressed interest in where I went for my weekends and for other vacation separations. He also wondered if I or other members of my family had taken photographs that were in my office. When I questioned him about this, he expressed an interest in whether my children went with my wife and me on vacations. In response to my pressing him further in this area, he noted that some of his happiest early memories were of being on vacation with his parents and sister during his early latency years. What seemed implicit in his inquiries, was the underlying question as to whether my wife and I also exposed our children to primal sexual scenes, as his had done.

By the end of the first year of the treatment, Charles had almost completely lost interest in his wife sexually. In this setting, she came home early from work one day to find her husband masturbating in bed while watching a pornographic tape. The behavior was so upsetting to her, because of the feelings of being excluded and rejected, that she decided to leave him. When I attempted to link his behavior toward his wife with his wishes for increased closeness with me in the transference, the patient became angered at what he felt was my attempt to convince him that he was a homosexual. From that point on, he became more and more addicted to the watching of the X-rated tapes.

When I questioned him about his behavior with the tapes, I became aware of the long history and the driven quality concerning his actions in this area. He had first started watching pornographic tapes in early adolescence and the cassettes he chose to watch then were ones which he had found in his parents' bedroom. Despite the fact that he felt sexually aroused and masturbated to orgasm while watching these tapes, by his own description Charles was aware of little overt pleasure in his voyeuristic pursuits. Rather, he sensed that he was looking for something else in the tapes, only he was uncertain of just what that was.

Throughout the second and third years of the treatment with me, Charles did not date at all. He worked hard at his job and was promoted and financially rewarded for his efforts. But the area he seemed to live for most, was the watching of the X-rated tapes. During this period, he informed me that he had watched many hundreds of such sagas. In probing for details, I found that much of the time when he watched the tapes, he felt bored, as if he were looking for something specific on them which did not happen. While he preferred certain tapes to others, most of them seemed to be interchangeable to him. After all, he noted, there were only so many different positions and variations that could be shown on the tapes. He did acknowledge, however, that he preferred tapes in which some variant of incestuous themes was played out. When I pressed for further details, I was usually put off with exclamations of my having a "dirty, one tracked mind" and that I was trying to "get off" at his expense.

Whereas Charles had initially been curious about me and my family, in the two-year period following his wife's leaving him, he rarely ever evinced any interest in me or my office at all. I should also note that he rarely spontaneously mentioned his wife again. When I commented to him on these phenomena, he angrily informed me that his wife had deserted him and did not deserve any further expenditure of emotion from him and I had not even attempted to forestall her departure, hence I was either unconcerned about his welfare or was ineffectual. In either case, he saw no reason to pay any further heed to me as well. I commented that he seemed to be indicting me for the crime which he really held his parents accountable for, the disappearance of his sister, and noted to him that her loss must have sorely troubled him. He burst into tears in response to my words and informed me that his sister, and to a lesser extent his wife, were the only people whom he had ever really cared about. He felt that his parents never really loved him or his sister at all. Otherwise they would not have treated them with such incredible indifference to their very existence and would not have disregarded them while pursuing their "disgusting activities in the bedroom."

After the session in which this material emerged, Charles missed his next three visits. On his return, he told me that he had been unable to force himself to go into work and had spent his days watching an endless assortment of pornographic tapes and masturbating himself into a state of insensibility. He spoke of feeling hopeless about his life and of being depressed, and even verbalized passive suicidal ideas that he would be better off dead. He said that his current feelings were simply an intensification of the empty feelings which he always felt, and that the only activities which ever offered him relief of any kind were watching the tapes and masturbating, being with his wife, or coming to his sessions with me.

I considered placing him on antidepressant medication at that time, but he quickly snapped out of his depressed mood and was able to resume going to work. His cassette viewing also tapered off and he became more involved in the analysis than he had been for years. "I think I get you confused with my parents, at times" he announced one day. "You're both so interested in sexual things and you both operate in a kind of bedroom setting." I agreed with him that he had confused us, and then commented that he, too, was quite interested in sexual things. "You're right," he said, "but I don't even know what I'm really looking for." I suggested to him that he seemed to be looking for two different things in the tapes. One had to do with gaining an understanding of the parents' sexual activities in the bedroom when he was a child and with not feeling excluded from them. The other was less certain to me, but I thought that perhaps he might be looking for his sister on the tapes. With this comment of mine, Charles groaned and doubled up on the couch as if I had kicked him in the stomach.

In the sessions that followed, he spoke of feeling sure that I was right about his looking for his sister on the tapes. He had never realized it consciously, but he reasoned that if his sister were still alive now, she likely would have gone into prostitution to support herself and perhaps would have become a part of the pornography industry as well. In his endless inchoate scanning of the videotapes, he had been seeking to refind the lost love object whom he felt had eased his anxiety when he had been excluded from the parental bedroom at the age of 5. He deeply missed his sister and was able to mourn for her loss at this time, as he had never mourned for her when he was 11 and she had run away. He made inquiries with the police from his home city, and employed a private detective agency to investigate the matter, but never obtained any further information on her.

At this writing, Charles' analysis is still progressing. While his tape watching and masturbation continues, it has diminished in intensity and in frequency. While Charles has become interested in watching tapes with a particular porno queen whom he feels resembles his missing sister, his viewing no longer can be characterized as having the driven, addictive quality which it had before. He has not, however, been able to form any important new object relationships in his life and has still had considerable difficulty in analyzing his feelings of dependency on me. We are proceeding, however, and the outlook is hopeful.

Discussion

In this paper, I have presented material from three male patients who exhibited sexually addictive behavior. Regardless of the objects chosen, the behavior itself had an intensely driven quality. In addition, though orgastic pleasure was a frequent by-product of the frantic forays of these three men, attempts to gratify needs other than sexual ones were also subsumed in their repetitive searches.

Alex's cruising, for example, served a number of different ends. Most conspicuous was his attempt to gain the love and adoration of other men (and unconsciously of his mother), through their admiration of his erect penis. In his repetitive attempts to accomplish this aim, Alex unconsciously endeavored to reverse the passively experienced childhood traumata associated with being exposed to his stepfather's erect phallus and to the invidious comparisons which he made at that time with his own organ. When he was able to get other men to admire either his own actual erect penis or the photograph of his engorged member, he was able for that moment to undo the lifelong feelings of humiliation and castration which he carried with him since childhood. These aspects of his behavior are similar to ones detailed by Socarides (1978), Calef and Weinshel (1984), and Willick (1988) in their works on homosexual cruising.

In addition, in "impacting" on the object by the means of having his penis admired, Alex managed to neutralize some of the enormous rage which he felt toward the rejecting, humiliating parental figures from his past. This function of his actions is consistent with the conceptualizations offered by Stoller (1975), about the genesis of certain perverse acts and is important in understanding the behavior of all three patients described by me in this paper.

Finally, Alex's need to "impact" on others also served a self-regulatory purpose geared toward overcoming feelings of anhedonia or depression. When he attempted to modify the frequency of his sexually addictive behavior, the patient became depressed and the adjunctive use of antidepressant medication (fluoxetine) was indicated. This autoregulatory function of sexually addictive behavior was important with my other two patients as well, and to my way of thinking, is one of the most important keys to the overall understanding of the genesis of such behavior.

If we consider Burton's case, aside from the obvious oedipal competitive wishes to triumph over his father in vying for the affections of the "prostitute"-mother, we can easily recognize that his interactions with prostitutes also served as an attempt to neutralize enormous increments of rage derived from his childhood interactions with both parents. Also, as I noted earlier, through the medium of his masturbation, Burton became for himself the comforting mother which he had never had as a child, via the unconscious identification between his total self and his phallus. Needless to say, this self-administered maternal ministration was also an attempt on his part to decrease the inordinate rage which he felt as a result of the inadequate mothering which he had received as a child in reality.

As I noted in the case history, however, when particular prostitutes refused to gratify the wish to sexually relieve Burton's intense underlying needs, he either became overtly enraged or markedly depressed. The former feeling propelled him into treatment and the latter, during a period of vacation separation from the analysis, led to his attempt to self-medicate his depression with cocaine and to my instituting treatment with a tricyclic antidepressant. Prior to my returning from vacation and beginning the medication, the patient still maintained the sexually addictive behavior with prostitutes in an effort to ameliorate the intense feelings of depression and anhedonia.

In Charles' case as well, the obligatory use of pornographic videotapes served to diminish the intense anger which the patient felt toward the indifferent parents. His incessant scanning of the tapes also served as a way for him to both understand and to not feel excluded from the parental sexual behavior which he had been exposed to in his years of being billeted in their bedroom, and as a means of searching for the missing sister. I should note here, that the sister was primarily viewed by the patient as someone capable of soothing his intense feelings of anxiety and anger, as when he was excluded from the parental bedroom as a child, and his feelings of depression and anhedonia when he felt unloved by his parents.

In closing, let me offer a few words on analytic treatment of patients with sexually addictive behavior. As you will note from my descriptions of these three men, treatment only effected modest changes in all of them. Alex still cruises for men and Burton for women, while Charles still quite frequently scans pornographic videotapes for his missing sister. Yet in all three, the dramatic intensity and frequency which characterized these behaviors at the beginning of their analyses has been markedly diminished. Alex, Burton, and Charles all experienced depression during the course of their analyses, and two of the three required the adjunctive use of antidepressant medication. It is my belief that this occurrence should be expected, given the presence of the underlying anhedonia, and should in no way deter us as therapists from continuing with such treatments. And finally, all three of my patients have become more productive in work and in their capacity for forming higher level object relationships. Needless to say, these are no mean accomplishments, though the end results are far from perfect.

SECTION II
THE DISCUSSIONS

Chapter 7

Psychic Helplessness and the Psychology of Addiction

Lance M. Dodes, M.D.

I will discuss the papers in this symposium from the perspective of the role in addiction of psychic helplessness and of the narcissistic rage it produces in addiction vulnerable individuals. I will begin by summarizing my views (Dodes, 1990). The essence of psychic trauma is a state of being helplessly overwhelmed by affects, which produces great anxiety. The maintenance of a sense of control over one's own affective state is therefore an essential self-regulatory mechanism, and may also be considered a central aspect of narcissism. Addictive behaviors are sought because they provide a way to achieve a sense of internal emotional control over psychic helplessness. Drugs, for example, are "a device *par excellence* for altering, through one's intentional control, one's affective state" (Dodes, 1990, p. 401). In addition, drugs are able to reestablish a sense of power without any pharmacologic effect having occurred, as in the commonly reported experience of alcoholics who feel relief at the point they order a drink, or the point of beginning to drink it. Something has been accomplished by the act alone of obtaining the drug. I've viewed this as a signal satisfaction (analogous to signal anxiety) of the drive to reestablish mastery. By starting the chain of events which will lead to alteration of one's affect, one has confirmed the ability to alter and control one's affective state. Since the use of drugs, and other addictive behaviors, have the ability to restore this central sense of internal omnipotence, they may function as a corrective when an addiction vulnerable person is flooded with feelings of helplessness or powerlessness. The addictive behavior then serves to restore a sense of control when there is a feeling of control or power having been lost or taken away. I have pointed out that experiences of helplessness or powerlessness are central in addicts, as seen for instance in the first step of the twelve steps of Alcoholics Anonymous (AA) and the other "twelve-step" programs, which focuses on the need to tolerate powerlessness: "We admitted we were powerless over alcohol . . . " (Alcoholics Anonymous World Services, 1952). Similarly, AA's "serenity prayer" centers on tolerating helplessness in its expression of the wish to be granted "serenity to accept the things we cannot change" (Alcoholics Anonymous World Services, 1975). This vulnerability to experiencing feelings of helplessness as traumatic may arise in addicts from any level of psychosexual development. This is consistent with the narcissistic significance of such a vulnerability since narcissistic injuries may arise at any developmental level. It is also consistent with the fact that addicts as a group have a wide range of overall psychological health. Finally, addictive behavior demonstrates a powerful, relentless drive. This drive is clearly aggressive in nature, and is in the service of remedying a sense of helplessness and restoring a sense of internal power. This intense aggressive drive, arising as a result of narcissistic vulnerability, may be called narcissistic rage. In fact, the principal defining characteristics of addiction are identical to those of narcissistic rage. These include an intense drivenness which is not responsive to reality factors; a loss of ego autonomy in which other elements of the personality (other ego functions) are overwhelmed; a quality of turning a passively experienced situation (helplessness) into one that is actively pursued (in the addictive behavior); and the fact that, like narcissistic rage, addiction appears to have a particular quality of permanent risk of recurrence. To sum up, I view addiction as simultaneously the active conscious and unconscious effort to reestablish a sense of internal power and control when

faced with psychic helplessness, and the expression of the narcissistic rage which such overwhelming (traumatic) helplessness en-
genders.

Dr. Edith Sabshin (chapter 1) pointed out that addictive behavior is characterized by a "driven, demanding, insatiable, impulsive peremptory quality." Any theory which attempts to shed
light on addiction will have to explain this quality. Though recent
psychoanalytic thinking emphasizes the role of pain reduction in
addiction, there is no doubt that addicts actively seek something
through their behavior that is intensely gratifying, and this evi-
dently drive-gratifying, id-derived aspect of addiction must be addressed. In terms of my emphasis on the central importance of
rage in addiction, Dr. Sabshin's review of Simmel's (1927) paper
is particularly apropos, in its recounting of addicted patients'
breaking of branches off trees and killing and castrating the staff
in effigy. Dr. Sabshin also pointed out that there is considerable
variability in the severity of behaviors that are considered addictive. This variability must be considered in assessing the capacity of any individual to do analytic work, and should be explicable
by any formulation of addiction.

Dr. Krystal (chapter 4) referred to the importance in addiction of the "illusion of symbiosis" in the small child which permits
the infant to indulge the fantasy of omnipotence. If this illusion
is prematurely interrupted by long-lasting unrelievable distress,
the object representation (of the mother) becomes idealized, and
the self representation of the child is left without hope of soothing
or regulating itself, without even a sense of having the right or
power to regulate itself. However, while addicts may at times be
unaware of their affects, and may have the fantasy of an inability
to act which Krystal describes, they nevertheless continually act
to soothe themselves through their addictive behavior. The idea
that addicts are not in control, albeit unconsciously, of their behavior, but instead that the drug has power "over" them, is a
frequently encountered defense among addicts (Dodes, 1990). It
is an externalization which serves to deny addicts' own intense
feelings which are regularly enacted through the addictive behavior. Thus, while patients may experience themselves as forbidden
from soothing or comforting themselves, this may be primarily a

structural fantasy which serves to deny feelings of narcissistic injury and entitlement to restore what has been lost.

It should also be noted that the failure to experience ordinary affect, which is characteristic of alexithymia, is present in only a limited portion of the total population of addicts. For most addicts, affects *are* available, or at least are expressed in the behavior as I have described and are interpretable, can be experienced, and ultimately can be integrated. Therefore, if we are looking for the essence of an understanding of addiction, we cannot expect to find it in alexithymia itself. Krystal's emphasis on psychic trauma is significant, not in the form of overwhelming global catastrophe leading to alexithymia, but in the form of specific repeated traumatizations at various levels of psychosexual development that leave a legacy of narcissistic vulnerability to helplessness and rage. (The content about which one feels traumatically helpless will depend on the specifics of that person's development.) A consequence of the perspective I am suggesting is that addicts are in general more accessible to treatment than the severely limited patients who truly suffer with "pensée operatoire" or alexithymia.

Dr. Khantzian (chapter 2) also emphasized the treatability of many if not most addicts with a psychoanalytically oriented approach. He noted that one's view of the severity of psychopathology in addicts is a function of the population being studied. When he moved from working with patients in a methadone maintenance program to other settings, he was impressed with his patients' range of psychological capacities. My own similar observations have led me to feel that any formulation of addiction must involve a narrower kind of psychopathology than characterizes a personality disorder; the pathology in addiction is present in a wide variety of character structures.

In addition, how one approaches the population one treats will influence one's findings and conclusions. Failing to take a psychodynamic approach to addicts will result in not learning of their inner experience and the meaning of their use of addictive behavior; the result can be failure to help them to become abstinent. This has been a serious problem in treatment settings which do not address, or even actively avoid, a psychodynamic approach (Dodes, 1988, 1991). Vaillant (1981), for instance, working with treaters he called "psychodynamically naive," was led to the false conclusion that therapists could not manage their countertransference feelings or the issues arising in the therapy of alcoholics (Dodes, 1991). The contributions presented in this volume suggest that, contrary to Vaillant's view, it is essential for treaters of addicts to *not* be psychodynamically naive in order to understand the psychopathology and to address the treatment needs of this population (Dodes, 1991).

Dr. Khantzian focused on the self-medication aspect of drug use, pointing out the inner circumstances that might lead an addiction vulnerable person to select one type of drug over another. It is clear that this kind of selection process is at work for many addicts who do have a favorite drug. On the other hand, the fact that addicts frequently switch from one drug to another of an entirely different pharmacologic class, or use different classes of drugs in irregular combinations, means that the pharmacology of the substance can be of only limited significance in understanding addiction (Wurmser, 1974; Dodes, 1990). The quality of "addictiveness" of drugs is also overestimated as a factor in etiology or relapse of addiction (Dodes, 1990). For example, the common safe and social use of so-called addictive drugs (such as alcohol or even cocaine) by individuals who are not psychologically prone to addiction, suggests that the problem cannot be externalized to a quality inherent in the substance. But these points do not negate the usefulness of the self-medication idea, since it highlights the addict's search for a solution to an internal, psychological problem. The selection of a particular drug may be understood as an attempt to maximize the needed psychological effect. The self-medication concept is therefore compatible with a variety of formulations all of which have to do with managing an internal psychic function by drug use.

The role of self-care deficits which have been described by Khantzian (1978) and Khantzian and Mack (1983), raises the interesting question of the role of ego deficit psychology in addiction. Inherent in addiction is a paradox concerning being out of control. Addiction is clearly a phenomenon whose very nature, as a compulsive, driven behavior, is experienced by the addict as well as by those around him or her, as being out of control. Yet, most psychodynamic views of addiction describe the behavior as an effort to serve some purpose, whether the management of intolerable affect states, the search for an idealized object, the management of a punitive superego, or even, as I have emphasized, the retention of control itself. The resolution of this paradox is found in the conflict between unconscious aspects of the psyche and other aspects of the psyche that are temporarily overwhelmed. Addiction involves both the loss of control by certain of the ego's functions, that is, a loss of a degree of ego autonomy, and, simultaneously, seizure of control by unconscious ego defenses and drive derivatives resulting in enactment of the addictive behavior. This view of a balance of psychic forces in addiction allows for the expression of drive and drive gratification in addiction, as originally focused upon in psychoanalytic thought, without foregoing ego psychology (ego defensive function and defense deficit) and the significance of narcissistic issues. From this perspective, the role of deficits in self-care may be seen as one of the factors which affect the psychological balance within addicts, making them vulnerable to addictive behavior. Or, conversely, the presence of strong self-care functions may be protective against enacting otherwise peremptory forces within the psyche that would lead to addictive behavior. A deficit psychology may then be integrated with views of the active defensive functions of addiction, including the active aggression-driven corrective nature of addictive behavior which I have emphasized.

Another interesting point raised by Dr. Khantzian is the history of the debate between a disease model and what he termed a "symptom approach" to substance abuse. I agree with him that there is no need to pit one against the other. But integration of the two is possible only when the "disease" concept is defined in terms that allow coordination with psychodynamic work rather than as an explanation in itself. The disease concept is a good example of the confusion between description and explanation that Dr. Wurmser (chapter 3) addressed. I have suggested (Dodes, 1988) a model for an integrated approach, in which the "disease" is defined as having two components: first, a history of substance use that is repeatedly hurtful to the individual, and second, a permanent risk of repeating this behavior in the future. Taken together this model of a "disease" focuses attention on the seriousness of the illness and the corresponding need to be abstinent without shutting off psychodynamic exploration of the factors that contribute to the behavior. The "disease" in this definition is "an historical and psychological fact, not an explanation" (Dodes, 1988, p. 290).

For some, integrating psychodynamic therapy with a "disease" concept means that therapy be "sequenced" with an initial non-psychodynamic "disease" oriented therapy followed by psychodynamic therapy. The problem with this plan is that it risks failing to address the very issues which compel the patient to continue to use drugs. Addressing these factors may be necessary for the patient to become abstinent, or in some cases for the patient to be able to use other treatment modalities such as AA (Dodes, 1991). The major criticism of initial psychodynamic intervention has been the failure of some psychodynamic therapists to attend to the need for abstinence from the beginning of treatment, the need for "stability, containment, and control" as mentioned by Khantzian. But if safety factors are taken into consideration, then psychodynamic or psychoanalytic work from the beginning of treatment will often be useful and even essential (Dodes, 1991). The assessment of whether psychodynamic psychotherapy can continue in the presence of continued addictive behavior is an important technical question which is beyond the scope of this paper. In brief, the assessment in these cases needs to consider several factors: the realistic risks to the patient, the state of the transference, and the possibility of doing useful work in therapy while the patient is actively using the drug (Dodes, 1984).

Dr. Khantzian also emphasized the supportive, guiding role of AA and its focus on individuals' need for the help of others. It is clear that AA plays a critical role for many alcoholics. My own view has been that AA is *able* to serve in this ego prosthetic role because of the transference which many alcoholics bring to AA. As an organization it serves as an omnipotent object and through its "higher power" provides an omnipotent transitional object which many alcoholics make use of as a substitute for the internal omnipotence sought through alcohol use. As alcoholics "relinquish aspects of their own power (the sense of mastery and control) by acknowledging an inability to control their drinking and their lives, A.A. is assigned this potency, which lives on in the A.A. concept of the 'higher power' or in an idealized vision of

A.A. itself . . . Sobriety (in these cases) is achieved through willing surrender of the option to drink in exchange for the nurturance and protection of an idealized object" (Dodes, 1988, p. 289). This, then, is an object relations statement of the addict's effort to reestablish internal omnipotence (Dodes, 1990).

Finally, Dr. Khantzian cited an improvement in our ability to treat addicts psychotherapeutically. He mentioned improved recognition of patients' vulnerabilities, and corresponding modification of technique by therapists to provide greater "support, structure, empathy and contact." I would like to add some thoughts about the psychological function of a more active therapeutic stance. Such a stance may be understood as providing an object whose active, overt concern about the safety and well-being of the patient can be internalized, eventually providing the basis for an internal "self-care function" (Dodes, 1984), but whose immediate purpose may be to provide the omnipotent object whose power, borrowed in the transference, substitutes for the power achieved by the addictive behavior. For this purpose, while the therapist is active in expressing his or her concern about the importance of abstinence and the patient's safety, it is unnecessary for the therapist to attempt to actively create the transference role; it is the nature of transference that it is supplied by the patient. However, as Kris (1990) has recently pointed out, if the analyst takes a silent position with a patient who has significant punitive unconscious self-criticism, then the analyst's silence "is experienced as confirmation of the self-critical attitude" (p. 615), and therefore is not neutral from the standpoint of the patient's experience of the analyst. A more active position therefore does not have to mean a retreat to treatment by "suggestion," but on the contrary may be necessary to permit full analytic exploration by avoiding the unintended creation of unspoken unanalyzable negative transferences. Since many if not all addicts suffer with such unconscious self-criticism, a more active stance as described by Khantzian is often appropriate.

Dr. Wurmser (chapter 3) also emphasized the treatability of addicts, pointing to the fact that there is no fundamental gulf between addicts and other individuals with neurotic, or severely neurotic, disturbances. The difficulties of addicts are of the form familiar to us, namely, powerful inner forces embedded in layers of conflict, and outwardly expressed in destructive behavior. In considering this internal landscape, Dr. Wurmser focused on the role of drugs in overthrowing the superego's "burden-some . . . authority [and as a] flight from conscience." He described the deep shame and guilt of Victor, a man who witnessed, by sight or sound, the death of his father, then fled the scene. Dr. Wurmser referred to the conflict in this and similar cases as "the often irresistible tendency to spiral down into overwhelming affects and impulses versus the desperate effort at controlling them and the shame about losing such inner control—a control reestablished with those 'crazy,' compulsive actions." This reestablishment of control via compulsive activity agrees perfectly with my view. I would only add that the enraged reassertion of control in drug use often lies beneath the shame about not being in control, and is more denied. For example, when Victor left the house he was overwhelmed by his emotions and was also thereafter unable to tolerate them. His drug use was not only to relieve his shame and guilt, but was itself an action, like leaving the house, which was designed to calm him, to give him a sense of being stable and back in control. The patient improved when Dr. Wurmser helped him speak of this incident. In putting the event into words, it was exposed to the light of a benign prosthetic superego in the form of Dr. Wurmser, and the patient's punitive judgment about it was modified. With the dissolution of the affects forced on the ego by the superego judgments, that is, with the end of the experience of internal helplessness caused by being flooded with shame and guilt, there was no longer a need to act by taking drugs to reestablish internal control. In making this interpretation I want to be clear that it is critical in treatment to learn the specifics of what leads to the welling up of a feeling of helplessness in any given individual, and the specific factors which Dr. Wurmser described for Victor are essential to understanding the case. However, I am emphasizing the active corrective nature of the addictive behavior here.

The case of Burton, presented by Dr. Myers (chapter 6), is also illustrative. This man heralded his involvement in treatment by a rage episode, destroying the room of a prostitute who had refused to masturbate him. Likewise, he had rage outbursts when limited by the unavailability of cash machines, or of his analyst

during weekends and vacations. Myers described Burton as feeling at these times worthless and enraged, and said that his only
"solace" was in his repetitive encounters with prostitutes or in
compulsive masturbation. He also pointed out that Burton's sexual activities were fueled by "the desire to dampen aggressive
tensions and to overcome feelings of anhedonia." I would view
the sexual behavior as "solace" but in the sense that it dampened
aggressive tensions by expressing them, seizing a sense of power
through being able to totally control his access to sexual release,
thereby reversing overwhelming feelings of worthlessness. Likewise, I would see Burton's frantic masturbation later in the analysis, when he felt devalued by his dependency on the analyst, as
not only a means to relieve his depression, but also to reassert
his potency, fueled by the "impotent rage" which, Dr. Myers
pointed out, followed his distressing dreams of finding his penis
shrunken and unresponsive. Burton's overall improvement in
treatment was linked to his insight and lessening of his shame
(narcissistic injury), so that he had more capacity to tolerate his
feelings of abandonment and neediness without being overwhelmed by them, hence had less need to be enraged and less
need to have to restore his potency.

I will also comment briefly on the use of antidepressants in
this case. It appears to me that the occurrence of depression in
this case was a sign of improvement. It entailed an increased
tolerance of the patient's injured and devalued feelings without
having to immediately repair them with action. This is not to say
that antidepressant drug treatment may not have been indicated,
only that one would want to consider the fact that the shift in
affect and mood was an advance, in making the decision to intervene with a drug.

Charles, another of Dr. Myers' cases, was exposed to his parents' narcissistic investment in themselves at the expense of both
himself and his sister. As Dr. Myers wrote, the parents "treated
them with . . . incredible indifference to their very existence,"
which was linked to the parents having "disregarded them while
pursuing their 'disgusting activities in the bedroom.' " Charles
was placed in a helpless position, not only by the overt overexpo-
sure to his parents, but by his own desire which was stimulated
by the scene. We may assume he was also overexposed to his sister

with whom he shared a room between ages 5 and 11. Charles subsequently reverses his helpless role by taking an active position in which he himself controls his access and exposure to the incestuous scenes in the videotapes. Likewise, after the hour in which he burst into tears, Charles does not come to the next three sessions, stops going to work, and has a binge of watching pornographic tapes, "masturbating himself into a state of insensibility." We learn subsequently that he is unconsciously searching for his lost sister in the tapes, but the immediate form of this is an addictive frenzy. The aspect of this that is distinctively *addictive* is the intensely driven quality which overwhelms other aspects of his functioning and loses touch with realistic factors such as going to work. I would also stress that it is a turning of passive into active, via both the active behavior of the masturbating and the selection and viewing of the tapes, and via withdrawing from the analysis where he had just been again overwhelmed by exposure to his feelings of loss and valuelessness. His addictive behavior regained for him an immediate, repeated kind of mastery. Later, through the work of the analysis, his tendency to retraumatization by helplessness was reduced (through his increased insight into the origins of this sensitivity and the modification of his shame-induced superego), allowing him to better tolerate the previously overwhelming feelings of rage and grief. Consequently his tape watching and masturbation, although continuing as behaviors, lacked the fuel of an enraged reassertion of mastery over helplessness, that is, lacked the qualities of addiction.

Dr. Ornstein (chapter 5) presented Mrs. Holland, a patient who engaged in a repetitive, driven search for a man who would fulfill her fantasies. Mrs. Holland experienced herself as powerful, able to excite her father more than her mother could, and depended upon by him, but also and more deeply felt great shame, guilt, and devaluation. She was attracted to men who would confirm her sense of power via their capacity to be seduced by her and remain attracted and attached to her. Although Mrs. Holland was consciously aware of feelings of tenderness toward these men, the deeper level of her use of them as narcissistic objects (i.e., objects utilized to fulfill certain needed fantasies) became clear when she would abruptly abandon them once they failed to support her fantasy. On those occasions there was a "return of the denied," to use Wurmser's felicitous term, with a flood of feelings of "shittiness" and worthlessness. In the transference likewise, Mrs. Holland had fantasies of power over the analyst who could be seduced and helplessly excited, be "under her spell." This appeared to represent an enraged assertion of her power, turning the tables on the tormenting object, actually her own punitive superego, but in its projected form as the analyst in the transference. This dynamic was demonstrated by the reduction in Mrs. Holland's sadistic fantasy once she experienced her analyst as less judgmental; that is, once her own self-punitiveness was reduced in the course of the analysis she no longer projected it onto Dr. Ornstein and then no longer needed to be enraged with her and be powerful over her. Mrs. Holland had considerable narcissistic expectations, particularly in the transference where Dr. Ornstein at times could say nothing that was "good enough." These expectations reflected the underlying narcissistic injuries with which she suffered, shown in her feelings of worthlessness and emptiness, and defended against in restorative grandiosity and sadism, and in the addictive imperative which expressed these feelings. With a waning of the experience of being overwhelmed by her longings, her guilt, and her shame, there was less enraged drive to repeat the restorative addictive behavior.

I would like to note my disagreement with the idea expressed in Dr. Ornstein's paper that gambling and drug and alcohol use are "pseudo-excitements" used to overcome feelings of "deadness." In my view this raises the question of what the "deadness" feeling and fantasy are about and how the addictive behavior relates to these underlying issues. Is "deadness" for instance a way of describing giving up on having what is wanted? Is the addiction then an unconscious solution to this giving up through insisting on having a life? Joyce McDougall (1984) describes an infant struggling for "the right to exist" as one form of the struggle in addictive behavior to retake control of one's experience (Dodes, 1990). There is in fact a good deal in Dr. Ornstein's interesting paper that suggests that the addictive behavior had functions well beyond achievement of exhilaration.

Finally, I would like to offer some thoughts on the factors which define addiction. First of all, I would say that addictions are all compulsive, but that they represent a subset of compulsions; not all compulsions are addictions. The affect which arises when compulsions are prevented is predominantly anxiety, but when addictions are blocked, while there may certainly be anxiety, there is a preponderance of rage. In addition, compulsions are experienced as obligatory. Addictions are also obligatory, but unlike many compulsions they are also consciously sought out. Following from these and many other observations I suggest the following definition: addiction is a compulsively driven activity characterized by intense unremittingness, a relative loss of ego autonomy in which other aspects of the personality are overwhelmed (including responsiveness to reality factors and self-care ego functions), and in which there is a turning of passive into active. In my view these factors are all explicable by the presence in addiction of narcissistic rage which arises in the setting of a vulnerability to narcissistic injury as a result of the emotional experience of helplessness. The addiction is a transiently successful effort to both correct this internal helplessness and to express the narcissistic rage it produces. In any individual case, it will be necessary to analyze the specific factors which are critical for producing the traumatic state of helplessness. Such an analysis will finally also explain the roots of this sensitivity in the patient's development.

Chapter 8

A Child Analyst Looks at Addictive Behavior

Dale R. Meers, Ph.D.

A generation ago sexual promiscuity, delinquency, and alcohol and drug abuse were understood as symptomatic forms of acting out, forms of self-medication that were antithetic to psychoanalytic treatment. Clinical experience was persuasive: patients with impulse ridden character neuroses acted out their symptoms, rationalizing their conduct to defend against insight. Those who used alcohol and drugs added pharmacological insult to psychopathological impairment of ego functions since they biologically undermined reality testing in drug induced magical thinking.

A generation ago, in the years immediately preceding my child analytic training in London, and in the best tradition of Aichorn and Redl, I worked chaotic twelve-hour days with neurotic, delinquent, acting-out, working-class adolescent males. My retreat to quiet academic research and the elegance of training in analysis of (mere) symptom neuroses seemed a very reasonable trade-off for the fourteen-hour days that we who identified with Anna Freud shared with her at Hampstead.

In the early 1960s, Hampstead Heath's adolescent hangout, the Witch's Caldron, was haunted by some of London's more distinguished (if not first) flower children, including the older two brothers of my patient, Esther. While Esther was jealous of her mother's involvement in her brothers' drug use, she seemed even more envious of her mother's apparent voyeuristic interest in a girl who partied with the boys; the girl, not incidentally, was out of Freud's extended family. I included this in my weekly clinical notes that all candidates and staff completed and circulated to the Clinic's research groups. While I was well aware that my patient's older brothers were both in analysis, I had not appreciated, until my supervisor (Hansi Kennedy) advised me of the fact, that Anna Freud would terminate the brothers' treatment if she learned of their drug use.[1]

I returned to the United States a committed, if sheltered ego psychologist, ill prepared for the hysterical tarantellas bequeathed to that time by the returning dark ages. Conduct that had earlier characterized impulse disorders was becoming popularized and cross-culturally sustained. I began private practice in Washington in the midst of "Beatle-mania," fervent adolescent proselytizing of grass, of LSD tripping, and the extraordinary sexual revolution. As females demonstrated that they could be as promiscuous as males, and homosexuals came out of the closet—gonorrhea, syphilis, and the socialization of psychopathy were revitalized. Dejâ vu all over again! My private practice was preponderantly drug impaired, sexually promiscuous, acting out adolescents, only upper class this time.

The profound significance of political protests of that time were not infrequently obscured by the impulsive fervor of group sustained passions. President Kennedy was confrontational and also a catalyst; while he championed civil rights with the National Guard he also introduced the nation to the military morality of Vietnam. The assassinations of President Kennedy, Martin Luther King, Jr., and Robert Kennedy contributed to our national sense of urgency, that exploded in inner city ghetto riots. Orwell had arrived in Washington, DC, twenty years prematurely, with intimate TV coverage of the next generation, as in *Apocalypse Now*,

---

[1]Situated in one of London's most sedate residential areas, the Hampstead Clinic actively sustained clinical, psychoanalytic research in delinquent and borderline pathology. To secure annual relicensing, the Clinic had to defend its patients/status against community objections that were sometimes understandable.

as rock, drugs, and sex merged with civil rights and Vietnam war protests.

My new patients were black youngsters whose academic and intellectual impairments qualified them for research at Children's Hospital (Meers, 1970, 1972, 1973a,b, 1974). Naomi's mother was borderline and hospitalized three times during her child's analysis. It was over a year before I learned that Naomi's father, a chronic alcoholic, was living in her house. By age 8, Naomi allowed me to know that she gave her oldest brother blow-jobs in return for favors. Incidentally, she had been introduced to cunnilingus at age 5 when placed in a foster home during one of her mother's early hospitalizations.

Years later when she was troubled, Naomi found me again. She wondered if she had made a mistake in not telling me everything when she had been in treatment. Her father had always been drunk, and she had always blown him when he demanded, and he didn't pay her like her brother had. She had been too ashamed, not of herself but of her father, to tell me when she was a child. Naomi wanted to know if her childhood resistance to confession might have something to do with her own adolescent sexual anesthesia with the boyfriend she otherwise had come to love. In effect, Naomi belatedly asked for my absolution, as if my understanding might yet mitigate the damage she had suffered.

My second ghetto patient was 5 years old and lived with his mother and her parents. Virgil's uncle was serving a life sentence for manslaughter and his mom readily reminded the boy that he, his dad, and uncle were like peas in a pod. Virgil's mother was a clerk in a local school and usually came home for lunch if Virgil's grandmother went out to work for the day. The grandmother attempted to control her alcoholic husband who could sweet-talk Virgil's mother into getting a bottle for lunch if the grandmother went to work. If she did, the two would get so loaded that they often invited street drunks into the house.

A cab driver found Virgil's mother in a gutter, stripped and beaten. The hospital discovered that her assailant had injected her with heroin laced with rat poison—apparently for nonpayment of her bill. I then learned that she worked the streets for her heroin, taking her johns home when Virgil's grandmother was out. After she was discharged from the hospital, Virgil's mother accepted my recommendation to try a methadone clinic. The day following, she called me in profound misery. Someone at the clinic had recognized her and had maliciously called her school, and she had been summarily fired. I then reread Ibsen's *Wild Duck*, became considerably more humble, and managed all subsequent drug referrals with much greater care.

Child analysis was (and still is) an analytic mutant, without formal criteria to establish the legitimacy of either its parentage or methods. I had trained at the seat of orthodoxy, where analysis of impulsive borderline and mildly delinquent youngsters was formally built into Hampstead's research. If someone questioned whether an analysis was classical, the issue was diagnostic rather than a criticism of technical mismanagement.

The Baltimore-Washington Institute sustains a kind of quiet, protective humor in which some of us have always seen ourselves as the DAR of theoretical and clinical orthodoxy. Within the self-righteousness of my own orthodoxy, I found it quite implausible that all the sexual and drug related impulsivity that exploded in the 1960s originated in individual, unconscious conflicts. It had much more of a group psychological aura of shared hysteria. Talking of this with a friend Paul Gray, also a supervisor, he speculated, as I recall, that the prevailing sexual revolutionaries had produced their own culturally shared and gender reinforced ego ideal that was like a reaction formation to superego standards; that young women who then sought analysis presented sexual histories that a very little earlier would have defined them as suffering with unanalyzable, acting out character disorders.

At a Hampstead clinical conference in 1963, Anna Freud reflected somewhat sadly on the profession's clinical dedication to borderline, delinquent, and other severe forms of illness. She wondered that if all the effort that had gone into such well-intentioned research had been dedicated instead to the simple neuroses, we might understand them a little better.

I doubt that we understand the neuroses better today than Anna Freud did in the early 1960s. It is certainly apparent that psychoanalysts have shared in the prevailing ignorance of the causes of our national, cultural misadventures and miseries of pervasive drug use and sexual promiscuity. Professional historians may someday review whether that provocative climate that challenged national social and political orthodoxies also stimulated proliferating analytic interests in borderline and narcissistic character disorders that Klein and Kohut brought out of orthodoxy's closet. If there are significant trade-offs to compensate for the continuing incompleteness of our theoretical understanding of the neuroses, they undoubtedly derive from our clinical engagement with borderline and addictive character disorders.

We have six interesting papers that overlap and sometimes contradict each other conceptually, symptomatically, and clinically. Concurring that addiction is more a description than a diagnosis, they have presented patients of quite differing degrees of pathology, whom they treated in quite differing ways based upon different theoretical premises. Drs. Sabshin, Krystal, Khantzian, Wurmser, Myers and Ornstein have provided a very full menu that is sufficiently diverse to whet all appetites.

I suspect that the driven, destructive bondage of addictions contributes more to their pejorative denotation than does their purported, nominal hedonism. Addictions entail perversions of normality. Out of our shared romantic, prejudicial protectiveness, we exempt the most profound of human addictions, loving and sexuality, from that nomenclature. While we joke that our own love is blind, a temporary insanity and a fine madness, we are also awed and not infrequently clinically defeated by the imperative, driven, and dependent character of our patients' unbearable losses that Sabshin has referred to.

Ornstein cautioned against indiscriminate use of the term *addictive*. Perhaps her warning derives from analytic convictions of the imperative, repetitive dependencies we see in *all* forms of pathological behavior and much of normal human experience. While few clinicians accept Freud's convictions of a death instinct, fewer yet would doubt the profound and all too dramatic evidence of the ubiquitous, pathological compulsions our patients repeat.

Our panel concurs that addictions are adequately defined by their impulsive, imperative, peremptory, and self-destructive character and unconscious purpose. Wurmser's emphasis on the addict's self-destructive bondage leads me to ask if there is diagnostic merit in distinguishing between normative and pathological addictions. Common impulsive, imperative, peremptory types of gratifying sensuality strike me as *instinctively* addictive. Intimacy, love, and sexuality are circularly, richly, powerfully rewarding and self reinforcing; their addictive character is not apparent until a person is deprived of one or all.

Pathological addictions are also instinctive, yet are distinguished by: (1) the unconscious significance of the addictive substance or behavior that is unique to each patient; (2) the profound, self-deceptive, magical thinking that seduces addicts to rationalize their conduct; (3) the progressive bondage (Khantzian's "deadly amplification") of substance abuse that globally, neurologically exacerbates existing psychological ego dysfunctions; and (4) the dangers of decompensation or suicide that patients may suffer from therapeutic prohibitions that ignore the defensive purpose of an addiction.

Addictions readily expose theoretical differences. The panelists generally agree that psychological illness produces the primary misery of substance abusers and that continued use of drugs accelerates malfunctioning, thereby increasing depressive and suicidal potentials. Wurmser's case vignette illustrates his understanding that destructive substance addiction is a purposeful, superego type of self-punishment for unconscious guilt. Khantzian is less convinced that his addict's choice of damaging drugs is masochistic or self-punishing. His construction that addictive pain is sought as a price for actively mastering an infantile passive trauma has the sound of a preoedipal, Kohutian thesis. Such constructions are not mutually exclusive, but characterize disagreements that only patients can resolve.

Ornstein documents the object relations, self psychological theoretical perspectives that guide her in what she listens for and interprets to her patient. I found her clinical elaboration of her patient's addictive conduct most interesting. Her technical recommendations are so clear that they should be obligatory reading for students of classical psychoanalysis who would better understand the clinical consequences of Kohut's developmental theory. If this were a comparative technical seminar, Ornstein's case would be particularly fruitful to compare when, where, and why the defense analysis of ego psychology differs with self psychology.

I have seen only a few patients with presenting symptoms who knew directly and painfully that they were "addicted" to particular persons. Ornstein's experience seems typical, namely, that the addictive character of ego syntonic behavior is exposed by unanticipated breaches in a patient's defenses. The plasticity of Mrs. Holland's worst symptoms, her incipient depressive sorrow, abandonment, and depreciation, became dramatically evident with her repetitive initiation, destruction, and replacement of one love affair after another.

Ornstein did not report her patient, Mrs. Holland, as suffering from guilt for her chronic extramarital adventures. Mrs. Holland's borderline reality testing seems evident in her ego syntonic acceptance of quite remarkable crushes on unknown men. I would contrast this with a patient whom I saw diagnostically because of her profound misery with her ego *dystonic* addiction to a psychopathic lover.

Divorced from a miserable marriage, Mrs. X had delighted in a lover who sexually excited and fulfilled her as she had never dreamed possible. But he had a rather major character problem: he stole, cheated, lied, and was provocatively, sexually disloyal. As this became apparent, Mrs. X left him in both anger for his duplicity and sorrow for her loss. To her ensuing astonishment, Mrs. X discovered that she could not stop obsessing about the man she had left, and she became so profoundly depressed that she had no interest in looking for someone better. In her misery, Mrs. X had repeatedly returned to her lover, who on recognizing her vulnerability, humiliated her all the more. I suspect that Mrs. X, like Wurmser's patient, was driven by unconscious guilt—in her case for her newfound, extramarital, unbridled sexuality.

Ornstein is all too familiar with ego psychologists who continue to ask the questions she and Kohut have already tried to answer. She has undoubtedly heard our earlier protests that self psychologists bypass exploration of the unconscious origins of their patients' rages and offer transference cures in the name of transmuting internalization. Stated a bit differently, ego psychologists naggingly enquire about Ornstein's patient's openly expressed fury with the outrageous father of her childhood. The men Mrs. Holland seduced, passionately loved, then abandoned were presented as incidental victims rather than tortured paternal surrogates. Eventually abandoning her self-perpetuating miseries in the security of a comforting transference, Mrs. Holland is described as replacing a destructive, external, sexual addiction with a regressive, desexualized introject.

One purpose of the *Workshop Series* is to involve nonanalysts in the excitement of psychoanalysis. In our review of addictions, we have the opportunity to share some of our humor, exasperation, and respect for the theoretical and technical differences that we have yet to resolve with each other. Irrespective of whether one agrees with Ornstein's theoretical or clinical premises, her work demonstrates some of the miracle of psychological change, of the mutability of a patient's illusions and the elemental, psychotherapeutic modification of her symptomatology. Charcot's hypnotic extravagances introduced Freud to the extraordinary mutability of symptom formation. In our readiness to dispute with each other as to why this is true, we ignore the vulnerability of our patients to psychopharmacological incest with neuropsychiatry and the advertising media.

Myers presented synopses of three cases in which analyses of blatant, obsessed sexual dramas revealed their addictive character. One is not surprised with Myers' diagnosis of borderline pathology. Alex cruised incessantly for men with big penises, Burton for inexhaustible hookers, and Charles searched porn videos for his lost erections and for his sister. Therapy elaborated the idiosyncratic origins of each man's sexual obsession. As with Mrs. Holland, they separately documented a common sexual escape from a profound sense of worthlessness, emptiness, and incipient rage. While Myers links such emotions to histories of infantile abandonment, humiliation, and misery, his patients' were undeterred in their anachronistic perseverations in reliving the past.

In the brevity of his summaries, Myers does not explain the "neutralization" of his patients' "enormous rage." But he does note that Alex began to get better when he discovered his analyst's soothing presence and that Burton looked in his dreams to an older man to return his potency. That is, Myers seems to imply a Kohutian, nurturing clinical response to unconsciously motivated rage.

Medication is selectively prescribed to enhance reality testing, and from a patient's subjective vantage it should soothe and neutralize. Most borderline patients, I suspect, have no difficulty in accepting a pharmacological introject as a transitional comforter to manage anguish.

Each of us has had our first borderline patient. My Wolfman had a dramatic, wild, adolescent analysis that apparently saved him from institutionalization. A much later, extended analytic psychotherapy, that was sustained by medication, prepared him for analysis. My patient was deeply wounded that his referring psychiatrist, also an analyst, had abandoned him. He was ambivalent that depletion of his medication would require a consultation with his old therapist for a prescription refill, and he carried an extra pill in his shirt pocket for good luck.

After perhaps a year's explorations of fulminating anxieties and passive irascibility, my patient was delighted, indeed excited, by my interpretative question, namely: Could he imagine that his chronic passivity might be defensive? But humor turned to fear as my patient subsequently, anxiously questioned my diagnostic competence. What happens, said he, if you err, if I abandon passivity and my dreams are real? His most horrendous, repetitive nightmare entailed descending into a basement where he opened a deep-freeze with the certain knowledge of a Saran-wrapped, dissected female body. Though he had some nine years of previous therapy, we agreed that we should proceed with particular reserve and respect for passivity. But we also agreed that we might enquire about motives for preserving a woman so coldly, rigidly, and meticulously in the dark.

My patient subsequently discovered that he had forgotten to take his medication for some weeks. He found it quite humorous to experiment and discovered that even if he only carried his pill in his shirt pocket, it helped as much as if he had ingested it. Winnicott would have enjoyed my patient's joke, namely, that the pill he carried in his shirt pocket was his psychiatrist and that his psychiatrist was a pill!

Incipient rage, characteristic of borderline and narcissistic pathology, may prove unapproachable in the most tender of clinical inquiries. From that vantage, even ego psychologists accept transference cures as *most* acceptable alternatives to suicide or psychotic decompensation. In his technical management, Myers specifically noted that he tested that fragile possibility. From that context, he would appear to share Ornstein's theoretical premise that incipient rage should be neutralized, as by medication or unconditional acceptance, rather than elucidated and examined to clarify any archaic, illusory residues of childhood.

Krystal views substance addiction as originating in a defensive aftermath of a severe traumatic infantile episode. In his formulation, trauma precipitates a precocious loss of an infant's symbiotic illusion of omnipotence, leaving the baby with an eternal, paranoic fear. Krystal's hypothesis appears strikingly similar to Melanie Klein's paranoid-depressive conceptions of infancy. While Klein speculatively elaborated that infantile fears derive from a death instinct, Krystal perceives them as traumatic sequela. Postulating a primal ego defect that Krystal labels an "affect defense," such traumatized infants hypothetically are unable to discern differences in feelings, which sounds like a variation on Freud's hypothesis of a genetic, primal stimulus barrier.

Wurmser and Khantzian clearly share some of Krystal's interest in preconflictual, infantile origins of hypersensitivity. At that conceptual juncture, I suspect that their shared concerns arise from the very special ego impediments of borderline and narcissistic patients who, in this context, are incidentally also addicts. Our theorists belong to that honorable group of researchers who struggle to make sense of the elemental vulnerabilities of those babies we describe as atypical, psychosomatic, autistic, and psychotic.

Krystal's assumption of a primal ego defect appears to contribute to his clinical departure from classical, defense analysis. Since patients could hardly be expected to recall or remember a genetic defect or phylogenetic process, Krystal offers them educational insight into "aggression of extraordinary intensity." The subsequent relief Krystal's patients experienced should be something like Jung's, Freud's, or Klein's patients when they were respectively reassured that the woman in the deep-freeze was the victim of archetypal memory traces or a death instinct.

Wurmser writes as an ego psychologist and his brief outline of Victor's treatment is that of defense analysis. Victor's developmental miseries, symptoms, and addictions qualify him for a borderline diagnosis. But from Wurmser's ego psychological perspective, a borderline diagnosis is simply part of the general continuum of psychopathological fragility that necessitates infinite clinical tact and patience. Wurmser's therapeutic goal remains the gentle, meticulous clarification of past and present that strengthens a patient's explorations of his defenses (Gray, 1973).

From an ego psychological perspective, infantile pain and failures of nurture are far more than deprivational. Neonatal pain initiates genetic responses that we variously label as primary repression, projection, introjection, denial, or splitting. Such defenses are instinctive, nonselective, and contribute to distorted, nonveridical maturational awareness of both self and the object world. In that context, Klein's conceptions of neonatal paranoia, precocious ego development, and depressive restitution are far closer to ego psychology than Kohut's deficit version of Mahlerian theory. Kohut's conception of rage needs a better interpreter than I; his deficit theory of narcissistic wounds (that should be benevolently healed by introjective processes) has my total endorsement—and complete disbelief.

Krystal, Wurmser, and Khantzian readily affirm that most drug addicts are not in treatment, and that the small proportion who are seen at drug clinics are typically too severely impaired to use psychoanalysis. As analysts we lament that we are technically impotent in treating chronic drug abusers who damage themselves beyond our capacities to help. Our complaints with commercial seductions for analgesics, amphetamines, antidepressants, and a host of pharmacological addictions are ignored. And addicts of a commercial persuasion, whom we might more readily and effectively help, share in an extraordinary, communal denial that extends public rationalizations even of alcohol and tobacco addictions. With 60 million smokers in the United States and 400,000 related deaths per year, doctors (Krystal advises) write 100 million benzodiazepine prescriptions per year.

Millions of the general public treat their worries, pains, anger, and sorrows promiscuously with food, sex, alcohol, tobacco, and over-the-counter drugs. Krystal's and Sabshin's conclusions seem apt, namely, that we only get to see those addicts who fail at their own efforts at medication or, with Ornstein and Myers, when they incidentally reveal addictions disguised in ego syntonic behavior.

The research findings that derive from the treatment of chronic substance abusers is the most interesting to analysts because it appears to sustain our theoretical expectations. Yet these data seem egregiously tainted. The substances chronically abused, particularly alcohol, heroin, crack, and PCP, are so pervasively damaging to global ego functioning as to obscure and distort a patient's premorbid history. From a research perspective, such addicts appear the least reliable of all subjects for explorations of developmental contributions to their pathologies.

We admire but rarely envy those colleagues who return to the burdens of general psychiatry in the treatment of severely disturbed and addictive patients. Three of our panelists have introduced psychoanalytic perspectives into the drug abuse clinics and literature. Given the tortured relationships of present-day psychoanalysis, it would be helpful to learn if *any* analytic contributions still find acceptance with our neuropsychiatric, behavioristic colleagues.

Sabshin dated analytic reconceptualizations of addictions to the 1920s, to ego psychology and the structural theory. Jung worked extensively with severe pathology, and his most cogent criticism of Freud's pre 1914 ego-instinct, sexual instinct theory accurately demonstrated the internal contradictions that self-punishment and suicide could hardly derive from self-preservative ego instincts (Nagera, Baker, Edgcumbe, Holder, Laufer, Meers, and Rees, 1970). Freud's remarkable response (to Jung [Jones, 1955]) entailed the radical introduction of ego psychology/the structural theory (beginning with "On Narcissism" [1914]), the reformulation of anxiety as a signal (rather than transformed libido) (Strachey and Tyson, 1959), and the invention of the death instinct (Freud, 1920).

While Freud introduced ego psychology and defense analysis to psychoanalysis in the 1920s, Melanie Klein reintroduced a neo-Freudian id psychology in the 1930s. The Nazis tried to render European psychoanalysis extinct, and the 1940s brought psychoanalysis into the sphere of U.S. military psychiatry. Military and general psychiatry readily embraced dynamic conceptions of the traumatic neuroses, alcohol, and drug abuse—each of which proliferated during and after World War II. The European infusion of American psychoanalysis both enhanced and complicated notions of orthodoxy by disclaiming Kleinian adventures with borderline pathology, by readily abandoning preoedipal pathology to an emerging dynamic psychiatry, and by defining heresy as clinical dilution of psychoanalysis to treat disorders more severe than the neuroses. Leo Stone (1967) wrote that such institutional claims of purity were largely a clinical fiction; from the beginning of time, analysts have discovered and treated symptom neuroses that masked severe character disorders. Child analysts, Melanie Klein, Anna Freud, David Winnicott, René Spitz, Benjamin Spock, and Margaret Mahler undermined an aging pretention that oedipal pathology defined psychoanalysis. And adult analysts Melanie Klein, W. D. Fairbairn, Michael Balint, Heinz Kohut and, later, Otto Kernberg, linking borderline and narcissistic psychopathology to the earliest of developmental conflicts, undermined orthodoxy in refocusing analytic clinical interests back to some of its general psychiatric origins.

Child analysts sometimes joke that DSM-III ignored "adolescence" as *the* developmental neurosis that hits every family. While we shudder that Middle Eastern and U.S. adolescents wield AK47s and Uzis, we tend to ignore the fact that we also provide our young people with lethal wheels and sufficient access to alcohol and drugs to contribute significantly to our 25,000 auto deaths a year. It is less than clear whether we are more impotent than indifferent or collusive as we nurture our adolescents in our impulse-ridden society.

Adolescents of yesteryear survived alcoholism better than nicotine addiction, and most juggled sexuality guiltily with minimal venereal disease or pregnancies. But in our brave new world, we cannot protect our adolescents from their proselytizing buddies, particularly the all too friendly dealers Krystal alluded to. The power of adolescent peer group relations is most evident in their shared idealizations that what is cool is partly defined by opposition and negation of parental and adult values. The strength of groups is also their danger since group psychological processes encourage regressive disclaimers of personal responsibility that are as seductive as alcohol or marijuana.

Adolescents are the more vulnerable to addiction through casual drug use because their peer groups proclaim their maturity by opposition to adult warnings and conventions. Today's adolescents are also at greater risk, as Sabshin noted, because new drugs like crack are both more addictive and more lethal. I am reasonably sure that our young jocks have a greater investment in alcohol and cocaine than in the past, but I worry as much about their quieter sibs who are on grass and party, copulate, and procreate all too frequently.

Our panelists introduced four patients whose sexual behavior was a central part of an addictive process. The consequences of current adolescent sexuality suggests widely shared sadomasochistic motives and massive denial. Given the threat of autoimmune deficiency syndrome (AIDS), sexual education has never been more extended or explicit, yet venereal disease continues to escalate. Washington, DC, had the dubious honor of being the first metropolitan city where more babies were born out of wedlock than within it. Multiple pregnancies of unmarried, disadvantaged adolescents do not occur for want of understanding or condoms. Babies born to very young mothers have the highest risk of prematurity, mortality, and congenital defects. While the majority of child parents grow up familiar with street drugs, we might ask if they are like Ornstein's and Myers' patients, whether promiscuous sexuality is even more addictive than drugs.

Conclusions

We readily concur that substance abuse, as with heroin, cocaine, PCP, and alcohol, introduces what Khantzian has called a biological deadly amplification. Our deliberations have included those substance abusers who fail in their efforts at self-medication, hence are more apt to be seen at drug clinics. We do not find it exceptional that they are more often severely impaired borderline and narcissistic patients who found greater need for drugs and are then more imperiled by them. They clearly cannot be treated by psychoanalysis.

I am surprised with some treatment procedures, not merely because they are confrontational but because they are recommended by knowledgeable, sensitive analysts like Khantzian. Since we share a conviction that our patients defend against and then self-medicate to avoid such propensities as unconscious violence, why would therapists return to Freud's earliest mistakes and insist that patients acknowledge that which they mutilate their minds to avoid?

Ornstein's and Myers' patients present such dramatic secondary gains from their sexual obsessions that they appear to merit inclusion as sexual addictions. Not unlike clinic patients, however, Ornstein's and Myers' patients are borderline or narcissistically impaired, which is their significant and basic diagnosis. Their sexual conduct was impulsive, imperative, peremptory, and derived from unconscious motives, which satisfies all of our criteria that define addictions except that of self-destructiveness.

Their sexual obsessions contributed to searches in places and with persons who could have been personally quite dangerous; the obsessions were incapable of more than transient satiation, hence they were a barrier to continuity of relationships in real life. In that context, such behavior satisfied the last criterion, namely, that of bondaged self-destructiveness.

The starkness of these patients' sexual behavior tends to obscure the more elemental fact that it was obsessively manipulative. Sex and beauty were essential to Mrs. Holland in reducing her self-deprecating, suicidal miseries through a transient lover's nurture. Alex's primary concern was not with the sensuality of his own or his homosexual partners' sexuality. Sex was the come-on, the vehicle he used to try to neutralize his internal, eternal self-deprecation. Burton, like Alex, was never sated because his sexual demands could never secure his unconscious purpose of finding some inexhaustible source of reassurance for his incessant self-deprecation. And Charles was the least sexual of all in his impotent, masturbatory searching of porn videos.

Such manifest sexuality masked quite hostile and archaic demands. When we review their sexuality dispassionately, we might ask whether such patients are implicitly "plea bargaining" their diagnoses. It is more dramatic and understandable to confess that one is passionately driven, with imperative sexual needs, than to admit to paranoic obsessions with sexual manipulation of interchangeable objects, all designed to relieve archaic illusions of infantile reality.

While I am content with the diagnosis of addictive behavior, the cases presented by this group of authors found their addictions not in sensuality-sexuality but in the manipulative control of others. Which is to conclude that the common element of blatant sexuality contributes to misnaming the addiction. It would probably be more accurate to label such cases as sadomasochistic addictions.

The authors of the present work have many opportunities to critique our theoretical and technical differences with each other. But such deliberations belong in other volumes. We join each other here to invite the interests of other clinicians and researchers in the fascination of our discipline.

Finally, as tragic as street drugs and street people may be, the brave new world of neuropsychiatry and psychopharmacology troubles me even more. The addictive behaviors that we see and treat are but a ripple in the flood of addictive substances and behavior in the nation that are increasingly sustained by our new scientists and morality. I fear that as we fiddle, Rome burns; that as addictions proliferate, we fail to build a clinical consensus and professional forum that is sufficiently impressive to influence either legislators or the public.

Chapter 9

"Transitional" and "Autistic" Phenomena in Addictive Behavior

David M. Hurst, M.D.

A ddiction is an awesome social problem today; awesome in its prevalence, its destructiveness, and its tenacity. What have we as psychoanalysts learned in the first hundred years of our science about addiction, and what is the current state of our knowledge? In asking these questions, we are considering not only the treatment of alcohol and drug abuse, but the general psychology of addictive behavior, the depth psychology of addiction itself.

Addiction is the process of becoming psychologically enslaved to somebody, something, or some behavior: a substance, a job, a hobby, money, gambling, religion, physical exercise, or sex, to mention a few. The effects can be obvious or subtle, but an addicted person minimizes and denies his addiction, and those around him do the same. Addiction is remarkably ubiquitous, affecting many more people than is generally recognized. The characteristic that best distinguishes addictive behavior is expressed in the words of the first step of the Alcoholics Anonymous Program of Recovery: "We admitted we were powerless over alcohol."

How do people become enslaved and powerless? Do they get "hooked" by trying something that turns out to be irresistible? Some things in life have an inherently irresistible quality, and some chemicals are well known to be physiologically entrapping, but getting hooked seems to have more to do with the addict himself, and with the factors that predispose him.

It has been suggested that for such people the infant–mother bond either fails to develop adequately or is disrupted prematurely during early development. Since our species is notable for the extended, symbiotic, almost marsupial nature of early development, a caretaker is required to provide food, warmth, and body care, as well as needs of the soul: the need for a loving, caring, other person to hatch out the relational potential with which we are all endowed. Margaret Mahler (Mahler, Pine, and Bergman, 1975) referred to this hatching out process as the emotional birth of the human infant.

René Spitz (1945), in his studies of hospitalism, showed that without adequate contact with a warm enough caretaker, an infant develops anaclitic depression, a biopsychological withdrawal due to the lack of someone to lean on, to depend on. Left untreated, such an infant may develop marasmus, a condition of severe depression and withdrawal leading to death.

Donald Winnicott (1974) went so far as to say that so great were the needs of the infant that he was nothing by himself, that there is no such thing as an infant; only an infant and a mother. He meant mother and infant are a biopsychological system in which adequate unfolding of the infant's development requires an adequate caretaker.

Mahler (Mahler, Pine, and Bergman, 1975), describing this theme of symbiosis, observed and detailed the importance of the gradual separation and individuation that followed, with its tentative moves away from and back to the caretaker.

Winnicott pointed out the importance of transitional phenomena in this process. The child attempts to embody the caretaker in some personalized special symbolic object, like an old blanket, or a pacifier. The earliest transitional object may be the infant's thumb or fingers which he put into his mouth to delay distress while waiting for his mother to feed him.

The creation of the transitional object is an attempt to bring mother along as the child goes off on his own to explore the world. Such objects serve as reminders, reassurers, or talismans, representing warmth, security, and safety throughout life. Transitional objects help maintain the tie to a caretaking, loving object that provides a sense of security and well-being.

What happens if separation is not gradual, if there is no period of transition with the possibility of developing transitional objects? In such circumstances, Dr. Krystal describes a turning away from the mother to find something, anything, to provide solace against the flood of nameless affect. The infant does find something, if he survives at all, something fashioned out of the environment that does not involve a reminder of mother, but is instead of mother. Having nothing, the infant or child is as nothing; he has to fashion something to support survival that provides some solace in the retreat into his own private world. This object within the self system that functions not to remind the infant of the mother might best be described as an autistic object, in the tradition of Kleinian part objects, or Kohutian selfobjects within the self.

Many clinicians can remember from their training a film made by James Robertson (1952). A sick 2-year-old child is left by his parents to be cared for in a hospital. After the parents tear themselves away, we observe the child's insistence that they return; his anger when they don't; his immense protest, leading eventually to depression, then despair and helplessness, and finally sleep, a sleep of depletion, and escape into dreams. Engel and Schmale (1967) characterized such a state of despair as "hopeless, helpless."

Eventually the child in the film makes an adjustment of sorts out of the caretakers on the ward and objects fashioned from his environment that comfort him. Presumably these are not transitional objects, because at this point the mother seems lost forever, and her memory would not produce comfort but would be a reminder of grief and despair. He has lost his objects and has not yet found new ones. It may have been only a few days, but each minute passed in such a traumatic state must seem endless. The child attempts to comfort himself somehow, and lacking transitional objects and new objects, may use autistic objects at this point.

When the parents do return some four days later, the child seems not to recognize them. He turns away, as if they were a painful apparition, some cruel trick his mind is playing on him, a reminder of his despair. One can see how hard the child is trying to shut his parents out of his new world.

When he refuses to acknowledge them, they insist on forcing their presence upon him. Then, the child reacts with rage; they are the enemy, hurtful persecutors, not remembered as loved ones. But after a while, this view of them succumbs to remembering them as loved ones; he punishes them for being so cruel as to leave him all alone, thinking they would never return. Finally, after sufficient punishment, actually only a few minutes, the child accepts them back in a joyful reunion.

Melanie Klein's description of the paranoid-schizoid and depressive positions help us to understand this child's behavior. The paranoid-schizoid position is a closed, one-person system with part objects that play autistically designated roles. If they fail in these roles, they are spit out like poison milk, excluded, hated, regarded as persecutors in a paranoid way. This paranoid, autistic world is a useful model to keep in mind when treating people with deep narcissistic wounds. The big step for them is to let someone else back into their self system, to take the chance of trusting someone, to let them be important again.

Klein's depressive position is a two-person system. The mother, although dangerously separate, is acknowledged, needed, and longed for in what Spitz called the diatrophic attitude, to indicate that each influenced the other. This is called the depressive position because of the pain of disappointment in relationships, pain which leads to the ambivalence of hating the person you love the most, and the gradual softening of such hatred by retaining the memory of the loved qualities, rather than psychologically exterminating the object and withdrawing into the one-person paranoid-schizoid world.

Could it be that inadequate symbiosis with premature disruption of the bond turns the child toward the paranoid-schizoid position while, conversely, adequate symbiosis points the child toward the more healthy two-person depressive position? And could it be that the paranoid–schizoid position becomes the main system for people who have been traumatized extensively in their attempts to relate to a caretaker in their early years? Retreat to the paranoid–schizoid position would then be an attempt to adapt to the damage done to the emerging sense of self, and to the self in relation to other human beings, as described by Daniel Stern (1985).

These are people who were not well loved and did not learn to love themselves, to develop healthy self-esteem. Such early damage to the emerging self calls forth special defenses. They have to protect themselves against overwhelming feelings of being no good, worthless, or even nonexistent, except as useful to someone else. Leonard Shengold (1989) has described this early abuse and neglect as soul murder.

The rest of their development is experienced through the distorting lens of the paranoid–schizoid position. Autistic objects developed in such a system are relied upon in preference to human objects or transitional reminders of human objects. They can be controlled better, and do not disappoint and hurt as much.

Can we conclude from this that the autistic object is the precursor of the addictive object and is the prototype for it? We know how an addict's relationship with his addictive object consumes his time and energy; it is the center of his life, having replaced human relationships. He has little faith in himself or in others and retains the idea that he can control his world with his addictive object; he looks to it to provide him with what is missing inside himself.

But this is self-deception. He learns that he is fooling himself, that the addictive object is only transitorily comforting, but he has to deny that this is so. He has nowhere else to turn, except perhaps to a better addictive object, another drug, or another sex object.

This idealizing of objects, people, and behavior for a symbolic purpose and using them compulsively to control the world has some of the characteristics of a perversion. This is well demonstrated in all the cases described by Dr. Myers and in the way Dr. Ornstein's patient tried to use her relationships with men. The apparent purpose of the behavior may be genital, but the aim is turned (perverted) and compulsively used to meet some pressing pregenital need.

The turning or perversion of an ordinary object or behavior into an addictive object, is similar to a neurotic's avoidance of reality testing in the area of his symptoms. A compulsion neurotic's symptom of preventing some catastrophe by washing his hands is based on magical thinking. In both the neurotic's symptom and the addict's behavior, the individual knows he is being unreasonable, but feels compelled to do it anyway, for symbolic, magical reasons. The addict isolates his behavior from reality testing, and idealizes the addictive object as if his life depended on it. The neurotic does essentially the same. I like Dr.Wurmser's view of addicts as severe neurotics, with acting out and perverse features, rather than as borderline, probably because I find a diagnosis of "borderline' to be diagnostically meaningless and therapeutically nihilistic.

Through Dr. Sabshin's fine historical summary we can trace the idea that the addictive object cannot be taken away from the addict without risking suicide. Simmel (1927), Fenichel (1945), and Knight (1937) all subscribed to this idea, which runs counter to modern thinking about treatment. This tradition, however misguided, has legitimate roots in the observation that the addict has nowhere else to turn and is lost without the addictive object; that he needs something to replace it when he gives it up. This wisdom can be found in the Program for Recovery of Alcoholics Anonymous (AA) which expects the addict to stop drinking as he realizes the program has something else to offer: spirituality, and people who struggle with the same problem. And they only expect him to commit himself to abstinence one day at a time, realizing how difficult this step can be.

Step 2 and step 3 concern belief "that a Power greater than ourselves could restore us to sanity" and "a decision to turn our will and our lives over to the care of God as we understand him." The rest of the steps show how this higher power is turned to as a good parent. If we confess to him and turn our lives over to his care, he will remove our defects of character (step 6), and take away our shortcomings (step 7). By taking personal inventories of people we have harmed, by trying to make amends to them (steps 8 and 9), by continuing to survey or inventory ourselves, and by admitting when we are wrong (step 10), the alcoholic seeks to improve his conscious contact with God as he understands him (step 11). This leads to a relationship with a new (internal) object, a new loving and powerful parent figure. The twelfth, and final step describes, "a spiritual awakening as a result of these steps" and the attempt to "practice these principles in all our affairs."

Alcoholics Anonymous has been demonstrated to work very well for people who can embrace its principles. Perhaps the addictive object is replaced by a new external object and a new internalized object, in relation to which he experiences a new sense of himself as worthwhile and loveable.

Perhaps this is the way psychotherapy works. Instead of faith in God, we try to lead our patient into a treatment relationship that will be more reliable, more trustworthy, more forgiving, and less judgmental than previous relationships. We try to enter his one-person system and facilitate its gradual conversion to a two-person system. We want him to rely on us, and eventually on himself, not on a substance or some addictive practice. At first, we may be used as a new addictive object, but this is a step in the direction of becoming a new object to him in our own right. We hope by this to help the patient develop a faith in us, in other people, and most important, in himself.

Just as AA requires motivation and an acceptance and eventual devotion to its principles, so does psychotherapy require something similar of its participants. Both must realize they are getting into a long-term relationship that will be trying and often unrewarding in the short term, a relationship with all kinds of obstacles, limitations, and frustrations. The major developmental failures from which addictive behaviors arise yield only slowly and partially to efforts to change. Our therapeutic aim is to try to mend the perhaps unfixable early experiences by providing a human relationship that can be turned to for attunement, responsiveness, and caring.

Dr. Khantzian, in a balanced, attuned approach, emphasizes self-care which serves to underscore the importance of the caretaking atmosphere. Dr. Wurmser stresses the importance of analyzing underlying conflicts, especially superego conflicts, once a safe relationship has been established. This means establishing what he calls a rational alliance, a therapeutic atmosphere of kindness and tact, as well as auxiliary measures, because of the severity of affective intolerance and flooding. Several modalities almost always have to be added to the psychoanalytic therapy, including medication, marital or family therapy, self-help groups, and sometimes behavioral approaches.

I was struck with the similarity, or perhaps overlap, of this population of patients with adult patients who were abused as children and have posttraumatic stress disorders. They are similar not only in childhood history and adult symptomatology, but also in defensive style and personality organization. Dr. Krystal's work with alexithymia supports this view.

Bessel Van der Kolk (1989), among others, has identified addiction to trauma itself in many victims. He shows by statistics how often trauma is a repetitive reenactment and how a victim of persecution can become addicted to his persecutor and to the abuse. This is a crucial area for further research.

Some years ago I had an emergency phone call from Bert, the husband of Marjorie, a patient of mine who was a recovering alcoholic. With panic in his voice he told me that Marjorie, who had been dry for the past two years, had had a fight with him that morning. When he came home from work, he had discovered a suicide note next to an empty bottle of antidepressants and a half-empty bottle of Scotch. The note said she wanted to die because she had been drinking all day. She had threatened many times: "If I take a drink, that's it; I'll be humiliated and have to kill myself." Bert didn't know where she was, but was convinced that her intentions were lethal. There had been no previous suicidal behavior and she was not histrionic. We notified the police.

As I waited anxiously, I thought of our two-and-one-half year treatment. Marjorie, a hard-boiled nursing supervisor at a large general hospital, was well liked and respected for her fairness, supercompetence, and her "heart of gold." But she could also be angry, vindictive, and impulsive, and people at work had begun to suspect these traits were associated with heavy drinking. This behavior had only become problematic during the two years after her mother died of a barbiturate overdose. Going for professional help had been out of the question; Marjorie denied she had a drinking problem and had trouble trusting anyone. Bert, her gentle, passive husband of twelve years, had long been dominated by her and had shared in the denial of her alcoholism. A crucial issue was the shame she anticipated if exposed as an alcoholic like her mother, as a person out of control and in need of help from others.

She had been given my name by her internist and, after carrying it around for four months, had finally called following an episode of vomiting blood for which she had been hospitalized briefly with a diagnosis of gastritis. She wanted to get back in control of her drinking, she explained to me, and she wanted to keep her treatment short term. She did not need AA, she insisted, nor did she intend to stop drinking completely. She was dictatorial about the terms on which she was willing to enter treatment; being able to control her own treatment was a nonnegotiable prerequisite.

It soon became apparent to both of us that she could not control her drinking and would need to give it up entirely. She agreed most reluctantly, however, because her denial was still strong despite all the evidence of how alcohol was dominating her life, interfering with her health, her work, and her marriage.

When I recommended that we use Antabuse to help her abstain, she went along with it. But in order to prove that nothing and nobody could control her but herself, she took the Antabuse and drank anyway. Feeling wretchedly ill with an alcohol-Antabuse reaction, red-faced, vomiting, tachycardic, hypertensive, she went right on drinking. A few such experiences convinced me that these severe alcohol-Antabuse reactions were too dangerous. I could not control her, she explained, only she could. We stopped the Antabuse.

Having made her point, she set her prodigious determination to achieving abstinence. Soon she began having panic attacks. I wondered if the alcohol had been masking an underlying affective disorder. On tricyclic antidepressants, the panic disorder was better but she was still unable to remain abstinent.

Reluctantly she accepted the need to begin AA, and after some difficulty in finding the right group for herself she became totally abstinent and remained so until the night I am describing two years later.

To summarize the outpatient treatment regimen: In addition to psychotherapy, I met with Marjorie and Bert (who was active in Alanon, and Adult Children of Alcoholics) and continued to prescribe antidepressant medication. They received couples therapy with another therapist. She went to as many as seven AA meetings a week, participated regularly in a small study group with other AA members, and had a good relationship with her sponsor. Her internist occasionally consulted with us on medical questions.

Our psychotherapy appointment schedule was flexible, with a minimum of two appointments weekly. She knew she could reach me any time to talk on the phone and that I would schedule an appointment whenever she needed to see me. When I was out of town, I left her a number where I could be reached which she never used; still, it meant to her that I was accessible.

In the psychotherapy we addressed her denial, her need to control everything, her distrust, her parents' alcoholism, and her guilt, shame, and fear of exposure and humiliation. We worked on her isolation, her loneliness, her fear of having children, and her fear of remaining childless. We spoke of the obstacles to intimacy, of how substances had taken the place of relationships because they were easier to control and more reliable than people. We spoke of her inner need to fill some seemingly bottomless pit within herself. We were making progress in the building of a trusting treatment relationship.

Then she became suspicious that Bert had begun seeing another woman. He denied it to her and to me in one of our joint sessions. I thought she was displacing onto Bert the increasing vulnerability of allowing herself to depend on me. She accepted this idea but her suspicions continued. Finally Bert admitted the truth, begging for forgiveness, and promising to break off the affair.

These were the circumstances that led to the fight on the day of the drinking and the suicide note.

The phone rang. It was Bert, saying she had returned. She had vomited up the overdose and had returned to look for more pills. Bert had called the police; they arrived quickly and had taken her into custody. I felt tremendous relief, followed by an unexpected wave of hatred of her for scaring me so badly. Did I care too much, more than she cared for her own life? Had I become codependent? Or had my involvement helped her to get as far as she got, and my vulnerability was the price I had to pay if I wanted to treat someone in her situation?

I asked the police to bring her to the emergency room where I met them to evaluate her. At the hospital, she was severely intoxicated, menacing the staff, but happy to see me. Since she refused to sign in voluntarily, I put a mental health hold on her and transferred her to a locked psychiatric ward where I saw her daily. Despite her protests I continued to hold her involuntarily on the basis of continuing suicidal risk. I hoped that beyond my controlling her she would experience me as concerned and protective.

I tried to transfer her to a residential alcohol treatment program, which she refused. When I could no longer hold her involuntarily, she signed out of the hospital against medical advice and enrolled in an outpatient alcohol treatment program, making it clear that she was through with me. I tried by letters and phone calls to have her return to see me to discuss the rupture of our treatment relationship but her refusal was chillingly final.

She told me the treatment had been misguided because I gave her antidepressants, encouraging further reliance on a substance, and because I saw her in individual psychotherapy which interfered with AA, regardless of how much I supported its importance to her recovery program. Then I learned she had also broken off her relationships with her AA study group and sponsor.

I think her drinking was an attack on Bert for betraying her and on me for putting her in a dependent position where I could hurt her, too. Probably she did not want to die but to punish us, in which case my controlling her may have felt retaliatory or even sadistic. But I also wonder if her drinking meant to her she had failed me and her AA sponsor; that she was terribly ashamed. The feeling we had failed her may have been a projection of her own sense of failure. Was the involuntary hospitalization unbearable for her and irreparable? I feel it was required, given that the voluntary treatment tie had broken down when she took the overdose instead of calling me. The tie had not been sufficiently reestablished in the hospital for me to feel she would be safe in outpatient treatment.

Her personality was dominated by narcissistic defenses; grandiosity and overcompensatory perfectionism covered over what was missing inside her that made her feel bad and ugly. She was only comfortable helping others in need. She had felt betrayed and traumatized in childhood by unreliable, unpredictable, alcoholic parents and may have been abused sexually. Subsequent relationships with teachers or counselors had always been a disappointment, and she had always been thrown back upon herself for survival. We had reenacted this familiar scenario once again.

Was I in error to try to treat her in psychotherapy? Was the use of antidepressant medication appropriate? Had our treatment interfered with a total commitment to AA? Will she get beyond her anger and sense of failure with me, the reaction to having me take over the treatment and control her? Was the involuntary hospitalization avoidable? Could it have been accomplished without alienating and losing the patient?

Chapter 10

The Advantages of Multiple Approaches to Understanding Addictive Behavior

Jacob G. Jacobson, M.D.

The treatment of addiction, like all areas of treatment, has had its changing fashions. In a recent syndicated column, Ellen Goodman (1990, p. A25) quoted the opening line of Kitty Dukakis' autobiography, "I'm Kitty Dukakis and I'm a drug addict and an alcoholic." While admiring the fierce honesty of the book, Goodman lamented this self-description which collapses the complex personality she had once known and admired into a mere disease entity. Goodman says, "What troubles me . . . most . . . is what the culture of addiction treatment seems to demand of the troubled in this area. Your whole identity." Now there is no reason to expect Ellen Goodman to understand the ego supportive and healing aspects of the disease concept, or to comprehend the full significance of an addict finally confronting his or her denials and evasions; but at the same time she is voicing a concern which illustrates a changing fashion in the treatment of addictive problems.

There was a time in the history of psychoanalysis when patients and situations were viewed entirely in dynamic terms, and the deleterious effects of addictive substances were not adequately factored into personality assessment or treatment planning. Patients were given character diagnoses, and were then "treated," while they were in the throes of low grade chronic intoxication, with an earnest belief that the effects of the drug presented no special complications to either diagnosis or treatment. Expressive psychotherapy was indiscriminately idealized as the treatment of choice in all cases, and was unnecessarily viewed as mutually exclusive from such approaches as Alcoholics Anonymous (AA), which emphasized the efficacy of structure, control, and group support.

Over time we learned our lesson well and we do now afford the respect and priority which is their due to substance effects and to genetic and biological predisposition factors, to social factors, and to the special needs of this patient group. And we do understand how these factors join with psychological predisposing and precipitating factors in producing manifest addiction. Our former unwarranted skepticism of various control and containment approaches has been replaced by a humble seeking to understand the means by which they manage to do so well in helping addicts with whom we have struggled over so many years. But, now secure in our grasp of the disease aspect of substance abuse, human nature being as it is, we are, of course, in immediate danger of overidealizing those considerations, and falling into the arms of Charybdis as we lose our grasp of the individual identities and varying psychological needs of our patients with addictive symptoms. This is the warning being sounded by Ellen Goodman. The six authors have made clear our strivings to integrate the disease and psychodynamic approaches and to work appropriately, compatibly, and even comfortably, with the various twelve-step and self-help modalities.

Each of the authors emphasized the precious individuality of their patients. While interested in drawing useful generalizations about this group of difficult patients, they were equally interested in the poignant specialness of the struggles each was engaged in.

Two of the papers dealt with members of a group of individuals who appear to be addicted not to substances at all, but in a metaphoric sense to certain constellations of behaviors, of affects, of self states, or of interpersonal configurations, to be controlled or avoided at all cost. They manifest in their love relationships, in their sex life, in their modes of eating, or in specific activities such as gambling, behaviors which bear the stamp of being compulsory, obligatory, peremptory, and relentlessly driven, qualities which have earned them the label "addictive," even though no substance is involved.

In their descriptions, each speaker has, in different terms, pointed to the early, the archaic, the primitive, the preoedipal, the preverbal locus of the life-and-death struggles manifested by those engaged in these behaviors. This emphasis echoes Freud's line of argument in his exploration of traumatized individuals and demonic self-destructive repetitions in his 1920 book, "Beyond the Pleasure Principle." The world of wishes and their gratification does not become developmentally relevant, he argued, until a certain fundamental task has been accomplished. This task, which is what he defines there as lying beyond the pleasure principle, consists in binding potentially traumatic amounts of stimulation. Only after that task has been accomplished, "would it be possible for the dominance of the pleasure principle (i.e., wishes and their gratification) to proceed. Till then the other task of the mental apparatus, the task of mastering or binding excitations, would have precedence" (Freud, 1920, p. 35). In other words, he is saying, in the language of the time, that certain primal issues need to be resolved before coherent wishes, capable of satisfaction, can emerge. I think each of our speakers in individual ways has undertaken to describe the early tasks whose failure of resolution results in these repetitive, relentlessly driven behaviors we come to call "addictive," seeking from substances or from repetitive behavioral constellations, outside assistance with absent or failed internal functions.

Despite the passage I quoted from Freud's 1920 book, analysts and analytically oriented psychotherapists have for decades reached back to even earlier formulations, and misapplied, as several of our speakers have indicated, ill-fitting and naive early theoretical and technical approaches to addictive populations.

The shift over the years in our view of the addict, from pleasure-seeking hedonist to desperate self-medicator, is well illustrated in all six of the papers. Drs. Khantzian, Wurmser, and

Krystal are in agreement that the purpose of drug use is to relieve or change affects experienced as painful, unbearable, or overwhelming because of deficits in the individual's capacity to modulate or defend against them. The varying ways the particular substances are used by different individuals to provide the needed energizing, or calming, or socially facilitating effects were also catalogued for us.

Dr. Khantzian made a clear and comprehensive case for addictive behavior having as its primary goal neither suffering nor pleasure-seeking nor self-destruction; but, rather, as representing the outcome of major difficulties in self-regulatory functions manifesting themselves in the areas of feelings, self-esteem, object relations, and self-care. Drs. Ornstein and Myers describe similar efforts at self-ministration accomplished via repetitive sexual or seductive behaviors, rather than by substances. In both groups of patients, externalizations and repetitions are evident, which have as their goal the mastery of previous trauma by converting a former passive experience into one now actively controlled, even if the resulting scenarios are painful or self-destructive. An additional motive for these repetitions is a striving to retain the safety of the familiar, described by Dr. Krystal as a struggle to maintain the status quo in an effort to prevent the recurrence of the original infantile trauma. This was illustrated by Dr. Ornstein's patient's dream of clutching the rock as representing the least catastrophic solution of which she was capable. Dr. Krystal makes the point that addicts, like other traumatized individuals, live in a world of action, tending to impulsive action and somatic reactions, in place of being able to experience and describe affective experiences as meaningful psychological events, the situation he terms *alexithymia*. Dr. Khantzian's paper included a vivid example of this action language. I will offer some further vignettes of my own.

The first vignette is very brief. A 35-year-old man with addictive difficulties had been unable to react to any interruptions in his treatment. During the last hour before a vacation of mine he made his usual quite sincere denial of feelings about it. It simply made no difference to him, he said. He left, and my next patient came in chuckling and bemused. When I asked her about it, she said, "That guy has never spoken to me before. Today he came out and said to me, 'Well, I guess I'll see you in two weeks.' " He could handle the separation feelings only by a displaced enactment with the next patient, in which he played the active role.

The second vignette, this one in a bit more detail: Some years ago I encountered a family who lived in a world of action, with little direct recognition of their feelings. I was seeing a daughter of the family who, upon graduating from college, was overwhelmed by the unmanageable demands of moving into the adult world. Miss D began handling this by taking street drugs and by drinking, a solution widely shared within her family, and she became depressed and suicidal.

I recommended hospitalization at a particularly well-suited facility in another city. The patient readily accepted the recommendation, but warned me that convincing her family would be extremely difficult. This turned out to be wildly understated. Her jet set mother blew in the following day. Mrs. D heard out my findings and recommendations, barely waiting for the conclusion before presenting me with the question she had come a great distance to pose. "My daughter's uncle," she said, "has been sitting upstairs at his ranch for the past 12 years with a gun pointed at his head, shouting orders and threatening to shoot himself if they were not obeyed. *He* hasn't needed a psychiatrist, so why are you telling me my daughter needs one?" This last was said triumphantly, gesturing toward the patient. My keen clinical insight told me at once that this was going to be difficult. I explained once more the extremity of her daughter's pain, and the seriousness of her plight. We set an appointment for the following day to continue what gave every evidence of being an uphill battle. That evening I received a frantic call from Mrs. D. She had come over to her daughter's room moments before, to find her unconscious on the floor, with an empty pill bottle beside her. I had an ambulance bring them both to the local hospital, the daughter still unconscious. We pumped her stomach and obtained a fair amount of bourbon, but not a particle of pill remnants of any kind. Her vital signs were good and, as I was wheeling her gurney to a room to recover, she roused slightly and opened her eyes. I'll never forget how she looked, a blanket up to her chin, her dark eyes open in her quite pale face—and then she winked! And then I understood. She had not tried to kill herself in despair of getting through to her mother, as I had thought, nor had she drunk herself into a stupor to escape the pain of her plight; she was simply talking the family language—action, or perhaps we should call it alexithymese.

In current parlance, "You want guns to the head? I'll give you guns to the head." And the message got through. By the time I got to the waiting room, Mrs. D had only one question for me: "What's the best way to get to that hospital, Doctor," she asked me, "via Boston or Albany?" I had become a travel agent! Notice that this entire complex set of affectively highly charged life and death transactions took place without one explicit mention of feelings, on the part of mother, or daughter.

Edith Jacobson, in her 1964 book, *The Self and the Object World*, describes a set of observations related to this issue of nonaffective language. She contrasts "the wide and rich affective scale, the manifold and subtle shades of feeling, the warm and vivid emotional qualities of normal development and mature object love," with the limited range of feelings in the autistic–schizoid mode (meaning individuals traumatized, and therefore arrested at, a stage of development before full selfobject differentiation has been achieved). She describes the feelings of this traumatized group as being limited to a narrow range "of cold hostility, of anxiety, hurt, humiliation, of shame or pride, of security or insecurity, of high or low self-esteem, of grandeur or inferiority and guilt" (1964, pp. 85–86).

The six papers are replete with examples from this catalogue of constricted affects. And we were told that some addicts may use substances in an effort to move from that constricted range to the more open and varied spectrum of affective experiences. Dr. Krystal emphasizes the role of affect regression in the psychosomatic problems of the addictive group, and their use of substances as modifiers of their affects. Traumatized in their early relationships, they show, as Dr. Krystal has vividly put it: "A preference for short-acting intoxicants over taking a chance on a person." And we must bear in mind that when we attempt to initiate therapy with an addicted person, we are asking them to take a chance on us.

Dr. Wurmser demonstrated an intense focus on the affects and the lexicon of issues of shame, and the archaic and tormenting guilt of a primitive and brutal superego. The need for flexibility in approach was demonstrated in various ways in these presentations. Dr. Myers, for example, utilized psychotropic medications to assist in the soothing function he was attempting to provide for his patients, who had not developed that capacity for themselves. Dr. Khantzian emphasized the importance of integrating the disease concept of addiction, where the accent is on containment and control, with the psychodynamic concept, which addresses the specific vulnerabilities in self regulation. He is urging us, in other words, to stabilize the changing fashion of treatment approaches at an intermediate and integrative point. His concept of the primary care therapist is one way of attempting to address the multiple levels of need manifested by this group of patients.

Dr. Krystal treated us to an odyssey of his experiences as clinician and as theoretician. He pointed out past problems that had accrued as a result of having only one clinical tool to apply. Someone once constructed an apt aphorism: If a hammer is the only tool you have at your disposal, each problem you encounter will have an uncanny tendency to resemble a nail. And so, as Drs. Krystal, Sabshin, and others described, we struggled along for decades carrying a procrustean bed—or couch or hammer—along with us.

Oddly enough, as Dr. Krystal has pointed out in another context, even these misapplied treatments worked for a while until "beginners' luck," as he says, ran out. Each new chemical or psychological treatment in the mental health field tends to have this period of "beginners' luck," an exciting time during which therapeutic zeal provides a generous increment of results. This creates a false optimism, until eventually the placebo effect factors itself out and the actual efficacy and limitations become clear. The early idealization of fluoxetine is probably the best recent example of this shakedown process, as we have settled into a more sober appreciation of its true effectiveness, and its limitations.

So there was a time when we had our one hammer, and we did the best we could with it. Since the hammer didn't work reliably, therapists didn't like to treat addicts, and addicts were pleased to have us leave them alone. Over the past several decades, however, as psychoanalytic structural theory developed and expanded, it provided more accurate tools for understanding the details of such ego functions as delay, judgment, memory, modulations, and so forth, all of which are necessary for affect regulation. The signal model of anxiety, first presented by Freud in 1926, and later expanded to become a model for all affects, provided the basis for an experiential and empathic understanding of affect functioning.

Developmental and relational theories add further dimensions to structural theory which are necessary for understanding addictive phenomena. Margaret Mahler's studies on separation-individuation began to appear in the 1950s (e.g., Mahler, 1958) with the concept of symbiosis, from which psychological birth and individuation evolves. Soon after, the theories of Melanie Klein (1968), Winnicott (1960), and Fairbairn (1954) arrived in this country, adding new and valuable object relations conceptualizations. In the 1960s, Kohut began to present his theory of self-psychology (e.g., Kohut, 1968); the evolution of his theory is exemplified by Dr. Ornstein's presentation. Currently, many analysts use multiple theories to cover various aspects of the clinical phenomena which confront them, as exemplified in the work of John Gedo (1979), or in the "Four Psychologies" approach of Fred Pine (1988). Others have expanded structural theory by incorporating developmental, self-psychological, and object relations conceptualizations within it. Loewald (1960), Adler and Buie (1979), and others have broadened our base for understanding, conceptualizing, and empathically interpreting the phenomena of addictive behavior. Reflecting these approaches, Dr. Khantzian and others argued for the advantages of a multiple model approach.

An important and relevant clinical contribution, which has come to us from several quarters, lies in our having recognized the immense therapeutic impact of acknowledging, and validating to a patient, the reality of past and present trauma, abuse, and neglect. There was a time when such an acknowledgment might have been avoided out of concern that it might dilute a full understanding and working out of the fantasy elements involved. Such well-intentioned avoidance sometimes has the unfortunate effect of retraumatizing a patient, who experiences the failure to acknowledge and validate as disbelief, or even blaming of them; an unwitting repetition of the denial and deviousness which surrounded the original neglect or abuse within the family.

Failures of psychotherapies which were not appropriate for patients who had suffered severe early trauma suggested erroneously, as it has turned out, that dynamic psychotherapy was quite ineffective for addictive patients. This view is changing as approaches become more sophisticated and attuned on the basis of these newer understandings. There is a greater appreciation of the importance of flexibility, responsiveness, empathy, a nonjudgmental attitude, and an eye to the current reality in working with this group of patients.

Dr. Khantzian makes the point that addicts "need greater support, structure, empathy, and contact" than classical psychoanalytic patients. I believe we have been discovering over these same decades that all patients require the engagement with therapist or analyst in the room together, of which he speaks, and that most, perhaps all, require more empathic and responsive interaction for effective analytic and psychotherapeutic work than we at one time believed optimal. I believe that makes the findings and discoveries which emerge from treatment experiences with this particularly demanding group relevant and useful for our understanding of all our patients. In that sense, as Dr. Sabshin put it, "The history of the theory and the treatment of addictive behavior reflects the history of psychoanalytic thinking."

The difficulties experienced and displayed by this group of patients, and which we attempt to address therapeutically, seem to fall into three general areas of personality development and functioning.

Affect Regulation

We are in agreement that vulnerabilities, deficits, and defects in the capacity for affect regulation, which manifests as a failure of the individual's self-soothing and impulse control functions, constitute a crucial predisposing factor in these conditions. Issues of affect tolerance and affect regression are especially emphasized by Dr. Krystal. Dr. Myers' patients, Alex and Burton, clearly are spurred to their driven, ostensibly sexual behaviors in their efforts to prevent crises of dysregulation; and Dr. Ornstein's patient used masturbation to control a level of agitation which threatened disintegration.

The Self

The second area of difficulty has to do with the self: self experience, self structure, selfobject differentiation, and self-esteem. Dr. Khantzian put it most simply, "Addicts suffer because they do not feel good about themselves." He pointed out the abrupt alternation between selflessness and self-centeredness, which others have noted as vacillation between depreciated states of the self and exalted, entitled modes. He pointed out how substances "can serve as powerful antidotes to the inner sense of emptiness, disharmony, and lack of ease such people experience." These vacillations were clearly observable in Dr. Ornstein's patient, Mrs. Holland, who experienced a rotten self and an entitled self. Consistent with her self psychological theoretical orientation, Dr. Ornstein formulated the case entirely in terms of this second category, understanding the regulatory problems and repetitive behaviors in terms of selfobject and self-state dynamics. Dr. Wurmser speaks of blurring of selfobject boundaries by states of fusion with others, and in Dr. Myers' patient, Alex, the need to be admired was clearly an antidote to his early experiences of failures in attunement, which left him feeling minimized and insignificant.

Object Relations

The third category of observations is in the realm of object relations, referring to relationships between the self and the world of objects.

Each of the papers is replete with descriptions of and allusions to the relentlessly repetitive, often self-destructive constellations of self and object which so characterize the lives of this group of patients. With painful repetitiveness, Dr. Ornstein's patient needed to win a man with whom she had rapidly become ob-sessed, and secure from him the life-energizing, almost resuscitat-ing, response of passionate admiration within a fantasy of "lasting union," to be followed by the inevitable disappointment, deideali-zation, cold withdrawal, and then on to the next "lasting union."

A patient of mine with similar issues, as she was beginning to understand a sequence of this kind, reported one day with amazement that she had caught herself thinking, "I've got to have this man!" as she heard a friend's husband, to whom she was about to be introduced for the first time, walking down the hallway to join her and the friend. "I fall in love with footsteps!" she exclaimed in dismay, and with that had taken one small step on her way out of the endless repetition. Dr. Myers' patient, Alex, also had a very specific repetitive private mission during sexual encounters—his worthwhileness, and even his very existence, re-quired that he experience repeatedly the admiration of his erect penis by an other, who had become for the purpose momentarily significant. Similarly with Burton, who needed repeatedly to dem-onstrate that a woman would grant her sexual favors for financial gain, and with Charles, who was driven to find his parents and lost sister again and again in the videotapes. In all of these in-stances, the need to externalize the problem and repeat it in the attempt to convert passive infantile helplessness into active mastery is quite evident.

A former patient of mine, who will illustrate a repetitive pat-tern of this kind, crosses the boundaries of the kinds of patients under discussion; he showed addictive behaviors with and without substance abuse. He was a research scientist in his thirties, whose presenting complaints were migraine headaches and ritualized peremptory and anonymous homosexual encounters in public restrooms. He frequented the local hospital's emergency room for injections of Demerol for his headaches, rather liberally sup-plied by his family physician out of misplaced compassion for the patient's degree of suffering. After a few months in the analysis his headaches quietly disappeared as he became involved in the analytic process. He continued, however, to visit the emergency room at an only slightly reduced frequency, and it looked like we might have an iatrogenic Demerol addict on our hands. Except that, at my urging, he was readily able to request alternative non-narcotic medication from the E.R. physicians, which turned out to satisfy his "addictive" need just as well. During this period the traumatizing experiences behind his addiction to what we had come to think of as "the emergency room process," began to come to light. In the ordinary seeming lower middle class household of his childhood, titanic life and death struggles were enacted regularly by his parents, somewhat in the style of the family of Dr. Wurmser's patient, Victor. One memory which emerged through great pain and panic as an organizing forcus was a time when his father had threatened to jump from the family's fifth floor apartment window. In response, the patient's mother had walked purposefully over to the window, opened it wide, and invited him to do just that, as the distraught boy of 4 looked on in terror. The previously healthy child now developed headaches, which became the nucleus of a school phobia a year later, necessitating his mother's staying home from work and keeping him home from school to minister to him. She would make him a soothing cup of tea and lovingly spoon it out to him. These times became an oasis of peace, calm, and safety in the vortex of rage and fear in which this boy lived. The essentials of the later emergency room process forming in these experiences of being nursed by his mother are clear. As the patient began to understand this and to experience the analysis as ministrations of a different but related kind, the emergency room constellation, and the later, more complicated, "addictive" homosexual behavior, both dropped out and had not reappeared on follow-up ten years after termination. The good outcome in this case seemed to me conditioned on the severe trauma having occurred in later childhood, with apparently reasonable nurturance and care during infancy.

Obviously, each bit of clinical data can and should fit into all three areas: affect regulation, self and selfobject differentiation, and object relations. I believe that each of our currently available psychoanalytic approaches offers particular strength and clarity in understanding and addressing one or another of these dimensions of psychological functioning. And in a given situation one or another may be especially apt for grasping it or for gaining clinical access.

Our understanding of the interactional aspects of the therapeutic relationship has been enriched in recent years by infant and child observational studies. In digesting the issues raised in these papers, it occurred to me that review of one such observation of infant development might further our discussion of these matters. It can serve as a relatively simple paradigm, and offer at least a hypothetical prospective look at one kind of infantile situation we often find ourselves hypothesizing retrospectively in our work with older children or adult patients. I am thinking of the "stone face" or "still face" experiments of Brazleton and Tronick (1978), where normal mothers were instructed to present a "stone face," in place of their usual spontaneous smiling response, when their normal infants smiled engagingly and invitingly at them. The results were dramatic. The infant, confronted by this painful disruption of the interactional rhythm, would make repeated efforts to elicit the needed responsive smile from the mother. If we bear in mind the obvious survival value to the infant of this particular skill of engaging the caretaker, we can readily understand the intensity and the high biological stakes at issue here. But, even then, we might not be prepared for what is about to take place.

Very shortly, between repeated attempts to elicit the responsive smile, the infant begins to manifest distress, by fussing slightly and by looking away for relief. This is soon followed by yawning, startle responses, and jerky movements, grimaces, sober facial expression, and withdrawal to a head-down, curled position, sucking on fingers, and making rocking motions. None of the infants in the series of seven mother–infant pairs cried, although the investigators later demonstrated, in a *Nova* (1986) film *The First Year of Life*, the progression of this sequence to include a disintegration of regulatory capacities, an autonomic storm evidenced by hiccuping and drooling, and then total body involvement in all-out distressed crying. These alarming sequences occur in normal infants subjected to one episode of unresponsiveness to smiling by an otherwise loving and attentive mother. What of the infant who experiences this catastrophe many times a day, over long periods of time, because the mothering figure is depressed, or preoccupied with overwhelming realities, or narcissistically absorbed, or is psychologically absent on alcohol or drugs? I think of the cruel and dysfunctional environments described by Dr. Meers. Upon viewing films of this situation one cannot help wondering what such affective storms, if repeated frequently, and the ensuing helpless withdrawal, might do to the long-term capacity for affect regulation, for robustness of the self, and for basic trust in the world of objects. One wonders also what is happening within this beleaguered infant to norepinephrine, to dopamine, to serotonin, to the entire neural transmitter and receptor system. The effectiveness of the tricyclics and fluoxetine in panic as well as in depression, suggests an importance of such moments of psychophysiological breakdown in setting up vulnerabilities to both panic and depression. We then come full circle to the use of addictive substances as prosthetics for missing internal psychological functions.

In using this example, I am not positing a specific cause of addictive vulnerability, but rather using it to illustrate one kind of caretaker–infant interaction which can lead to severe difficulties in affect regulation shown by our adult patients. Discussion of this issue tends to return repeatedly to the possible organizing effects of the mother's responsive gaze and to the possible disorganizing effects of its absence.

How might we view the "stone face" episode through the three lenses of affect regulation, self and selfobject differentiation, and object relations?

1. Affect dysregulation is obvious in this situation. It is interesting in pointing up how infant neglect can lead to an intermediate step we sometimes overlook, of traumatic overstimulation, en route to the protective withdrawal and consequent states of emptiness and deadness we see clinically. While each of our theories postulates its own set of *causes* of affective dysregulation, the many years of research and study of regulatory ego functions under the aegis of structural theory have provided more detailed understandings of the dysregulation itself than have other points of view.

2. Second, from the standpoint of self development and selfobject differentiation. A developmental point of view might focus here on the failure of attunement, on the premature phase-inappropriate traumatic disruption of what Dr. Krystal called "the illusion of symbiosis," and which Mahler and others have posited

as a crucial developmental step. An ego psychologist might focus on the failure of the caretaker to provide a model of regulatory functions, which the infant could internalize through identification. The self psychologist would see here a failure of the mirroring function of the selfobject interfering with transmuting internalization. A Winnicottian point of view might see an interaction of this kind as a failure of the facilitating maternal environment, in response to which a false self is likely to be formed, isolated from inner feelings which have come to threaten a repetition of the potentially traumatic overstimulation. For Balint (1968), it would represent the first fissure in what is to become a "basic fault." However differently each of our currently available systems of psychoanalytic conceptualization might formulate such an episode, each of them does deal with it in its own way, and with its consequences to the formation of self-structure and sense of self. And each highlights an important and clinically useful nuance of the experience, which is the value of a multiple model approach.

3. Third, the view from an object relations standpoint. Less obvious in the direct infant observation, but predictable as a later unfolding, would be the repetitive, typically self-destructive efforts of the individual, either to engineer the repetition of such an infantile traumatic state, or to seek its antidote. Dr. Ornstein's patient seemed to be in the grip of efforts to repeat and to master an early crisis of understimulation and disregard by seeking out passionate attachments as energizing antidotes to her inner deadness. One can readily imagine an infant, confronted repeatedly by an equivalent of the stone face, needing, as Dr. Ornstein's patient needed, to produce at any cost the look of intense involvement and passionate gaze which Mrs. Holland would secure from the men she seduced. In Dr. Ornstein's words, the man had to be "completely focused on her." It also would not surprise us that the man's enraptured look would not resolve such a massive infantile deficit in a definitive way, that sooner more likely than later his intensity would wane momentarily, and the traumatic lack of responsive gaze would threaten to be repeated. And it would not surprise us that he would then loom as the hated and feared stone face all over again, requiring her to destroy his importance by finding fault and deidealizing him, and that she

would then need to move on to the next conquest and the next enraptured look. One can understand in similar terms Dr. Myers' patient Alex's search for the enraptured look in his homosexual partner of the moment. In both instances, other persons have become drawn in as players in a repeated psychological drama whose purpose is to supply missing internal structure.

A variant of what I have been describing is seen in the parent who will provide something of the responsiveness and attunement needed by the child, but who needs first to be activated by the child to draw him or her out of some form of depression or narcissistic preoccupation. One may find oneself as therapist being inflated or idealized by such a patient, who has learned that only if he or she succeeds in completing us in this way may there be any hope of obtaining some of what they are missing inside. It is a sort of sad trickle-down theory of human interaction they grow up with, and it constitutes one form of the codependency situation so commonly emphasized in many self-help approaches.[1]

I have tried to sort out some of the common themes of the six papers, to illustrate them with clinical examples, and to group them in ways which I thought might facilitate understanding. I also presented a simple illustrative bit of infant observation data, to function as a paradigm for discussing the kinds of infantile trauma many of us believe predispose to addictive behaviors.

---

[1]I applied these still-face observations to the broader issue of the therapeutic relationship in psychoanalysis and psychotherapy in Jacobson (1993).

References

Abend, S., Porder, M., & Willick, M. (1983), *Borderline Patients: Psychoanalytic Perspectives.* New York: International Universities Press.

Abraham, K. (1908), The psychological relation between sexuality and alcoholism. In: *Selected Papers of Karl Abraham.* New York: Basic Books, 1960.

———— (1916), The first pregenital stage of the libido. In: *Selected Papers on Psychoanalysis*, Vol. 1. New York: Basic Books, 1954.

———— (1924), The influence of oral eroticism on character formation. In: *Selected Papers on Psychoanalysis*, Vol. 1. New York: Basic Books, 1954.

Adler, G., & Buie, D. (1979), Aloneness and borderline psychopathology: The possible relevance of child developmental issues. *Internat. J. Psycho-Anal.*, 60:83–86.

Alcoholics Anonymous World Services (1952), *Twelve Steps and Twelve Traditions.* New York: Alcoholics Anonymous World Services.

———— (1975), *Living Sober.* New York: Alcoholics Anonymous World Services.

———— (1976), *Alcoholics Anonymous*, 3rd ed. New York: Alcoholics Anonymous World Services.

American Psychiatric Association (1994), Diagnostic and Statistical Manual of Mental Disorders, 4th ed. (DSM-IV). Washington, DC: American Psychiatric Press.

Archibald, W. C., Long, D. M., Miller, C., & Tuddenham, R. D. (1962), Gross stress reaction to combat: Fifteen year follow-up. *Amer. J. Psychiatry*, 119:317–322.

———— & Tuddenham, R. D. (1965), Persistent stress reaction after combat. *Arch. Gen. Psychiatry*, 12:475–481.

Arvanitakis, K. (1985), The third *Soter* who ordaineth all. *Internat. Rev. Psychoanal.*, 12:431–440.

191

Balint, M. (1968), *The Basic Fault: Therapeutic Aspects of Regression.* London: Tavistock.

Blatt, S. J., Berman, W., Bloom-Feshback, S., Sugarman, A., Wilber, C., & Kleber, H. (1984), Psychological assessment of psychopathology in opiate addicts. *J. Nerv. Ment. Dis.,* 172:156–165.

Blumenthal, S. (1988), A guide to risk factors, assessment and treatment of suicidal patients, *Med. Clin. N. Amer.,* 72:937–971.

Bowlby, J. (1961), Processes of mourning. *Internat. J. Psycho-Anal.,* 42:317–340.

——— (1969), *Attachment and Loss,* Vol. 1. New York: Basic Books.

——— (1977), The making and breaking of affectional bonds. *Brit. J. Psychiatry,* 130:201–210.

——— (1980), Information processing approach to defense. In: *Attachment and Loss,* Vol. 2. New York: Basic Books, pp. 44–74.

Brazelton, T. B., & Cramer, B. G. (1990), *The Earliest Relationship.* Reading, MA: Addison Wesley Publishing.

——— Tronick, E. (1978), The infant's response to entrapment between contradictory messages in face-to-face interaction. *J. Amer. Acad. Child Psychiatry,* 17:1–13.

Breasch, L. D. (1990), Book review of "Integration and Self-Healing." *Psychoanal. Quart.,* 49:157–159.

Brenner, C. (1982), *The Mind in Conflict.* New York: International Universities Press.

Brill, A. H. (1922), Tobacco and the individual. *Internat. J. Psycho-Anal.,* 3:430–444.

Brill, N. Q., & Beebe, G. W. (1955), A Follow-Up Study of War Neuroses. *Veterans Administration Medical Monograph.* Washington, DC: U.S. Government Printing Office.

Brown, S. (1985), *Treating the Alcoholic: A Developmental Model of Recovery.* New York: John Wiley.

Calef, V., & Weinshel, E. M. (1984), Anxiety and the restitutional function of homosexual cruising. *Internat. J. Psycho-Anal.,* 65:45–53.

Campbell, J. (1989), *The Hero with a Thousand Faces.* Los Angeles, CA: Audio Renaissance Tapes.

Cohen, J. (1980), Structural consequences of psychic trauma: A new look at beyond the pleasure principle. *Internat. J. Psycho-Anal.,* 61:421–454.

———— (1987), Trauma and repression. *Psychoanal. Inqu.*, 5:163–189.

———— Kinston, W. (1984), Repression theory: A new look at the cornerstone. *Internat. J. Psycho-Anal.*, 65:411–422.

de M'Uzan, M. (1974a), Analytical process and the notion of the past. *Intern. Rev. Psycho-Anal.*, 1:461–480.

———— (1974b), Psychodynamic mechanisms in psycho-somatic symptom formation. *Psychother. Psychosom.*, 23:103–110.

Deri, S. K. (1984), *Symbolization and Creativity.* New York: International Universities Press.

Desmers-Derosiers, L. A. (1982), Influence of alexithymia on symbolic function. *Psychother. & Psychosom.*, 38:103–120.

Dodes, L. M. (1984), Abstinence from alcohol in long-term individual psychotherapy with alcoholics. *Amer. J. Psychother.*, 38:248–256.

———— (1988), The psychology of combining dynamic psychotherapy and Alcoholics Anonymous. *Bull. Menninger Clinic*, 52:283–293.

———— (1990), Addiction, helplessness, and narcissistic rage. *Psychoanal. Quart.*, 59:398–419.

———— (1991), Psychotherapy is useful, often essential, for alcoholics. *Psychodynamic Letter*, 1(2):4–7.

———— Khantzian, E. J. (1991), Individual psychodynamic psychotherapy. In: *Clinical Textbook of Addictive Disorders*, ed. R. J. Frances & S. I. Miller. New York: Guilford Press.

Dorpat, T. L. (1985), *Denial and Defense in Therapeutic Situations.* Northvale, NJ: Jason Aronson.

Dorsey, J. M. (1971a), *Psychology of Emotion: Self Discipline by Conscious Emotional Continence.* Detroit, MI: Wayne State University Press.

———— (1971b), *Psychology of Language: A Local Habitation and a Name.* Detroit, MI: Wayne State University Press.

Dorus, W., & Senay, E. (1980), Depression, demographic dimension and drug abuse. *Amer. J. Psychiatry*, 137:699–704.

Dowling, S. (1977), Seven infants with esophageal atresia: A developmental study. *The Psychoanalytic Study of the Child*, 32:215–256. New Haven, CT: Yale University Press.

———— (1986), Discussion of the various contributions. In: *The Reconstruction of Trauma*, ed. A. Rothstein. Madison, CT: International Universities Press, pp. 205–217.

Duffy, E. (1951), The concept of energy mobilization. *Psychol. Rev.*, 58:30–40.

—— (1957), The psychological significance of the concept of "arousal" or "activation." *Psycholog. Rev.*, 64:265–275.

—— (1972), Activation. In: *Handbook of Psychophysiology*, ed. M. S. Greenfield & R. A. Steinback. New York: Holt, Reinhart & Winston.

—— Freeman, G. L. (1933), The facilitative and inhibitory effects of muscular tension on performance. *Amer. J. Psychol.*, 45:17–52.

—— —— (1948), *The Energetics of Behavior*. Ithaca, NY: Cornell University Press.

—— Malmo, R. B. (1959), Activation: A neurophysiological dimension. *Psychol. Rev.*, 66:367–386.

—— Pribram, K. H. & McGuinnes, D. (1975), Arousal, activation, and effort in the control of attention. *Psychol. Rev.*, 32:116–140.

Dukakis, K., with J. Scovell (1990), *Now You Know*. New York: Simon & Schuster.

Edgecumbe, R. (1983), On learning to talk to oneself. *Bull. Brit. Psychoanal. Soc.*, 5:1–13.

Engel, G. L. (1962a), Anxiety and depression-withdrawal: The primary affects of unpleasure. *Internat. J. Psycho-Anal.*, 43:89–98.

—— (1962b), *Psychological Development in Health and Disease*. Philadelphia: Saunders.

—— (1963), Toward a classification of affects. In: *Expression of Emotion in Man*, ed. P. H. Knapp. New York: International Universities Press, pp. 262–293.

—— (1967), Ego development following severe trauma in infancy. *Bull. Assn. Psychoanal. Med.*, 6:57–61.

—— Reichsman, F. (1956), Spontaneous and experimentally induced depression in an infant with gastric fistula. *J. Amer. Psychoanal. Assn.*, 4:428–453.

—— Schmale, A. (1967), The giving-up given-up complex illustrated on film. *Arch. Gen. Psychiatry*, 17:135–145.

Fairbairn, W. R. D. (1954), *An Object Relations Theory of the Personality*. New York: Basic Books.

Fenichel, O. (1931), Outline of clinical psychoanalysis. *Psychoanal. Quart.* 2:583–591, 1933.

——— (1945), *The Psychoanalytic Theory of the Neuroses.* New York: W. W. Norton.

Fingarette, H. (1988), *Heavy Drinking: The Myth of Alcoholism as a Disease.* Berkeley, CA: University of California Press.

Freeman, G. L. (1948), *The Energetics of Behavior.* Ithaca, NY: Cornell University Press.

Freud, A. (1965), Normality and pathology in childhood: Assessments of development. *The Writings*, Vol. 6. New York: International Universities Press.

Freud, S. (1893–1895), Studies on Hysteria. *Standard Edition*, 2:1–240. London: Hogarth Press, 1955.

——— (1905), Three essays on the theory of sexuality. *Standard Edition*, 7:125–243. London: Hogarth Press, 1955.

——— (1911), Psycho-analytic notes on an autobiographical account of a case of paranoia. *Standard Edition*, 12:9–82. London: Hogarth Press, 1958.

——— (1914), On narcissism. *Standard Edition*, 14:67–102. London: Hogarth Press, 1957.

——— (1916), Some character types met with in psychoanalytic work. *Standard Edition*, 14:309–333. London: Hogarth Press, 1957.

——— (1920), Beyond the pleasure principle. *Standard Edition*, 18:3–64. London: Hogarth Press, 1955.

——— (1924), Neurosis and psychosis. *Standard Edition*, 19:149–156. London: Hogarth Press, 1961.

——— (1926), Inhibitions, symptoms, and anxiety. *Standard Edition*, 20:77–175. London: Hogarth Press, 1959.

Frosch, W. (1970), Panel: Psychoanalytic evaluation of addiction and habituation. *J. Amer. Psychoanal. Assn.*, 18:209–218.

Gadini, R. (1975), The concept of the transitional object. *J. Amer. Acad. Child Psychiatry*, 14:731–736.

——— (1987), Early care and the roots of internalization. *Intern. Rev. Psycho-Anal.*, 14:321–333.

Gawin, F. H., & Kleber, H. D. (1984), Cocaine abuse treatment. *Arch. Gen. Psychiatry*, 41:903–908.

——— ——— (1986), Pharmacological treatment of cocaine abuse. *Psychiatric Clin. N. Amer.*, 9:573–583.

Gay, P. (1988), *Freud: A Life for Our Time*. New York: W. W. Norton.

Gedo, J. (1979), *Beyond Interpretation*. New York: International Universities Press.

———— (1986), *Conceptual Issues in Psychoanalysis: Essays in History and Method*. Hillsdale, NJ: Analytic Press.

Glover, E. (1931), The prevention and treatment of drug addiction. *Brit. J. Inebriety*, 29:13–18.

———— (1932), On the etiology of drug addiction. In: *On the Early Development of Mind*. New York: International Universities Press, 1956.

———— (1949), *Psycho-Analysis*. New York: Staples Press.

Goodman, E. (1990), The missing picture of Kitty Dukakis. *Boston Globe*, September 16, p. A25.

Gottschalk, L. A. (1978), Content analysis of speech in psychiatric research. *Comprehen. Psychiatry*, 19:387–392.

Gray, P. (1973), Psychoanalytic technique and the ego's capacity for viewing interpsychic activity. *J. Amer. Psychoanal. Assn.*, 21:474–494.

———— (1986), On helping analysands observe intra-psychic activity. In: *Psychoanalysis: The Science of Mental Conflict. Essays in Honor of Charles Brenner*, ed. A. Richards & M. Willick. Hillsdale, NJ: Analytic Press.

———— (1987), On the technique of analysis of the superego—An introduction. *Psychoanal. Quart.*, 56:130–154.

———— (1990), The nature of therapeutic action in psychoanalysis. *J. Amer. Psychoanal. Assn.*, 38:1083–1097.

———— (1991), On transferred permissive or approving superego functions: Analysis of the ego's superego activities. Part II. *Psychoanal. Quart.*, 60:1–21.

Greenspan, S. I. (1981), *Psychopathology and Adaptation in Infancy and Early Childhood*. New York: International Universities Press.

———— (1987), Early care and the roots of internalization. *Internat. Rev. Psychoanal.*, 14:321–333.

Grünbaum, A. (1984), *The Foundations of Psychoanalysis*. Berkeley, CA: University of California Press.

Hadley, J. (1983), The representational system: A bridging concept for psychoanalysis and trauma physiology. *Internat. Rev. Psychoanal.*, 10:13–30.

———— (1985), Attention, affect, and attachment. *Psychoanal. & Contemp. Thought,* 8:529–550.

Hering, A. M. (1987), *Alexithymia: A Developmental View Using a Differentiation Model of Affect Maturity.* Unpublished doctoral dissertation, University of Michigan.

Hesselbrock, M. N., Meyer, R. E., & Keener, J. J. (1985), Psychopathology in hospitalized alcoholics. *Arch. Gen. Psychiatry,* 42:1050–1055.

Hofer, M. A. (1978), Hidden regulatory processes in early social relationship. In: *Perspectives in Ethology,* Vol. 3, ed. P. G. Bateson & P. H. Klopfer. New York: Plenum Press.

———— (1981a), Toward a developmental basis for disease predisposition: The effect of early maternal separation on brain, behavior, and cardiovascular system. In: *Brain, Behavior, and Bodily Disease,* ed. H. Werner, M. A. Holdes, & A. J. Stunkard. New York: Raven Press.

———— (1981b), *The Roots of Human Behavior.* San Francisco: W. H. Freeman.

———— (1982), Some thoughts on "the transduction of experience" from a developmental perspective. *Psychosom. Med.,* 44:19–28.

———— (1983), On the relationship between attachment and separation processes in infancy. In: *Emotion: Theory, Research and Experience: Emotions in Early Development,* Vol. 2, ed. R. Pluchik. New York: Academic Press.

———— (1990), Early symbiotic processes: Hard evidence from a soft place. In: *Pleasure Beyond The Pleasure Principle,* ed. R. A. Glick & S. Bone. New Haven, CT: Yale University Press, pp. 55–78.

———— Weiner, H. (1971), The development and mechanism of cardio-respiratory responses to maternal deprivation in rat pups. *Psychosom. Med.,* 33:353–363.

Hoppe, K. D. (1977), Split brain and psychoanalysis. *Psychoanal. Quart.,* 46:220–244.

———— (1978), Split brain—Psychoanalytic findings and hypotheses. *J. Amer. Acad. Psychoanal.,* 6:193–213.

———— (1984), Severed ties. In: *Psychoanalytic Reflections on the Holocaust: Selected Essays,* ed. S. A. Luel & P. Markus. New York: Ktav Publishing House, pp. 113–133.

Horton, P. L., & Sharp, S. L. (1981), *Solace: The Missing Dimension in Psychiatry.* Chicago: University of Chicago Press.

—— —— (1984), Language, solace, and transitional relatedness. *The Psychoanalytic Study of the Child,* 39:167–194. New Haven, CT: Yale University Press.

—— Gewirtz, H. E., & Kreutter, K. L., eds. (1988), *The Solace Paradigm.* Madison, CT: International Universities Press.

Jacobson, E. (1964), *The Self and the Object World.* New York: International Universities Press.

—— (1971), *Depression: Comparative Studies of Normal, Neurotic and Psychotic Conditions.* New York: International Universities Press.

Jacobson, J. G. (1993), Developmental observation, multiple models of the mind, and the therapeutic relationship in psychoanalysis. *Psychoanal. Quart.,* 62:523–552.

Joffe, W.G. (1969), A critical review of the status of the envy concept. *Internat. J. Psycho-Anal.,* 50:533–545.

Jones, E. (1953), *The Life and Work of Sigmund Freud,* Vol. 1. New York: Basic Books.

—— (1955), *The Life and Work of Sigmund Freud,* Vol. 2. New York: Basic Books.

Jones, J. M. (1982), Affects: A nonsymbolic information processing system. Paper presented at the American Psychoanalytic Association as a precirculated paper, December.

Kernberg, O. (1975), *Borderline Conditions and Pathological Narcissism.* New York: Jason Aronson.

—— (1976), *Object-Relations Theory and Clinical Psychoanalysis.* New York: Jason Aronson.

—— (1984), *Severe Personality Disorders.* New Haven, CT: Yale University Press.

Khantzian, E. J. (1972), A preliminary dynamic formulation of the psychopharmacologic action of methadone. *Proceedings of the Fourth National Methadone Conference,* San Francisco.

—— (1974), Opiate addiction: A critique of theory and some implications for treatment. *Amer. J. Psychotherapy,* 28:59–70.

—— (1975), Self selection and progression in drug dependence. *Psychiatry Digest,* 10:19–22.

—— (1978), The ego, the self and opiate addiction: Theoretical and treatment considerations. *Internat. Rev. Psychoanal.,* 5:189–198.

—————— (1985a), The self-medication hypothesis of addictive disorders. *Amer. J. Psychiatry*, 142:1259–1264.

—————— (1985b), Psychotherapeutic intervention with substance abusers—The clinical context. *J. Substance Abuse Treatment*, 2:83–88.

—————— (1986), A contemporary psychodynamic approach to drug abuse treatment. *Amer. J. Drug Alcohol Abuse*, 12(3):213–222.

—————— (1987), Substance dependence, repetition and the nature of addictive suffering. Typescript.

—————— (1988), The primary care therapist and patient needs in substance abuse treatment. *Amer. J. Drug Alcohol Abuse*, 14(2):159–167.

—————— (1989), Substance dependence, repetition and the nature of addictive suffering. Typescript.

—————— (1990), Self-regulation and self-medication factors in alcoholism and the addictions. In: *Recent Developments in Alcoholism*, Vol. 8, ed. M. Galanter. New York: Plenum, pp. 225–271.

—————— (1991), Self-regulation factors in cocaine dependence—a clinical perspective. In: *The Epidemiology of Cocaine Use and Abuse*, ed. S. Schober & C. Schade. Research Monograph #110. Rockville, MD: National Institute on Drug Abuse, pp. 211–226.

—————— Halliday, K. S., & McAuliffe, W. E. (1990), *Addiction and the Vulnerable Self: Modified Dynamic Group Therapy for Substance Abusers (MDGT)*. New York: Guilford Press.

—————— Mack, J. E. (1983), Self-preservation and the care of the self–ego instincts reconsidered. *The Psychoanalytic Study of the Child*, 38:209–232. New Haven, CT: Yale University Press.

—————— —————— (1989), Alcoholics Anonymous and contemporary psychodynamic theory. In: *Recent Developments in Alcoholism*, Vol. 7, ed. M. Galanter. New York: Plenum, pp. 67–89.

—————— —————— (1994), How AA works and why clinicians should understand. *J. Substance Abuse Treatment*, 11:77–92.

—————— Treece, C. (1985), DSM-III psychiatric diagnosis of narcotic addicts: Recent findings. *Arch. Gen. Psychiatry*, 42:1067–1071.

—————— Wilson, A. (1993), Substance abuse, repetition, and the nature of addictive suffering. In: *Hierarchical Conceptions in*

Psychoanalysis, ed. A. Wilson & J. E. Gedo. New York: Guilford Press.

Kinston, W., & Cohen, J. (1986), Primal repression: Clinical and theoretical aspects of the mind: The realm of psychic states. *Internat. J. Psycho-Anal.,* 67:337–355.

——— ——— (1987), Primal repression and other states of the mind: The realm of psychostatics. Paper presented to the German Psychoanalytic Association.

Kleber, H. D., & Gold, M. S. (1978), Use of psychotherapeutic drugs in the treatment of methadone maintained narcotic addicts. *J. Amer. Acad. Sci.,* 331:81–98.

Klein, M. (1946), Notes on some schizoid mechanisms. *Internat. J. Psycho-Anal.,* 27:99–110.

——— (1968), *Contributions to Psychoanalysis 1921–1945.* London: Hogarth Press.

Knight, R. (1937), The dynamics and treatment of chronic alcoholic addiction. *Bull. Menninger Clinic,* 1:233–250.

Kohut, H. (1968), The psychoanalytic treatment of narcissistic personality disorders. *The Psychoanalytic Study of the Child,* 23:86–113. New York: International Universities Press.

——— (1971), *The Analysis of the Self.* New York: International Universities Press.

——— (1972), Thoughts on narcissism and narcissistic rage. *The Psychoanalytic Study of the Child,* 27:360–400. Chicago: Quadrangle.

——— (1977), *The Restoration of the Self.* New York: International Universities Press.

——— (1984), *How Does Analysis Cure?* Chicago, IL: University of Chicago Press.

——— Wolf, E. S. (1978), The disorders of the self and their treatment: An outline. *Internat. J. Psycho-Anal.,* 59:413–425.

Kris, A. O. (1990), Helping patients by analyzing self-criticism. *J. Amer. Psychoanal. Assn.,* 38:605–636.

Krystal, H. (1959), The physiological basis of the treatment of delirium tremens. *Amer. J. Psychiatry,* 116:137–147.

——— (1961), The management of alcoholism in medical practice. *Mich. State Med. Soc.,* 60:73–78.

——— (1962), The opiate withdrawal syndrome as a state of stress. *Psychoanal. Quart.,* (Suppl.) 36:53–65.

———— (1963), Social forces and the management of alcoholic patients. *Mich. State Med. Soc.*, 62:500–505.

———— (1964), Therapeutic assistants in psychotherapy with regressed patients. In: *Current Psychiatric Therapies*, ed. J. Masserman. New York: Grune & Stratton, pp. 230–232.

———— (1966), Withdrawal from drugs. *Psychosomatics*, 7:199–302.

———— (1968), Studies of concentration camp survivors. In: *Massive Psychic Trauma*, ed. H. Krystal. New York: International Universities Press, pp. 256–276.

———— (1970), Trauma and the stimulus barrier. Paper presented to meeting of American Psychoanalytic Association, New York.

———— (1971), Trauma: Consideration of its intensity and chronicity. In: *Psychic Traumatization*, ed. H. Krystal & W. G. Niederland. Boston: Little, Brown, pp. 11–28.

———— (1974), The genetic development of affects and affect regression. *The Annual of Psychoanalysis*, 2:98–126. New York: International Universities Press.

———— (1977a), Aspects of affect theory. *Bull. Menninger Clinic*, 41:1–26.

———— (1977b), Self-representation and the capacity for self-care. *The Annual of Psychoanalysis*, 6:209–246. new York: International Universities Press.

———— (1977c), Self and object-representation in alcoholism and other drug dependence: Implications of therapy. In: *Psychoanalytic Memos of Drug Dependence*, ed. J. D. Blaine & D. A. Julius. NIDA Research Management 12. Washington, DC: Department of Health, Education and Welfare/U.S. Public Health Service, pp. 98–100.

———— (1978a), Trauma and affect. *The Psychoanalytic Study of the Child*, 33:81–116. New Haven, CT: Yale University Press.

———— (1978b), Catastrophic psychic trauma and psychogenic death. In: *Psychiatric Problems in Medical Practice*, ed. G. U. Balis, L. Wurmser, E. McDaniel, & R. G. Grenell. Boston: Butterworth, pp. 79–97.

———— (1978c), Self representation and the capacity for self care. *The Annual of Psychoanalysis*, 6:209–246. New York: International Universities Press.

———— (1979), Alexithymia and psychotherapy. *Amer. J. Psychother.*, 33:17–31.

———— (1981), The hedonic element in affectivity. *The Annual of Psychoanalysis*, 9:93–115. New York: International Universities Press.

———— (1982a), The activating aspect of emotions. *Psychoanal. & Contemp. Thought*, 5(4):605–642.

———— (1982b), Adolescence and the tendencies to develop substance dependence. *Psychoanal. Inqu.*, 2:581–617.

———— (1982–1983), Alexithymia and the effectiveness of psychoanalytic treatment. *Internat. J. Psychoanalytic Psychother.*, 9:353–388.

———— (1985), Trauma and the stimulus barrier. *Psychoanal. Inqu.*, 5:131–161.

———— (1987), The impact of massive trauma and the capacity to grieve effectively: Later life sequelae. In: *Treating the Elderly with Psychotherapy*, ed. J. Sadavoy & M. Leszcz. New York: International Universities Press, pp. 67–94.

———— (1988a), *Integration and Self-Healing: Affect, Trauma, Alexithymia.* Hillsdale, NJ: Analytic Press.

———— (1988b), Book review of A. Rothstein (ed.), *The Reconstruction of Trauma, Its Significance in Clinical Work. J. Nerv. & Ment. Dis.*, 176:641–642.

———— (1988c), On some roots of creativity. In: *Hemispheric Specialization*, ed. K. Hoppe. Philadelphia: Saunders, pp. 475–492.

———— Niederland, W. G. (1968), Clinical observations of the survivor syndrome. In: *Massive Psychic Trauma*, ed. H. Krystal. New York: International Universities Press, pp. 327–348.

———— ———— eds. (1971), *Psychic Traumatization.* Boston: Little, Brown.

———— Raskin, H. (1963), Addiction and pain. Mimeographed.

———— ———— (1970), *Drug Dependence, Aspects of Ego Functions.* Detroit: Wayne State University Press.

———— ———— (1981), Drug dependence: Aspects of ego functions. In: *Classic Contributions in the Addictions*, ed. H. Shaffer & M. Burglass. New York: Brunner/Mazel, pp. 161–172.

Krystal, J. H. (1988), Assessing alexithymia. In: *Integration and Self-Healing*, ed. H. Krystal. Hillsdale, NJ: Analytic Press, pp. 286–310.

Kubie, L. S. (1937), The fantasy of dirt. *Psychoanal. Quart.*, 6:338–425.

—— (1947), The fallacious use of quantitative concepts in dynamic psychology. *Psychoanal. Quart.*, 16:507–518.

—— (1954), The fundamental nature of the distinction between normality and neurosis. *Psychoanal. Quart.*, 23:167–204.

—— (1978), Symbol and Neurosis. Selected Papers of Lawrence S. Kubie, ed. H. J. Schlesinger. *Psychological Issues,* Monograph 44. New York: International Universities Press.

Lacey, J. I. (1967), Somatic response patterning and stress: Some revisions of activation theory. In: *Psychological Stress: Issues in Research,* ed. M. H. Appley & R. Trumbull. New York: Appleton-Century-Crofts, pp. 14–42.

Lagerkvist, P. (1966), *Pilgrimen.* Stockholm: Bonniers.

Levy, L. (1925), The psychology of the effect produced by morphia. *Internat. J. Psycho-Anal.*, 6:313–316.

Lichtenberg, J. D.(1983), *Psychoanalysis and Infant Research.* Hillsdale, NJ: Analytic Press.

Lifton, R. J. (1968), Observations on Hiroshima survivors. In: *Massive Psychic Trauma.* H. Krystal. New York: International Universities Press.

—— (1976), *The Life of the Self.* New York: Simon & Schuster.

—— (1979), *The Broken Connection.* New York: Simon & Schuster.

Loewald, H. (1960), On the therapeutic action of psychoanalysis. *Internat. J. Psycho-Anal.*, 41:16–33.

Luborsky, L., Woody, G. E., Hole, A., & Velleco, A. (1977), *A Treatment Manual for Supportive-Expressive Psychoanalytically Oriented Psychotherapy: Special Adaptation for Treatment of Drug Dependence.* (Unpublished manual, 4th ed., 1981).

Mack, J. E. (1981), Alcoholism, A.A. and the governance of the self. In: *Dynamic Approaches to the Understanding and Treatment of Alcoholism,* ed. M. H. Bean & N. E. Zinberg. New York: Free Press, pp. 128–162.

MacLean, P. D. (1949), Psychosomatic disease and the "visceral brain." *Psychosom. Med.*, 11:338–353.

Mahler, M. S. (1958), Autism and symbiosis: two extreme disturbances of identity. *Internat. J. Psycho-Anal.* 39:77–83.

——— Pine, F., & Bergman, A. (1975), *The Psychological Birth of the Human Infant.* New York: Basic Books.

Marty, P., & De M'Uzan, M. (1963), La pensee operatoire. *Rev. Psychoanalytique* (Suppl.) 27:345–356.

——— ——— David, C. (1963), *L'investigation Psychosomatique.* Paris: Presses Universitaires Paris.

McDougall, J. (1974), The psychosoma and psychoanalytic process. *Internat. Rev. Psychoanal.*, 1:437–454.

——— (1984), The "dis-affected" patient: Reflections on affect pathology. *Psychoanal. Quart.*, 53:386–409.

Meers, D. R. (1970), Contributions of a ghetto culture to symptom formation. *The Psychoanalytic Study of the Child*, 25:209–230. New York: International Universities Press.

——— (1972), Crucible of ambivalence: Sexual identity in the ghetto. *The Psychoanalytic Study of Society*, 5:109–135. New York: International Universities Press.

——— (1973a), Psychiatric ombudsmen for day care. In: *Headstart, Child Development Legislation,* Joint Hearings (March 17, 1972) before the Subcommittee on Children and Youth and the Subcommittee on Employment, Manpower and Poverty of the Committee on Labor and Public Welfare, United States Senate, Ninety Second Congress, 1973.

——— (1973b), Psychoanalytic research and intellectual functioning of ghetto-reared, black children. *The Psychoanalytic Study of the Child*, 28:395–417. New Haven, CT: Yale University Press.

——— (1974), Traumatic and cultural distortions of psychoneurotic symptoms in a black ghetto. *The Annual of Psychoanalysis*, 2:368–386. New York: International Universities Press.

Menninger, K. A. (1938), *Man Against Himself.* New York: Harcourt, Brace.

Milkman, H., & Frosch, W. A. (1973), On the preferential abuse of heroin and amphetamine. *J. Nerv. Ment. Dis.*, 156:242–248.

Minkowski, E. (1946), L'anesthesie affective. *Ann. Medicopsychologique*, 104:8–13.

Mirin, S. M., Weiss, R. D., Solloqub, A., & Jaqueline, M. (1984), Affective illness in substance abuse. In: *Substance Abuse and Psychopathology*, ed. S. M. Mirin. Washington, DC: American Psychological Press Clinical Insights, pp. 57–78.

Modell, A. H. (1984), *Psychoanalysis in a New Context*. New York: International Universities Press.

Myers, W. A. (1990), A case of photoexhibitionism in a homosexual male. In: *The Psychotherapeutic Treatment of the Homosexualities*, ed. V. Volkan & C. Socarides. Madison, CT: International Universities Press.

Nagera, H., Baker, S., Edgcumbe, R., Holder, A., Laufer, M., Meers, D., & Rees, K. (1970), *Basic Psychoanalytic Concepts of the Theory of Instincts*. London: George Allen & Unwin.

Nemiah, J. C. (1970), The psychological management and treatment of patients with peptic ulcer. *Adv. Psychosom. Med.*, 6:169–173.

——— (1975), Denial revisited: Reflections on psychosomatic theory. *Psychother. & Psychosom.*, 26:140–147.

——— (1977), Alexithymia: Theoretical considerations. *Psychother. & Psychosom.*, 28:199–296.

——— (1978), Alexithymia and psychosomatic illness. *J. Continuing Ed. Psychiat.*, October 18, pp. 25–37.

——— Sifneos, P. E. (1970a) Affect and fantasy in patients with psychosomatic disorders. In: *Modern Trends in Psychosomatic Medicine*, ed. O. W. Hill. London: Butterworth.

——— ——— (1970b), Psychosomatic illness: A problem in communication. *Psychother. Psychosom.*, 18:154–160.

——— ——— (1977), Affect and fantasy in psychosomatic disorders. In: *Modern Trends in Psychosomatic Medicine*, Vol. 2, ed. O. W. Hill. London: Butterworth.

Niederland, W. G. (1961), The problem of the survivor. *J. Hillside Hosp.*, 10:233–247.

——— (1964), Psychiatric disorders among persecution victims: A contribution to the understanding of concentration camp pathology and its aftereffects. *J. Nerv. Ment. Dis.*, 139:458–474.

NIH Consensus Statement (1991), Treatment of panic disorder. NIH Consensus Dev. Conf. Concens, Statement September 25–27, 1991; 9(2). Bethesda, MD: Office of Medical Applications of Research, NIH.

Nova (1986), *Life's First Feelings*. Boston: WGBM.

Novick, K. K., & Novick, J. (1987), The essence of masochism. *The Psychoanalytic Study of the Child*, 42:353–384. New Haven, CT: Yale University Press.

————— ————— (1991), Some comments on masochism and the delusion of omnipotence from a developmental perspective. *J. Amer. Psychoanal. Assn.*, 39:307–332.

Overbeck, G. (1977), How to operationalize alexithymic phenomena: Some findings from speech analysis and the Giesen Test (GT). *Psychother. & Psychosom.*, 28:106–117.

Person, S. E. (1988), *Dreams of Love and Fateful Encounters.* New York: W.W. Norton.

Pine, F. (1988), The four psychologies of psychoanalysis and their place in clinical work. *J. Amer. Psychoanal. Assn.*, 36:571–596.

Rado, S. (1926), The psychic effect of intoxicants: An attempt to evolve a psychoanalytic theory of morbid craving. *Internat. J. Psycho-Anal.*, 7:396–413.

————— (1933), The psychoanalysis of pharmacothymia. *Psychoanal. Quart.*, 2:1–23.

————— (1964), Hedonic self-regulation of the organism. In: *The Role of Pleasure in Behavior*, ed. R. Heath. New York: Harper & Row, pp. 257–264.

————— (1969), The emotions. In: *Adaptational Psychodynamics: Motivation and Control.* New York: Science House, pp. 21–30.

Rangell, L. (1963a), The scope of intrapsychic conflict: Microscopic and macroscopic considerations. *The Psychoanalytic Study of the Child*, 18:75–102. New York: International Universities Press.

————— (1963b), Structural problems in intrapsychic conflict. *The Psychoanalytic Study of the Child*, 18:103–138. New York: International Universities Press.

————— (1974), A psychoanalytic perspective leading currently to the syndrome of the compromise of integrity. *Internat. J. Psycho-Anal.*, 55:3–12.

————— (1980), *The Mind of Watergate.* New York: W. W. Norton.

Richter, C. P. (1957), On the phenomena of sudden death in animals and men. *Psychosom. Med.*, 19:191–198.

Robertson, J. (1952), Film: *A Two-Year-Old goes to Hospital.*

Rothstein, A., ed. (1986), *The Reconstruction of Trauma.* Workshop series of American Psychoanalytic Association, Vol. 2. New York: International Universities Press.

Rounsaville, B. J., Weissman, M. M., Crits-Cristoph, K., Wilber, C., & Kleber, H.(1982a), Diagnosis and symptoms of depression in opiate addicts: Course and relationship to treatment outcome. *Arch. Gen. Psychiatry*, 39:151–156.

———— ———— Kleber, H., & Wilber, C.(1982b), Heterogeneity of psychiatric diagnosis in treated opiate addicts. *Arch. Gen. Psychiatry*, 39:161–166.

Ruesch, J. (1948), The infantile personality: The case problem of psychosomatic medicine. *Psychosom. Med.*, 10:134–142.

Savitt, R. (1963), Psychoanalytic studies on addiction: Ego structure in narcotic addiction. *Psychoanal. Quart.*, 32:43–57.

Schafer, R. (1960), The loving and the beloved superego. *The Psychoanalytic Study of the Child*, 15:163–188. New York: International Universities Press.

Schiffer, F. (1988), Psychotherapy of nine successfully treated cocaine abusers: Techniques and dynamics. *J. Subst. Abuse Treatment*, 5:133–137.

Schmale, A. H., Jr. (1964), A genetic view of affects. *The Psychoanalytic Study of the Child*, 3/4:253–270. New York: International Universities Press.

Schur, M. (1953), The ego in anxiety. In: *Drives, Affects, Behavior*, ed. R. Lowenstein. New York: International Universities Press, pp. 67–104.

———— (1955), Comments on the metapsychology of somatization. *The Psychoanalytic Study of the Child*, 10:119–164. New York: International Universities Press.

———— (1972), *Freud: Living and Dying*. New York: International Universities Press.

Seligman, M. E. R. (1975), *Helplessness*. San Francisco: W. H. Freeman.

Shands, H. C. (1958), The infantile personality: The case problem of psychosomatic medicine. *Psychosom. Med.*, 10:134–142.

———— (1971), *The War with Words: Structure and Transcendence*. The Hague: Mouton.

———— (1976), Suitability for psychotherapy I: Transference and formal operations. Paper presented at 10th Congress of the International College for Psychosomatic Medicine, Paris.

———— (1977), Suitability for psychotherapy II: Unsuitability and psychosomatic diseases. *Psychother. & Psychosom.*, 28:28–35.

Shengold, L. (1989), *Soul Murder*. New Haven, CT: Yale University Press.

Sifneos, P. (1967), Clinical observations on some patients suffering from a variety of psychosomatic diseases. *Acta Med. Psychosom.*, Proceedings.

——— (1967), Clinical observations on some patients suffering from a variety of psychosomatic diseases. In: *Proceedings of the Seventh European Conference on Psychosomatic Research*. Basel: S. Karger.

——— (1972), The prevalence of "alexithymic" characteristics in psychosomatic patients. In: *Topics in Psychosomatic Research*, ed. H. Freyberger. Basel: S. Karger.

——— (1972–1973), Is dynamic psychotherapy contraindicated for a large number of patients with psychosomatic diseases? *Psychother. & Psychosom.*, 21:133–136.

——— (1973), The prevalence of "alexithymic" characteristics in psychosomatic patients. *Psychother. & Psychosom.*, 22:255–262.

——— (1974), A reconsideration of psychodynamic mechanisms in psychosomatic symptom formation in view of recent clinical observations. *Psychother. & Psychosom.*, 14:151–155.

——— (1975), Problems of psychotherapy with patients with alexithymic characteristics and physical disease. *Psychother. & Psychosom.*, 26:65–70.

Simmel, E. (1927), Psychoanalytic treatment in a sanatorium. *Internat. J. Psycho-Anal.*, 10:70–89.

——— (1930), Morbid habits and cravings. *Psychoanal. Rev.*, 17:48–54.

——— (1948), Alcoholism and addiction. *Psychoanal. Quart.*, 12:6–31.

Socarides, C. (1978), *Homosexuality*. New York: Jason Aronson.

Southwick, S. H., & Satel, S. L. (1990), Exploring the meaning of substance abuse: An important dimension of early work with borderline patients. *Amer. J. Psychotherapy*, 44:61–67.

Spitz, R. A. (1945), Hospitalism. *The Psychoanalytic Study of the Child*, 1:53–74. New York: International Universities Press.

——— (1946), Hospitalism: A follow-up report. *The Psychoanalytic Study of the Child*, 2:113–117. New York: International Universities Press.

Spotts, J. V., & Shontz, F. C. (1987), Drug induced ego states: A trajectory theory of drug experience. *Soc. Pharmacol.*, 1:19–51.

Stern, D. N. (1974), Mother and infant at play: The diadic interaction involving facial, vocal and gaze behavior. In: *The Effect of the Infant on Its Caregiver*, ed. M. Lewis & L. Rosenblum. New York: Wiley.

———— (1983), Implications of infancy research for psychoanalytic theory and practice. In: *Psychiatry Update II*, ed. L. Greenspoon. Washington, DC: American Psychiatric Press, pp. 8–12.

———— (1985), *The Interpersonal World of the Infant. A View from Psychoanalysis and Developmental Psychology*. New York: Basic Books.

Stoller, R. J. (1975), *Perversion. The Erotic Form of Hatred*. New York: Pantheon Books.

———— (1985), *Observing the Erotic Imagination*. New Haven, CT: Yale University Press.

Stone, L. (1967), The psychoanalytic situation and transference: Postscript to an earlier communication. *J. Amer. Psychoanal. Assn.*, 15:3–58.

Stowasser (Der kleine Stowasser) (1940), Lateinisch-deutsches Schulwörterbuch, bearb. v. M. Petschenig. Berlin: Freytag.

Strachey, A., & Tyson, A. (1959), Editor's introduction to inhibition, symptoms, and anxiety. *Standard Edition*, 20:77–86. London: Hogarth Press.

Taylor, G. J. (1977), Alexithymia and the countertransference. *Psychother. & Psychosom.*, 28:141–147.

———— (1984), The boring patient. *Can. J. Psychiatry*, 29:217–222.

———— (1986), The psychodynamics of panic disorder. Paper presented at the Annual Meeting of the American Psychiatric Association, Washington, DC, May, 1986.

———— (1989), *Psychosomatic Medicine and Contemporary Psychological Analysis*. Madison, CT: International Universities Press.

———— Doody, K. (1982), Psychopathology and verbal expression for psychosomatic and psychoneurotic patients. *Psychother. & Psychosom.*, 38:121–127.

Taylor, G. T. (1984), Alexithymia: Concept, measurement, and implications for treatment. *Amer. J. Psychiatry*, 141:725–732.

Ten Houten, W. D., Hoppe, K. D., Bogen, J. E., & Walter, D. O. (1985a), I Alexithymia and the split brain. II Sentential-level content analysis. *Psychother. & Psychosom.*, 44:1–5.

———— ———— ———— ———— (1985b), Alexithymia the split brain III. Global level content analysis of fantasy and symbolization. *Psychother. & Psychosom.*, 44:89–94.

———— ———— ———— ———— (1985c), Alexithymia and the split brain IV. Gotschalk-gleser content analysis, an overview. *Psychother. & Psychosom.*, 44:113–121.

Thompson, A. E. (1981), *A Theory of Affect Development and Maturity. Applications to the Thematic Apperception Test.* Unpublished doctoral dissertation, University of Michigan, Ann Arbor, MI.

Traube-Werner, D. (1990), Affect deficit: a vicissitude of the phenomenon and experience of affect. *Internat. J. Psycho-Anal.*, 71:141–150.

Tustin, F. (1980), Autistic objects. *Internat. Rev. Psychoanal.*, 7:30–38.

———— (1981), *Autistic States in Children.* London: Routledge & Kegan Paul.

Ullman, R. B., & Brothers, D. (1988), *The Shattered Self: A Psychoanalytic Study of Trauma.* Hillsdale, NJ: Analytic Press.

Vaillant, G. E. (1981), Dangers of psychotherapy in the treatment of alcoholism. In: *Dynamic Approaches to the Understanding and Treatment of Alcoholism*, ed. M. H. Bean & N. E. Zinberg. New York: Free Press.

Valenstein, A. F. (1962), The psychoanalytic situation: Affects, emotional reliving, and insight in the psychoanalytic process. *Internat. J. Psycho-Anal.*, 43:315–324.

Van der Kolk, B. (1989), The compulsion to repeat the trauma. *Treatment of Victims of Sexual Abuse*, 12:389–411.

Von Rad, M., ed. (1983), *Alexithymie.* Berlin: Springer.

Waelder, R. (1951), The structure of paranoid ideas. In: *Psychoanalysis: Observation, Theory, Application.* ed. S. A. Guttman. New York: International Universities Press, 1976.

Weiss, K. J., & Rosenberg, D. J. (1985), Prevalence of anxiety disorder among alcoholics. *J. Clin. Psychiatry*, 46:3–5.

Weiss, R. D., & Mirin, S. M. (1984), Drug, host and environmental factors in the development of chronic cocaine abuse. In:

Substance Abuse and Psychotherapy, ed. S. M. Mirin. Washington, DC: American Psychiatric Press.

———— ———— (1986), Subtypes of cocaine abusers. *Psychiatric Clinics N. Amer.*, 9:491–501.

———— ———— Griffin, M. L., & Michaels, J. K. (1988), Psychopathology in cocaine abusers: Changing trends. *J. Nerv. Ment. Dis.*, 176(12):719–725.

Westerlundh, B., & Smith, G. (1983), Percept genesis and the psychodynamics of perception. *Psychoanal. & Contemp. Thought*, 6:597–640.

Wieder, H., & Kaplan, E. (1969), Drug use in adolescents. *The Psychoanalytic Study of the Child*, 24:399–431. New York: International Universities Press.

Willick, M. S. (1988), Dynamic aspects of homosexual cruising. In: *Fantasy, Myth and Reality. Essays in Honor of Jacob A. Arlow, M.D.*, ed. H. Blum, Y. Kramer, A. K. Richards, & A. D. Richards. Madison, CT: International Universities Press, pp. 435–449.

Wilson, A., Passik, S. D., Faude, J., Abrams, J., & Gordon, E. (1989), A hierarchical model of opiate addiction: Failures of self-regulation as a central aspect of substance abuse. *J. Nerv. Ment. Dis.*, 177:390–399.

Winnicott, D.W. (1960), Ego distortion in terms of true and false self. In: *The Maturational Processes and the Facilitating Environment.* New York: International Universities Press, 1965.

———— (1965), *The Maturational Processes and the Facilitating Environment.* New York: International Universities Press.

———— (1971), Mirror-role of mother and family in child development. In: *Playing and Reality.* New York: Basic Books

———— (1974), *Through Paediatrics to Psychoanalysis.* New York: Basic Books.

Woody, G. E., O'Brien, C. P., & Rickels, K. (1975), Depression and anxiety in heroin addicts: A placebo-controlled study of doxepin in combination with methadone. *Amer. J. Psychiatry*, 132:447–450.

———— McLellan, A. T., Luborsky, L., & O'Brien, C. P. (1986), Psychotherapy for substance abuse. *Psychiatric Clin. N. Amer.*, 9:547–562.

Wurmser, L. (1974), Psychoanalytic considerations of the etiology of compulsive drug use. *J. Amer. Psychoanal. Assn.*, 22:820–843.

—— (1978), *The Hidden Dimension. Psychodynamics in Compulsive Drug Use.* New York: Jason Aronson.

—— (1980), Phobic core in the addictions and the addictive process. *Internat. J. Psychoanal. Psychother.*, 8:311–337.

—— (1981a), *The Mask of Shame.* Baltimore: Johns Hopkins University Press.

—— (1981b), The question of specific psychopathology in compulsive drug use. *Annals NY Acad. Sci.*, pp. 33–43, 1982.

—— (1984a), More respect for the neurotic process. *J. Subst. Abuse Treatment*, 1:37–45.

—— (1984b), The role of superego conflicts in substance abuse and their treatment. *Internat. J. Psychoanal. Psychother.*, 10:227–258.

—— (1987a), Shame: The veiled companion of narcissism. In: *The Many Faces of Shame*, ed. D. L. Nathanson. New York: Guilford Press, pp. 64–92.

—— (1987b), *Flucht vor dem Gewissen. Analyse von Über-Ich und Abwehr bei schweren Neurosen.* Heidelberg: Springer.

—— (1987c), Flight from conscience: Experiences with the psychoanalytic treatment of compulsive drug abusers. *J. Subst. Abuse Treatment*, 4:157–179.

—— (1988a), *Die zerbrochene Wirklichkeit. Psychoanalyse als das Studium von Konflikt und Komplementarität.* Heidelberg: Springer.

—— (1988b), "The Sleeping Giant": A dissenting comment about "borderline pathology." *Psychoanal. Inqu.*, 8:373–397.

—— (1989), "Either-Or": Some comments on Professor Grünbaum's critique of psychoanalysis. *Psychoanal. Inqu.*, 9:220–248.

—— (1990), *Die Maske der Scham. Die Psychoanalyse von Schamaffekten und Schamkonflikten.* Heidelberg: Springer.

—— (1993), *Das Rätsel des Masochismus.* Heidelberg: Springer.

—— Zients, A. (1982), The "return of the denied superego"—A psychoanalytic study of adolescent substance abuse. *Psychoanal. Inqu.*, 2:539–580.

Zetzel, E. (1949), Anxiety and the capacity to bear it. In: *The Capacity for Emotional Growth.* New York: International Universities Press, 1970, pp. 33–52.

———— (1955), The incapacity to bear depression. In: *The Capacity for Emotional Growth.* New York: International Universities Press, 1970, pp. 82–114.

Zinberg, N. E. (1975), Addiction and ego function. *The Psychoanalytic Study of the Child,* 20:567–588. New York: International Universities Press.

Name Index

Subject Index

Absoluteness of experience, 56–57, 63
Abstinence, 8
Addiction. *See also* Alcoholism; Narcotic
    addiction; Sexual addiction; To-
    bacco addiction
  in adolescents, 159–160
  definition of, 163
  disease concept of, 34, 36–38, 138–
    139, 175
  disease model of, 34
  etiology of, 7
  factors defining, 144–145
  one-disease model of, 10
  psychic helplessness and, 133–145
  theory of, 8–9
  treatability of, 138–139, 140–141
Addictive behavior
  in child analysis, 147–162
  compulsiveness in, 58–60
  core conflicts in, 60–63
  core phenomena of, 56–58
  emotional disorders in, 65–100
  of Freud, 13–15
  judgmentalness and, 63–64
  layers of specificity of, 45–47
  multiple approaches to, 175–190
  neurotic process in, 56–58
  problem of, 43–45
  psychoanalytic studies of, 3–15
  spectrum of, 3
  superego analysis for, 47–56
  transitional and autistic phenomena
    in, 163–174
  treatment theory for, 4
Addictive disorders
  self-regulation vulnerabilities and, 18–
    41

  suffering and, 17–18
Addictive drugs, classes of, 28
Addictive mechanisms, 76
Addictive personality, 43–44
Addictive vulnerabilities, 18–19, 187–188
  clinical perspective on, 20–22
  data on, 19–20
  diagnostic and empirical findings on,
    22–23
Addicts. *See also* Alcoholics; Drug addicts;
    Substance abusers
  shifting view of, 177–178
  unsuccessful, 95–96
Addictus, 44
Adolescents, vulnerability of, 159–160
Adult catastrophic trauma, 68–69, 87–88
Adultery, compulsion to commit, 58–60
Affect. *See also* Emotion; Feelings
  activating aspect of, 76–81
  adult catastrophic trauma and, 67–69
  cognitive and expressive aspect of, 70
  components of, 69–73
  defense defect of, 27
  difficulties with modulating, 23
  dysregulation of, 188
  expressive *vs.* activating aspects of, 77–
    78
  hedonic element of, 75–76
  information processing view of, 71
  narrowed, 179–181
  physiological aspect of, 72–73
  regression of, 67–69, 88
  regulation of, 183–184
  self-regulation vulnerabilities and, 26–
    29
  tolerance of, 73–75, 86–87
Affective anesthesia, 67

Perception, complexity of, 99
Pharmacothymic crisis, 95
Phobic core, 45
Pleasure
  in addiction, 76
  versus gratification, 75
Polarization, 63
Pornography, 129
Posttraumatic stress disorder, 68–69
Powerlessness, 163–164
"The Prevention and Treatment of Drug
    Addiction," 11
Primary care therapist, 34–35
Promethean complex, 85–86
Pseudo-excitements, 144
Psychic closing off, 87–88
"The Psychic Effects of Intoxicants, an
    Attempt to Evolve a Psychoana-
    lytic Theory of Morbid Crav-
    ings," 8–9
"The Psychoanalysis of Pharmocothy-
    mia," 10
"Psychoanalytic Considerations of the Eti-
    ology of Compulsive Drug Use,"
    13
"Psychoanalytic Studies on Addiction,
    Ego Structure and Narcotic Ad-
    diction," 12–13
"Psychoanalytic Treatment in a Sanato-
    rium," 10–11
Psychodynamic approach, 136–137
  with disease concept, 139
  therapies of, 4–5
Psychomatic illness, 67–68
Psychopathology, *versus* vulnerability, 23–
    24
Psychophobia, 45
Psychotherapeutic relationship, 20–22
Psychotherapy
  for alcoholic patient, 171–174
  inappropriate, 183
  self-regulation vulnerabilities and, 20–
    22, 38–40
Psychothymis, 10
Psychotropic drugs, 98

Rage
  impotent, 141–142
  incipient, 155–156
  Kohutian theory of, 157
  neutralization of, 154–156
Recovery, Inc., 80
Regressive alcoholic, 12
Relational theories, 182
Relationships
  difficulties with, 17
  self-regulation vulnerabilities and, 24–
    25
Repetition, destructive, 184–186
Ressentiment, 62
Romantic love, 113

Schreber case, 9
Sedative-hypnotics, 28
Self, 184
  development of, 188–189
  disorders of, 110–111
The Self and the Object World, 180
Self object differentiation, 188–189
Self psychology, 4, 5, 188–189
  defense analysis of, 152
  on self-esteem maintenance, 25
  in sexual addict therapy, 110–114
"Self Representation and the Capacity for
    Self Care," 90
Self-care, 86, 169–170
  basis for, 140
  capacity for, 18
  deficits of, 137–138
  difficulties with, 17
  inhibition of, 89, 100
  self-regulation vulnerabilities and, 29–
    31
Self-cohesion, 5
Self-criticism, 8
Self-destructive repetitions, 177
Self-destructiveness, 10, 30, 151–152, 161,
    184–185, 189
Self-esteem, 5
  difficulties with, 17
  self-regulation vulnerabilities and, 24–
    25

Self-governance, 37
Self-help groups, 80, 97–98
Self-image, incomplete, 92
Self-medication, 28, 137
 failure of, 157
Selfobject, 165
 experience of, 107–108
Self-other problems, 25
Self-psychology, 182
Self-regulation vulnerabilities, 178
 areas of, 39–40
 case vignette of, 31–33
 causes of, 24–29
 psychopathology *versus*, 23–24
 self-care and, 29–31
 treatment implications of, 33–41
 understanding of, 18–23
Self-soothing, 86
Separation-individuation
 versus belonging, 62
 transitional object in, 165
Sexual addiction, 58–60, 101–114, 184–
  185
 analytic treatment of, 130
 clinical cases of, 115–127
 function of, 128–129
 secondary gains from, 161
 treatment of, 152–154
Sexuality, alcoholism and, 9
Sexualization, function of, 111–112
Shame
 versus guilt, 61
 issues of, 180–181
Smile, responsive, 187–188
Social change, 11
Solacing, 93, 142
Soul murder, 94
Specificity, layers of, 45–47
Splitting, 57
Stimulants, 28
Subjective experience, 72
Substance abusers, 17–41
Success, need to destroy, 47–49
Suckling, 93–94
Suffering, 17–18, 75
Suicide attempt, 179–180

Superego
 analysis of, 47–56
 core conflicts and, 61–63
 prosthetic, 141
 punitive, 138, 180–181
 tormenting, 8
Support groups, 35
 for alcoholics, 36–38
Support structures, 183
Symbiosis, 164
 illusion of, 90–91, 135–136, 188–189
 inadequate, 166–167
Symptom approach, 138–139

Tense depression, 10
Tension
 episodes of, 50
 need to release, 120
 regulation of, 111
 unbearable, 12–13
Therapeutic alliance, 35
 rational, 169–170
Therapeutic problems, 98–100
Therapeutic relationship, interactional,
  187
Thing orientation, 69, 92
"Three Essays on the Theory of Sexuality," 9
Tobacco addiction, 14–15
Transference
 ambivalent, 98
 idolatrous, 83–86, 100
 problems of, 82–83
 in sexual addicted patient, 107–110,
  121–123
Transitional affect precursors, 94
Transitional object, 94
 creation of, 165
 omnipotent, 139–140
 precursors of, 93
Transitional phenomena, 163–174
Transmuting internalization, $110n$
Trauma
 acknowledgement of, 182–183
 adult catastrophic, 68–69, 87–88
 childhood, 170